BRITISH LEGAL REFORM

An Agenda for Change

Edited by
Catherine Atkinson, Thom Brooks and
David Drew

First published in Great Britain in 2024 by

Policy Press, an imprint of
Bristol University Press
University of Bristol
1–9 Old Park Hill
Bristol
BS2 8BB
UK
t: +44 (0)117 374 6645
e: bup-info@bristol.ac.uk

Details of international sales and distribution partners are available at
policy.bristoluniversitypress.co.uk

ISBN 978-1-4473-7541-8 paperback
ISBN 978-1-4473-7542-5 ePub
ISBN 978-1-4473-7543-2 ePdf

Cover design: Robin Hawes
Front cover image: iStock/antova
Bristol University Press and Policy Press use environmentally
responsible print partners.
Printed and bound in Great Britain by CPI Group (UK) Ltd,
Croydon, CR0 4YY

Contents

Notes on contributors

Bren Albiston is a solicitor and specialist litigator at a City law firm, and Co-Chair of the Society of Labour Lawyers' Constitution Group. He is interested in constitutional reform, particularly questions of institutional reform. Bren has contributed to the wider debate on constitutional reform, and contributed to the work of the Commission on the Future of the UK, led by Gordon Brown.

Grahame Anderson is a barrister at Littleton Chambers specialising in employment law, particularly high value statutory and High Court cases. He co-chairs the Society of Labour Lawyers' employment law group. He is joint editor of Butterworths Employment Law Handbook and writes regularly on employment law topics.

Catherine Atkinson is the Labour Member of Parliament for Derby North and a barrister at 9 Gough Chambers and Chair of both the Society of Labour Lawyers and Socialists Societies Executive. She has written for *The Guardian* and *New Law Journal*.

Adrian Berry is a barrister at Garden Court Chambers, London. He is presently a Patron of the Immigration Law Practitioners' Association and was formerly its Chair. His practice includes not only case work in courts and tribunals but also policy work for institutions on immigration Bills, Home Office policy and mobility treaties. He specialises in British nationality law, statelessness, international mobility treaties, complex asylum cases, international co-ordination of social security, homelessness and social welfare law. In 2023, he was part of one of the legal teams in the Rwanda asylum-seeker case before the Supreme Court.

Thom Brooks is Professor of Law and Government at Durham University's Law School and currently Visiting Fellow at Yale Law School. He was the 112th President of the Society of Legal Scholars and a former executive board member of the Fabian Society and Society of Labour Lawyers. His award winning work includes *New Arrivals: A Fair Immigration System for Labour* (Fabian Society, 2022), *Reforming the UK's Citizenship Test* (Bristol University Press, 2022) and *Becoming British* (Biteback Publishing, 2016).

Grace Cullen is a practising barrister, specialising in family and employment law. She is Co-Chair of the Access to Justice Group of Society of Labour Lawyers. Chapter 5 draws on the pamphlet produced by the Access to Justice Group of the Society of Labour Lawyers 'Towards a national legal service, new visions for access to justice', 2023.

Liz Davies is a KC at Garden Court Chambers, specialising in housing and homelessness. She is co-author of *Housing Allocation and Homelessness* (Luba, Davies, Johnston and Buchanan, LexisNexis, 6th edn, 2022) and *Domestic Abuse and Housing* (Davies, James, McCurley and Sergides, LAG, forthcoming). She writes the monthly column 'Recent Developments in Housing Law' with Sam Madge-Wyld for *Legal Action* magazine. She is a Honorary Vice-President of the Haldane Society of Socialist Lawyers and co-convenes the Housing and Levelling Up Sub-group of the Society of Labour Lawyers.

Rosalee Dorfman Mohajer is a barrister specialising in housing and financial services law. She practices at 4–5 Gray's Inn Square Chambers. As the Equality and Diversity Officer, she focuses on strengthening the support provided to new parents in Chambers. She is a member of the Labour Party in the Putney, Southfields and Roehampton constituency.

David Drew is General Counsel at an investment fund. He specialises in complex litigation, cross-border investigations and asset recovery as well as corporate, regulatory and commercial matters. He also has extensive experience in government and legislative affairs, having worked for both the Chief Secretary to the Treasury and the Shadow Attorney General.

Ceri Edmonds is a barrister at Tanfield specialising in a wide range of work including leasehold enfranchisement, service charges, rights of first refusal, forfeiture, mortgages, possessions and real property. Before coming to the Bar, Ceri enjoyed a successful career as a civil servant working in the UK and abroad. She has extensive experience in advising ministers and senior officials and in drafting reports and submissions on complex and sensitive issues.

Hannah Gomersall is a barrister at Coram Chambers and a specialist in public and private children law. She is secretary of the Society of Labour Lawyers, Co-Chair of the Family Law Group and her publications include 'The voice of the vulnerable: achieving fairness for parents with learning disabilities or cognitive impairments', [2023] *Fam Law* 387; 'The liberty protection safeguards: the solution to a bureaucratic nightmare?', [2017] *Fam Law* 533; 'Kinship care conference', [2016] *Fam Law* 126; 'Children case update: public law', [2016] *Fam Law* 991.

Tristan Goodman is an artificial intelligence policy professional, having previously practised as a solicitor at a City law firm. He has recently written on the role of standards in the enforcement of the EU AI Act, published in the *LSE Law Review* (2023).

David Green is a barrister at 12 KBW specialising in industrial disease and employment law.

Stephen Hockman is a KC at 6 Pump Court, Temple, London, specialising in environmental, planning and health and safety law. He is a former chair of the Society of Labour Lawyers and edited the previous set of essays published by the Society, *Law Reform 2015*. He co-convenes the Housing and Levelling Up Sub-Group of the Society of Labour Lawyers.

Michael Horton is a KC, arbitrator and mediator in practice at Coram Chambers, and a specialist in financial remedies, international family law and family property law. He is a member of the Society of Labour Lawyers and his publications include: *Compromise in Family Law: Law and Practice* (Lexis Nexis, 2016); contributing editor responsible for chapter 21 (family property) of Rayden and Jackson on *Relationship Breakdown, Finances & Children* (Lexis Nexis, 2024).

Sally Hughes is a social scientist by training with a wide-ranging career including academia, policy and parliamentary work at Legal Action Group and Mind, journalism, editing and legal practice. Sally is qualified as both barrister and solicitor and her legal practice focused onmental capacity, mental health and convention rights issues. She served Executive Committee of the Society of Labour Lawyers Executive from 1995 to 2005, editing *Justice for All* and leading on legislative matters working on legislative matters relating to the housing of women affected by domestic violence. She is currently collaborating with Professor Nigel Duncan on a legal educational approach to the challenge of corruption to the practising profession.

Laura Janes is Lecturer at London South Bank University, within the Law Department. She is also a consultant solicitor. She has a particular expertise in community care, criminal justice, youth justice and mental health. Between 2005 and 2022 she worked at the Howard League for Penal Reform. She has a professional doctorate in youth justice. Her publications include articles and chapters on human rights, young adults, youth justice, prison and children's rights.

Daniel Jones is Senior Associate at DLA Piper, with experience of advising states, international organisations and corporate clients on a wide range of contentious and non-contentious international trade and public and international law matters. He previously worked as a policy and legal advisor to the Shadow Business & Trade team and sits on the Executive Committee of the Society of Legal Lawyers.

Jemima Lovatt is a barrister at 6 Pump Court, practising in criminal, regulatory and public law. She co-chairs the Society of Labour Lawyers' Constitution Group where her interests have focused on ethics and standards in public life. Previously she campaigned for a wider statutory definition of domestic abuse which was codified into law through the Domestic Abuse Act 2021. Other research interests include legal redress for harm caused by air pollution, the role of judicial review in outsourced public contracts and decriminalising abortion law.

Joseph K is a New York-qualified Associate in Public International Law, ESG and Business and Human Rights. He holds a MSc in Behavioural Economics, an LLM in Law (Harvard), and received the Clive Parry prize for International Law from Cambridge University. He was named the UK's 'Future Legal Mind of the Year 2020' for his advocacy in decriminalising homelessness. He is currently Chair of the Junior Labour Lawyers, and applying to be Labour's parliamentary candidate for Mid-Buckinghamshire.

Jamie McGowan is a caseworker at Hammersmith & Fulham Law Centre, a tribunal advocate at Justice for Tenants, and has worked for a Labour Member of Parliament since 2016.

George Peretz is a KC at Monckton Chambers and co-chair of the Society of Labour Lawyers Business and Trade Group and member of the Society of Labour Lawyers executive. He is a member of the Law Library of Ireland, chairs the Bar Council's working group on retained EU law, and is a member of the executive of the Administrative Law Bar Association. He specialises in regulatory, trade, and competition law. He has a free Substack (The Political Lawyer) and has written for *Prospect*, the *Guardian*, and the *Fabian Review* on Brexit and constitutional law issues, as well as co-authoring Blackstone's *Guide to the UK Internal Market Act 2020* and contributing to legal textbooks on Brexit and energy law, the law of the Ireland/Northern Ireland Protocol, competition law and state aid.

Wendy Pettifer is a retired solicitor. She was a legal aid lawyer for over 30 years, retiring in 2018 having worked mainly with migrants on destitution issues in the public law context fighting for social justice. She has lived in Hackney for over 40 years and is active in her local community. Since retirement, she has volunteered with Migrants Organise, Care4Calais and London Renters Union. She is a member of the Labour Party and joined the Society of Labour Lawyers in 2021. She is a member of the Housing and Levelling Up Sub-group and co-chair of the Immigration Sub-Group. She has a Masters in Refugee studies.

Andrew Pratten is a solicitor specialising in construction and engineering law. He practices at Osborne Clarke LLP acting for developers, employers, registered providers, contractors and sub-contractors across multiple sectors, including the built environment, mobility and infrastructure, and energy and utilities. Andrew is currently a member of the Adjudication Society, former secretary for the Bristol North West CLP, and is acting as agent (having also acted in 2021) for Labour's candidates in the Avonmouth & Lawrence Weston ward in the 2024 local council elections.

Jacob Turner is a barrister at Fountain Court Chambers. He is the author of *Robot Rules: Regulating Artificial Intelligence* (Palgrave Macmillan, 2018). He regularly advises public and private parties in different jurisdictions on the law and governance of artificial intelligence (AI). He has acted in several pieces of world-leading AI litigation, including the 'AI inventor case', *Thaler v Comptroller-General* in the UK Supreme Court, and the 'robo-firing case' *Drivers v Uber and Ola Cabs* in the Amsterdam Court of Appeals. He is on the Attorney-General's Panel of Counsel and has advised the UK government on matters of AI law and policy

David Watkinson MA, LLB (both Cantab), barrister (retired 2013) and accredited mediator, practised as a barrister for 40 years, mostly as a member of Garden Court Chambers, in housing and planning law, conducting cases in courts and tribunals at all levels from Magistrates and County to House of Lords (Supreme Court) and the European Court of Human Rights. Positions held included membership of the Civil Justice Council (advising the Lord Chancellor /Minister for Justice on law reform) and Chair of its Housing and Land (Property) Committee; Vice-Chair Housing Law Practitioners' Association; Lecturer in Housing Law, University of Warwick; currently member of the Society of Labour Lawyers' Housing and Levelling Up Sub-group. Publications include contributions to *Squatting: The Real Story* (Bay Leaf Books, 1980) and all three editions of *Gypsy and Traveller Law* (Legal Action Group, 3rd edn, 2020).

David Wolfe is a KC at Matrix specialising in judicial review challenges to the decisions of, among others, government, regulators (including environmental and professional regulators), local authorities, schools and health bodies. His clients include individuals and numerous environmental non-governmental organisations. He has previously held the position of Chair of the Recognition Panel established by the Royal Charter in the light of the Leveson Inquiry into the culture, practices and ethics of the news publishers. David was also a Commissioner (non-executive director) at the Legal Services Commission and a Board Member of the Legal Services Board and a part-time Chair of the Special Educational Needs and Disability Tribunal. His publications include Matrix's Noddy Guide to SEN Law; *Governance of Academies in England: The Return of 'Command and Control'* (British Journal of Education Studies, 2024), co-authored with Basma Yaghi; *Secondary Schools (Academies and Maintained Schools) in England: Issues of Governance and Autonomy* (Clare Market Papers (24), London School of Economics and Political Science, 2022), co-authored with Anne West and Basma Yaghi; *Government Policies Have Fragmented the UK State Secondary School Landscape* (London School of Economics, 2022), co-authored with Anne West; and *Governance of Schools: Current Issues and an Alternative Vision*, with Anne West in Renewing public education: proposals for an inclusive, democratic and joyful system (a FORUM ebook publication in association with Lawrence Wishart, 2024).

Foreword

Lord Charles Falconer,
PC, KC, former Lord Chancellor
and Secretary of State of Justice

The publication of *British Legal Reform: An Agenda for Change* could not have happened at a more pressing time. It is a very significant contribution to the discussion about how the law and the legal system need to adapt to the unprecedented challenges facing the country. The Society of Labour Lawyers has a track record of producing major works on legal reform at moments of great challenge in British political history. This book is no exception. It arrives at the dawn of a new Labour government and contains a great many proposals and ideas that can contribute to a serious programme of transformational and positive change.

The law has always been a powerful instrument for shaping society, removing injustices and fostering progress. However, the range of issues and emergencies that now need to be addressed is staggering. This book is a very serious effort to grapple with some of the most complex issues facing the new government. The breadth of the work is impressive, providing proposals on subjects ranging from the crises in the family courts and criminal justice system, to the UK's relationship with Europe and its role in international affairs, to averting environmental disaster and facing the rising power of artificial intelligence.

The authors of this book are highly respected experts in their fields and have produced something which is more than a lose collection of essays. It is a call to action underpinned by a commitment to the rule of law, access to justice and the principle that the legal system can be a force for good. That call is directed at policy makers, legislators, lawyers and members of the public and asks that they see the legal system as an essential tool navigating difficult times. It is a reminder that considered, constructive and well-designed law and legal policy are essential to delivering just, equitable and lasting change.

Introduction

Catherine Atkinson, Thom Brooks and David Drew

By any standards, the Conservative tenure since 2010 has been an appalling period of government. It has left the country poorer and more divided, with dilapidated public services, demoralised civil servants and degraded institutions. A failure of basic administrative competence has been combined with contempt for some fundamental principles of good governance. These have been particularly concerning in relation to the government's attitude towards the rule of law. A properly functioning court system, an independent judiciary and legal constraints on the use of executive power are essential in any truly democratic society. In the UK however each of these elements have been severely tested, strained and damaged in recent years.

This book provides a legal perspective (or more accurately, multiple legal perspectives) on some key policy challenges affecting the UK. The subject matter is broad, ranging from family law to Brexit and from environmental protection to artificial intelligence. However, the book does not provide a comprehensive review of government activity. Instead, it focuses on some essential policy areas in which law plays an unusually prominent role, often in managing complexity and changeability or the application of broad principles to unique individual circumstances. Some proposals may be contentious, but any serious agenda for change will require stepping into disputed territory.

The contributors to this book propose major reforms to both policy and the approach to policy making. A consistent theme is the need for an improvement in the quality of new law by bringing more rigour to the legislative process and for ministers to focus on the operation of law in practice. Both are essential for developing successful solutions to long-term, multidimensional problems. More broadly, however, we argue that the new government should reprioritise and revitalise some fundamental legal principles as a matter of urgency: access to justice; an independent judiciary; a properly functioning court system; and respect for the rule of law. These principles are the backbone of good governance and democratic accountability and run through every chapter of this book.

A challenging inheritance

Like much of the world, the UK seems to be in a state of permanent crisis. The financial meltdown followed by the programme of government austerity, national divisions over Brexit, the COVID-19 pandemic, war in Ukraine, horrific scenes in Israel and Palestine, the return of double digit inflation and the sharply rising cost of living have caused enormous shifts in the national and international political economy. This has been a uniquely challenging period for governments around the world. In the UK, however, the previous governing party's own internal chaos amplified the sense of national crisis. There were a bewildering number of changes in leadership, strategy, policy and plans, while major challenges were left unaddressed or sometimes actively made worse. The last few years have been marked by insubstantial, politically expedient policy announcements which quickly unravelled under scrutiny. More worryingly, certain policies were used as a purely political tool with their symbolic value trumping any positive practical effect. This approach to government was profoundly *unprincipled*, that is, lacking a coherent moral or intellectual framework. The result was a national government unable to deliver meaningful, positive and lasting change.

Nowhere was this more apparent than in the previous government's approach to the legal system. Since 2010, it has been damaged to the point of collapse by poor policy and severe underfunding. The deep cuts to legal aid and the wider Ministry of Justice budget have removed the ability of many to obtain legal advice, driven many lawyers out of the profession and created a dysfunctional and in some cases literally crumbling court system. Since 2016, following certain high-profile cases relating to the politically radioactive issues of immigration and Brexit, the independent judiciary has faced severe criticism both by elements of the press and, much more worryingly, parts of the government, including some of its senior law officers.

The new government faces enormous and potentially overwhelming challenges and the limits on public spending are a significant constraint on a transformative agenda. Indeed, many of the immediate issues facing the country, including a number which are highlighted in this book, are the result of 14 years of cuts and constraints in current spending and a lack of long-term investment. This is as true of the National Health Service, local government and the Ministry of Defence as it is of the court system, legal aid and the Ministry of Justice. So while policies affecting the rule of the law and access to justice are a particular concern of this book, the authors are fully aware that there is a sense of crisis gripping almost every area of public policy.

The scope of this book, however, ranges beyond just the functioning of the legal system. Whether the challenge is rehabilitating broken public services, reimagining the UK's international trading arrangements or tackling the dizzying advances in information technology, the solutions will require a sound legal basis, grounded in core legal principles and ultimately the ability for individual rights to be enforced in a functioning court system. Where there are occasional proposals for additional public spending in this book, there are accompanying proposals for revenue raising or costs saving. However, even with a grounded approach, the process for rehabilitating the public realm will be long and difficult.

The book and its structure

The year 2024 is a momentous one for elections across the globe. In the UK, there has been the first change of government for 14 years. The following chapters bring together lawyers who are experts in their field to provide analysis from a legal perspective on some key challenges for the government in the years ahead. Many of the authors have spent a number of years advising the

Labour Shadow Front Bench on legal and policy matters and this book is an effort to distil some of their thinking on the subjects in question. The book is divided into three parts, starting with fundamental domestic matters and moving outwards through complex policy challenges to the international sphere. Despite the division into three parts, as the chapters make clear, there is often significant overlap in the local, national and international issues covered.

Part I, 'Foundational issues', covers four of the most essential elements of government policy: housing; employment; family law; and crime. The section ends with a chapter on access to justice, both an important policy area in its own right and a central principle which sits at the core of the book. Chapter 1 (housing and homelessness) sets outs proposals to reform the private rented sector, improve housing standards, reduce homelessness and increase access to justice. It is impossible to separate the national housing crisis from the impact of social security policy and the funding of local authorities and although outside the scope of the chapter, these issues are also touched on. Chapter 2 (employment) discusses Labour's proposed New Deal for Working People alongside existing employment protections. The chapter argues that new rights will only make a difference in practice if they can be enforced and outlines proposals to address the challenges currently facing the courts and employment tribunal system in this area. Chapter 3 (family law) also considers the overburdened court system and its impact on children, families and the care system. It analyses some key lessons from the Family Drug and Alcohol Court and how it may serve as a model for other areas of the family justice system. Chapter 4 (criminal justice) considers the concept of 'restorative justice' and the need to prevent crime with a particular focus on violence against women and girls. Chapter 5 (access to justice) provides a survey view of the increasing problems people encounter in seeking access to justice, including the state of legal aid funding, court delays and the problems accessing adequate advice. It offers a review of the key issues raised in the previous four chapters and proposes a solutions-based approach to tackling them including the creation of a National Legal Services (discussed further below).

Part II, 'Emerging challenges', looks at five areas which are central themes of the political agenda but which, in practical terms, cut across a range of policy areas and government departmental responsibility. Creating effective policy in these areas will require a holistic approach which brings together those different strands. Chapter 6 (planning and levelling up) looks at the politically fraught issue of planning reform from the perspective of its impact on the disparity in living standards and economic productivity between different parts of the country (often referred to in broad terms as 'levelling up'). As noted earlier, this chapter should be read as a companion piece to the earlier chapter on housing. Chapter 7 (constitutional reform) addresses the large amount of 'unfinished constitutional business' in the UK, including reforming the current anachronistic elements of the legislature and how to overhaul and improve the system ensuring high standards in public life. Chapter 8 (devolution) sets out the fundamental principles that should underpin the reform of the UK's insecure devolution settlement along with a series of practical recommendations to address the current constitutional uncertainty. Chapter 9 (environment) provides a 'menu' of policy ideas for improving the UK's approach to climate change and ecological preservation. These ideas range from low-cost, easy-to-implement solutions that would have a dramatic effect to more radical rights for citizens to take action against polluters. Chapter 10 (artificial intelligence) argues that the professionalisation of the artificial intelligence industry can operate as an additional 'bottom-up' method of regulation, instilling a sense of shared values in the individuals creating and designing the systems we will come to rely on in our everyday lives.

Part III, 'The global context', looks at four areas where global factors have a direct impact on the domestic sphere and have become highly contentious areas of policy debate. Chapter 11 (asylum law) discusses asylum and irregular migration policy, the failures of the government's record and a series of practical policy recommendations that would transform the approach and deliver an asylum system that was fit for purpose in an era of mass migration. Chapter 12 (immigration and nationality) outlines a series of ambitious but deliverable immigration and nationality law policies to rebuild trust in the system and deliver progressive policies in a way that meaningfully speaks to the public's priorities. Chapter 13 (EU and trade) discusses how improving the UK's relationship with the EU can help Labour achieve its mission for growth and delivering clean energy. The chapter outlines the many technical issues that impede this goal and proposals for improvements which can open up a path for steadily increasing cooperation between the two parties over time. Chapter 14 (international law) discusses the UK's historically significant role in developing the rules-based international order and how it might refocus and revitalise its efforts to support an international order based on the shared rules which are so crucial to our supply chains, preventing environmental harms and ensuring that consumers do not accidentally support human rights abusers.

A tradition of legal reform policy

The Society of Labour Lawyers, which has produced this book, has a record of making important contributions at critical moments in British political history. Over the years, the Society has developed many policy ideas – some quickly implemented by incoming governments, others taking longer to arrive. Many structural improvements proposed by the Society are now pillars of the UK's legal architecture. For example, as far back as *The Reform of the Law* which was published in 1951 (edited by Glanville Williams) the Society was recommending the creation of a separate ministry of justice to deliver a more forward looking legal system. *Law Reform Now* published in 1964 (edited by Gerald Gardiner and Dr Andrew Martin) recommended the permanent law commission responsible for reforming English law which was established by the newly elected Labour government the following year.[1] *Legal Services For All*, written by Society members and published by the Fabians in 1968, proposed a comprehensive network of law centres and an expansion of legal aid. *Law Reform For All* published in 1997 (edited by David Bean) proposed a judicial appointments commission, improvements to the tribunal

---

[1] The Law Commission was established by the Law Commissions Act 1965.

system and the domestication of the European Convention on Human Rights – all changes ushered in by the Labour government of 1997–2010. Most recently, *Law Reform 2015* published just ahead of the 2015 election (edited by Stephen Hockman) set out, amongst many recommendations, ideas for integrating new technology into legal service delivery to drive improvements in an era of constrained public spending.[2] That progressive vision of the potential to harness technology to improve public services has been adopted as a key theme of this book.

British Legal Reform: An Agenda for Change draws from the principles underpinning the Society's significant body of work. It is a collection of chapters which can be read together or on their own except Chapter 1 (housing and homelessness) and Chapter 6 (planning and levelling up) where there is significant crossover in both contributors and content. Perhaps the main 'structural' proposal in the book, in line with the Society's previous proposals for a ministry of justice, a law commission or a judicial appointments commission, is the idea of a National Legal Service (discussed at length in Chapter 4 [access to justice]). The National Legal Service would be a strategic coordinating body designed to deliver a comprehensive system of legal advice and representation across a range of providers. There are many more policy proposals in this book. Some are straightforward, others are radical and none on their own will provide a complete solution. They are however all designed to be practical, realistic and achievable and focussed on solving some of the deep-seated problems of a highly damaged public sphere.

The chapters in this book are designed to help shape Labour's policy platform. They were originally written under the Conservative government but have been amended to reflect Labour's recent election win and the party's emerging agenda for change.

---

[2] This paragraph draws heavily from a speech by Sir Ross Cranston (Chair of SLL from 2003 to 2006) which was delivered at the Society of Labour Lawyers' 70th Anniversary AGM in December 2017.

PART I

Foundational issues

1

Housing and homelessness

*Liz Davies, Rosalee Dorfman Mohajer, Ceri Edmonds,
Stephen Hockman, Sally Hughes, Jamie McGowan,
Wendy Pettifer, Andrew Pratten and David Watkinson*

Introduction

Ambitious reform, and resources, are necessary so that all three
housing sectors – homeownership, the social rented sector and
the private rented sector (PRS) – become accessible, affordable
and safe. These sectors cannot be considered in isolation from
one another. The proposals to enhance the rights of renters and
homeless applicants considered in this chapter will be of limited
practical benefit without measures to significantly increase the
availability of all forms of housing, considered in Chapter 6.

The core value of any Labour programme for housing and law
reform should be a commitment to housing as a human right.
This would mean that Labour will respect and implement Article
11 of the International Covenant on Economic, Cultural and
Social Rights: '[T]he right of everyone to an adequate standard
of living for himself and his family, including adequate food,
clothing and housing, and to the continuous improvement of
living conditions.'[1]

---

[1] We note that the Welsh government has consulted on *Securing a Path
Towards Housing Adequacy and Fair Rents* (Green Paper, issued 6 June 2023,
consultation closed 15 September 2023) as part of the implementation of
the Co-operation Agreement (2021) between the Labour Party and Plaid

The rights we propose are meaningless if they cannot be enforced. The legal aid sector is in a crisis of sustainability and Law Society research shows that 26 million people do not have access to a local legal aid housing lawyer.[2] This chapter concludes with proposals to significantly increase the availability of advice and representation for people experiencing housing issues.

Private rented sector

After 40 years of little or no regulation of the PRS, the government published, on 17 May 2023, the Renters' (Reform) Bill, implementing its pledge to abolish s.21 'no fault' evictions[3] four years after having committed to do so. At the time of writing, the Bill had (on 15 May 2024) passed its Second Reading in the House of Lords. It is now doubtful when it will come into force owing to amendments from Conservative MPs, which have been accepted by the government, and which postpone implementation until the Lord Chancellor has assessed the operation of the process for obtaining possession orders in the County Court.[4] Abolition of s.21, along with the establishment of a PRS Ombudsman and a database for residential landlords are welcome and we support them. However, a number of the new mandatory grounds for possession are open to abuse.

We are concerned at the new mandatory Ground 8A, ground for possession. This means that a tenant who has accrued eight weeks' rent arrears three times over the previous three years will face eviction. The mandatory ground applies even where arrears resulted from events beyond the tenant's control, such as delays

---

Cymru. Acknowledging that housing is a human right would commit the government to progressive realisation of the goals of eliminating homelessness and providing for adequate housing. See Labour Housing Group and Labour Campaign for Human Rights, *Housing is a Human Right*, 2022, at https://labourhousing.org/wp-content/uploads/2022/03/Housing-is-a-Human-Right-digital-version.pdf.

[2] Law Society, 'Housing legal aid providers on the brink of collapse', 14 February 2024, at https://www.lawsociety.org.uk/contact-or-visit-us/press-office/press-releases/Housing%20legal%20aid%20providers%20on%20the%20brink%20of%20collapse.

[3] Housing Act 1988, s 21.

[4] These doubts have since been confirmed as the Bill fell with the dissolution of Parliament following the calling of a General Election for the 4th July 2024.

in payment as a result of precarious employment, or simply life events, and those arrears were subsequently paid off. Labour should commit to implementing the abolition of s.21, if not yet abolished, as soon as it comes into government.

We believe that grounds for possession against tenants should always be discretionary, permitting the court to take into account a tenant's position. This is particularly important in the case of the existing mandatory Ground 8 (eight weeks' rent arrears), the new proposed Ground 8A (discussed earlier) and the new proposed mandatory Grounds 1 and 1A (landlord's intention to sell or to move into the property). If those grounds are not discretionary, we suggest that they are open to abuse, not least because the Renters' (Reform) Bill contains very weak enforcement measures.[5] Legislating to ensure that all grounds for possession are discretionary, rather than mandatory, would not prevent a court making a possession order but it would allow a court to balance the needs of the tenant and the landlord.

With reference to the new Grounds 1 and 1A, specific evidence from the landlord as to their intention to sell or move in should be required before an order for possession is made, in order to prevent abuse. Labour should also consider enabling Rent Repayment Orders (RROs) as a sanction for the new proposed offences of relying on these grounds in circumstances where the landlord does not intend to sell or move in. Further, the period of three months during which the landlord is prohibited from re-letting (if the tenant leaves after receipt of a notice) is insufficient and should be extended.

Currently, there are defences available where a landlord is seeking possession following service of a s.21 notice (no fault eviction).[6] A s.21 notice cannot be relied on if the landlord has failed to comply with his or her legal obligations: to protect a tenancy deposit, to give the tenant a gas safety certificate or an energy performance certificate, to give the tenant information about 'how to rent' or to install a smoke or carbon monoxide alarm. Additionally, a s.21 notice cannot be used to initiate a 'retaliatory eviction': where a

---

[5] The only means of enforcement being a financial penalty imposed by a local housing authority if satisfied beyond reasonable doubt that the landlord served a notice of intention to seek possession on a tenant relying on a ground for possession to which the landlord was not entitled, and the tenant left, without an order for possession being made (clause 15, Renters' (Reform) Bill 2024).

[6] Housing Act 1988, ss 21A and 21B.

s.21 notice is served after a tenant complains to a local authority regarding the condition of a property and the local authority has served a notice on the landlord.[7] Those defences only apply to claims for possession based on a s.21 notice and so would be abolished along with it. The Bill provides that a failure to protect a deposit is a defence to nearly all possession claims, and this is welcome.[8] However, the other defences currently available to s.21 are important tools regulating and enforcing compliance by landlords with legal obligations. We consider that they should be enacted as defences to all grounds for possession. We would not expect local housing authorities or private registered providers (housing associations) to be in breach of those requirements, but the defences should be available nevertheless, for consistency and compliance.

We consider that the defence of 'retaliatory eviction' should be extended, so that it applies where a landlord seeks possession in response to *any* complaint of disrepair from his or her tenant, rather than the current requirement that it only applies where a tenant has complained to a local authority. If, contrary to our previous submission, mandatory grounds for possession are to remain, it would be particularly important to make this defence available for mandatory grounds for possession.

Private rented tenancies are the most expensive housing across the three tenures and rents continue to increase. Shelter research in January 2024 found that 66 per cent of people in England reported pressures on housing in 2023, in the form of struggling to pay housing costs, worrying about evictions or cutting back on other essentials to pay housing costs, and 40 per cent believed that their situation would worsen in 2024.[9]

Labour should legislate to provide a system of rent regulation, so that proposed rents, or proposed rent increases, can be considered by a locally based expert tribunal. The tribunal would take into account all relevant factors including the age of the dwelling, its condition and state of repair, its locality and the facilities provided, including

---

[7] Deregulation Act 2015, s 33.

[8] The exclusions are Ground 7 (tenancy devolved on death of tenant) and Ground 14 (anti-social behaviour).

[9] Shelter, 'Shelter and HSBC UK's new research reveals 40% of people fear housing pressures will get worse in 2024', 26 January 2024, at https://blog.shelter.org.uk/2024/01/shelter-and-hsbc-uks-new-research/.

furniture if any, and the effect of any scarcity of dwellings in the area. Labour should also consider the case for regional authorities to have powers to limit rent increases, as called for by the Mayor for London.

Local housing allowance should be reformed so as to cover rents in the 50th percentile or below, locally. The benefit cap and the bedroom tax, both of which require a tenant to pay the shortfall between the actual rent and benefits, should be abolished, along with other restrictions on benefits which are not related to means, such as the two child limit. Controlling rents would save public money as less housing benefit or the housing element of universal credit (in effect a rent subsidy) would be paid by central government.

The 'right to rent' legislation in the Immigration Act 2014 turns landlords into immigration enforcement officers and is applied in a discriminatory manner.[10] Labour should repeal it.

Local authorities should be resourced and encouraged to enforce the minimum housing standards in Housing Act 2004 (Housing Health & Safety Rating System [HHSRS]) against private landlords. These housing standards should be maintained and improved so that cases such as the tragic death of Awaab Ishak, who died from prolonged exposure to mould, are not repeated. All private landlords should be registered on a public register that is open for inspection and contains addresses of all properties let and any enforcement action taken against the landlord (as is in the case in Wales). We understand the PRS Database proposed in the Bill will contain that requirement, but if it does not, Labour should introduce it. We also support calls by Generation Rent to enable RROs to be made against landlords who fail to register on the database.[11] The wider use of these effective sanctions would divert a degree of the inspection and enforcement burden from local authorities and, by extension, the public purse, into the hands of tenants.[12]

---

[10] *R (JCWI) v Secretary of State for the Home Department* [2020] EWCA Civ 542, [2021] 1 W.L.R. 1151, CA, where the court found that some landlords were discriminating on the basis of nationality but dismissed the claim that it was contrary to human rights on the basis that the scheme was capable of being applied lawfully.

[11] https://www.generationrent.org/2023/12/18/why-rent-refunds-are-the-key-to-fixing-the-rental-market/#:~:text=Generation%20Rent%20believes%20that%20tenants,the%20council's%20instruction%20to%20register.

[12] Clause 88 of the Renters' (Reform) Bill would enable RROs to be made against landlords who fail to register on the Private Rented Sector Database

Summary of key proposals for the private rented sector

- Repeal 'no fault' and mandatory possession grounds without delay.
- Extend the current 'no fault' eviction defences (including retaliatory eviction) to all PRS tenancies.
- Establish a tribunal system to independently review proposed rent increases.
- Strengthen the Housing Benefit system so that housing costs are better met.
- Repeal the 'right to rent' legislation.
- Make available sufficient funding to enable enforcement of the environmental health and safety legislation.

The scourge of homelessness

Labour should develop and implement a Plan to End Homelessness.[13] This is best achieved by preventing homelessness from occurring. Plans to build 150,000 social homes for rent each year, and to legislate for indefinite and affordable private rented tenancies should mean that more homes are available for rent and everyone looking for a home is able to find one, without experiencing homelessness.

Homelessness assistance from councils should always be a last resort. Where someone is threatened with homelessness, councils should provide practical assistance, including financial assistance, at an early stage to find alternative accommodation, so avoiding homelessness. Early intervention and prevention is best.

Where someone does become homeless (because they do not have a safe and secure place to live which they have a legal right to occupy and which is reasonable for them to live in), they should be provided with emergency accommodation by councils, regardless of any test of eligibility, priority need or

---

only when they have already received a penalty or been convicted in respect of the breach (Clause 59(1), (2) and (3)), placing an upfront inspection and enforcement burden on local authorities.

[13] See Crisis, *Plan to End Homelessness*, 2018, at https://www.crisis.org.uk/ending-homelessness/plan-to-end-homelessness/.

'becoming homeless intentionally'.[14] Following the Scottish and Welsh governments, Labour should legislate to abolish the tests of eligibility for assistance, priority need and the 'becoming homeless intentionally' test.[15] Every homeless person, having been provided with emergency accommodation, should receive an offer of suitable accommodation.[16]

Councils should be funded so as to improve the amount of, and standards of, emergency accommodation. Councils should be required to apply the 'Housing First' model for applicants who have multiple and complex needs, so that they are provided with accommodation and support to retain that accommodation.[17] The practice of routinely making offers of accommodation out of district to homeless people should cease, and only be available in very unusual and specified circumstances.

---

[14] This proposal would make emergency accommodation available to all those who are homeless. In practice, however, it is envisaged that the numbers of people would be limited, since the approach of homelessness services will be to help an applicant find his or her own accommodation *before* he or she becomes homeless (prevention) and the increase in supply of available accommodation in both the social rented sector and affordable private rented accommodation should assist that task. Similarly, an increased supply will make it quicker for an applicant to move on from emergency accommodation into longer-term accommodation, so those who do need emergency accommodation will occupy it for shorter periods than the current months or years. See *Still Living in Limbo* (Shelter, 2023, at https://england.shelter.org.uk/professional_resour ces/policy_and_research/policy_library/still_living_in_limbo), which found that 'six in ten (61%) households have spent a year or more living in temporary accommodation, increasing to more than two thirds (68%) of families'.

[15] Priority need has been repealed in Scotland (Homelessness (Abolition of Priority Need Test) (Scotland) Order 2012). In Wales 'intentional homelessness' is not applied to families and young people (Housing Wales Act 2014, s 75(3)) and local authorities can choose not to apply it to other homeless applicants. Both Scotland and Wales are considering repealing other parts of the statutory tests. See the Welsh government's *White Paper on Ending Homelessness in Wales*, October 2023, at https://www.gov.wales/ending-homelessness-white-paper.

[16] The accommodation might be of social housing (accessed through the council's allocation scheme) or of PRS accommodation. In all cases, accommodation secured through homelessness must be suitable for the applicant, which means that it must be affordable.

[17] See Crisis, *Home for All: The Case for Scaling Up Housing First in England*, September 2021, at https://www.crisis.org.uk/media/245740/home-for-all_the_case-for-scaling-up-housing-first-in-england_report_sept2021.pdf.

Labour supported the repeal of the Vagrancy Act. Labour should not circumvent that repeal by permitting Public Space Protection Orders or other measures, such as those of 'nuisance begging' and 'nuisance rough sleeping' contained in the government's Criminal Justice Bill 2024 to be used against those sleeping rough or begging. Labour should commit to repealing any such provisions if passed in the 2023–2024 Parliament.

Labour should amend s.204A Housing Act 1996 so as to give courts a broad discretion to order that councils should provide temporary accommodation during the process of an appeal against a homelessness decision.[18]

Summary of key proposals for homelessness

- Develop a plan to end homelessness, including the provision of 150,000 social homes for rent each year.
- Enable councils to provide for early intervention to prevent homelessness.
- End the requirements of eligibility, priority need or intentionally homeless tests, which bar assistance to the homeless.
- Provide investment for homelessness hostels and enable the 'Housing First' model to assist those with complex needs.
- Restrict councils accommodating homeless persons outside their area.
- Empower courts to order councils to accommodate homeless persons during legal disputes.
- Repeal the Vagrancy Act and restrict the use of Public Space Protection Orders against homeless people.
- Repeal the provisions in Criminal Justice Bill (if passed) criminalising 'nuisance begging' and 'nuisance rough sleeping'.

---

[18] At present the courts have that power, but its exercise is severely restricted, see s 204A(5) and (6) Housing Act 1996 which provide that on appeal to the County Court against a negative homelessness decision, the court may only order accommodation pending appeal if the court is satisfied that failure to order accommodation would substantially prejudice the applicant's ability to pursue the appeal. The circumstances in which an appellant's ability to pursue the main appeal is prejudiced are limited, since the appeal rests solely on a point of law and legal submissions.

Housing standards

The death of Awaab Ishak from prolonged exposure to mould was described by the coroner as a 'defining moment' for the housing sector.[19] His shocking death highlighted the national scandal of unfit homes in the social sector and PRS. The Housing Ombudsman's annual complaints review for 2022–3 shows that property condition remains the biggest area of complaint about social landlords and more action is needed by social housing landlords to improve the quality of homes and service.[20] In the PRS, 23 per cent of properties are non-decent homes, and 11 per cent have problems with damp. Private rented dwellings have the lowest scores for energy efficiency.[21]

Tackling appalling housing standards requires resources for enforcement and investment to improve properties. The legislative framework already provides that all rented homes must be fit for human habitation, which would include that they are free from damp and mould and other Category 1 hazards.[22]

The government's response to Awaab Ishak's death was 'Awaab's Law', requiring social landlords to remedy certain defects within specified time limits (to be introduced by subordinate legislation (subject to a consultation process which closed on 5 March 2024).[23] This is an understandable reaction to the tragedy and adds to the existing armoury by which tenants can enforce their rights (through litigation for breach of contract and/or complaint

---

[19] 'Awaab Ishak death: the coroner's verdict in full', *Inside Housing*, 16 November 2022, at https://www.insidehousing.co.uk/login?Refdoc=https%3A%2F%2Fwww%2Einsidehousing%2Eco%2Euk%2Finsight%2Faw aab%2Dishak%2Ddeath%2Dthe%2Dcoroners%2Dverdict%2Din%2D full%2D79122.

[20] Housing Ombudsman, *Annual Complaints Review 2022–2023*, at https://www.housing-ombudsman.org.uk/annual-complaints-review-2022-23/.

[21] ONS, *English Housing Survey 2021 to 2022*, at https://www.gov.uk/government/statistics/english-housing-survey-2021-to-2022-headline-report/english-housing-survey-2021-to-2022-headline-report.

[22] Housing Act 2004 and Homes (Fitness for Human Habitation) Act 2018 (which inserted s 9A into Landlord & Tenant Act 1985).

[23] New sections 10A and 10B Landlord & Tenant Act 1985, inserted by Social Housing (Regulation) Act 2023.

to the Housing Ombudsman). We observe that the time limits do not apply to the PRS and that they should do so.

Our main point, however, is that the problem is not so much a lack of adequate legal remedies, but resources. Labour should commit to investing so that all social housing is renovated to the Decent Homes Standard and private rented landlords are subject to enforcement where their properties contain Category 1 or Category 2 hazards. These standards should be maintained and improved so that cases such as that of Awaab Ishak are not repeated.

Enforcement and investment are necessary in both the social sector and PRS. Local authorities lack resources to bring properties up to legal standards or to invest in improvements. Moreover, local authorities cannot be held to account under Housing Act 2004 for breach of the HHSRS in their own properties.[24] So only individual tenants can bring enforcement proceedings, as a claim for breach of their tenancy conditions, or by complaint to the Housing Ombudsman. Putting the onus on the individual tenant does not represent a holistic solution to systematic problems. If a tenant is to contemplate court action, he or she is dependent upon the postcode lottery of finding a specialist housing solicitor and the very limited availability of legal aid. This gives additional force to our proposals presented in the section on 'Access to justice'.

In the PRS, enforcement by tenants is even more difficult, despite the legislative framework. Although there is a restriction on 'retaliatory evictions', that only applies in certain circumstances[25] and so tenants who complain about breach of their tenancy can be evicted. We propose that the defence of 'retaliatory eviction' should be extended to all possession claims, and should include a wider range of complaints, such as complaining directly to

---

[24] *R v Cardiff City Council ex parte Cross* (1983) 6 H.L.R. 1, CA. We consider that this decision of the Court of Appeal could be overturned by legislation, so that local housing authorities would be able to investigate the condition of their own stock or, alternatively, each other's stock.

[25] As a defence to a claim for possession under s 21 Housing Act 1988, rather than to all claims for possession, and only where the tenant has complained to the local authority and the local authority has served an improvement notice. See the section on the PRS in this chapter.

the landlord. Local authorities have extensive powers to enforce HHSRS against private landlords under Parts 1–4 Housing Act 2004 but use of those powers is discretionary and environmental health departments are under-resourced.

Labour should be investing in local authority environmental health and tenancy relations officers, so as to take enforcement action against private landlords who let unfit properties, breach tenancy conditions or unlawfully evict their tenants.

Summary of key proposals for housing standards

- Apply the timescales being introduced by Awaab's Law for carrying out repairs in the social housing sector to the private rented sector.
- Ensure that all social housing is renovated to the Decent Homes Standard.
- Ensure that private landlords are required to carry out remedial works when Category 1 and Category 2 hazards (as defined by the Housing Act 2004) are identified.
- Ensure that failure to comply with the above leads to enforcement by local authorities (including extending the retaliatory eviction defence to protect tenants who complain about housing conditions) and make provision for the funded legal advice and representation that will be required. This applies to both the private and social housing sectors.
- Enable enforcement by local authority environmental health officers and tenancy relations officers in the private and social housing sectors.

Access to justice

Legal rights that cannot be enforced are meaningless to people who cannot locate advice or pay for legal services.

Any new legislation and regulation planned by an incoming Labour government will be a dead letter unless it can be used and enforced by individuals (through several avenues, including effective complaints procedures, complaints to the relevant Ombudsman and litigation in the courts). Enforcement means that those needing to use an adversarial legal system must be enabled to do so in terms of obtaining adjudication in the courts or tribunals when necessary.

The Legal Aid, Sentencing and Punishment of Offenders Act 2012 (LASPO) came into force in 2013 and made significant changes to civil legal aid provision, reducing the scope of legal aid and the means-test. In the area of housing law, legal aid for disrepair claims was restricted to cases where there is a serious and present risk of harm to the health or safety of any occupier.[26] Legal aid is therefore not available for cases where any disrepair has been remedied but the tenant is still entitled to compensation.

Most egregiously of all, LASPO removed the provision of early legal advice in the area of welfare benefit law. As a result, legal aid is not available for an adviser to help a tenant who has rent arrears recoup any money by resolving benefit issues. Nor is legal advice available for debt. The government has recently realised that omission and has funded a Housing Loss Prevention Advice Service, for advice, including advice on welfare benefits, for tenants facing possession proceedings before and at court.[27]

We believe that early legal advice should be available, subject to means, regardless of the area of law for which advice is sought. Most importantly, it should be urgently restored for cases of welfare benefits and debt advice. Early legal advice can resolve disputes, prevent litigation, and produce economic and social benefits for the individual involved and for the public.[28]

---

[26] LASPO, Sched 1, para 35.

[27] https://www.gov.uk/government/consultations/housing-legal-aid-the-way-forward.

[28] In 2010, Citizens Advice calculated that £1 of housing advice saved the state £2.34; The Law Centre Network policy document *Funding for Law Centres* (2014) estimated direct savings of between £212 and £247 million as a consequence of annual public expenditure costs, associated with debt, temporary accommodation, homelessness, stress, anxiety and ill health. See *Right Time, Right Place: Improving Access to Civil Justice* (Social Market Foundation, May 2022) setting out the personal cost of litigation to unrepresented litigants of stress, financial loss and ill health. See also J. Kelen, 'How to fund it: the economic case for civil legal aid' (in *Towards a National Legal Service*, Society of Labour Lawyers, 2023, pp 27–34), showing that funding civil legal aid in housing cases can reduce the state's resources spent on homelessness by a quarter, prevent reductions in house prices and increase stability in employment, all resulting in significant savings.

In addition, legal aid should be extended to include all claims for damages by a tenant against a landlord for disrepair.

The legal aid sector is experiencing a crisis of sustainability and requires intervention if it is to continue to exist. Legal aid rates of pay have remained static since 1996 and must be increased. The Law Society's interactive map shows graphically that the number of solicitors firms or law centres providing housing legal aid has significantly diminished since LASPO.[29] Forty-one per cent of the population do not have access to a housing legal aid lawyer in their local authority area. Legal aid has become increasingly uneconomic, despite the dedication of legal aid lawyers and their wish to work in that sector.

A Labour government, besides investing in early advice to resolve problems and restoring legal aid for all housing litigation, must invest in legal aid remuneration rates in order to ensure that legal aid advice and representation continue to be available to the public. The establishment of a National Legal Service should be considered. This will require the cooperation of the legal profession. It should not be an alternative to a properly funded legal aid service but an additional part of it.

We consider that the existing forum of the County Court is the best system for the resolution of housing disputes, rather than a specialist housing tribunal.[30] Whatever the forum, the principle that the government should adopt to any dispute resolution system should be that of 'equality of arms', so that tenants and other occupiers are funded and represented. Housing law is an area of law in which a tenants (or homeless person's) opponent in court (their private landlord or local authority) is significantly better resourced. There must be a level playing field, with adequately funded legal advice, early intervention and representation at all stages.

---

[29] https://www.lawsociety.org.uk/campaigns/civil-justice/legal-aid-deserts/housing.

[30] A proposal which we note *A Fairer Private Rented Sector* (White Paper, DLUHC, 2022) rejects, in our view, for good reason: see p 41.

Summary of key proposals for access to justice

- Take steps to ensure that remedial legislation (current and pending) can be enforced and/or that disputes are resolved, whether by complaints procedures, Ombudsmen, alternative dispute resolution and, if necessary, litigation.
- To that end, the restrictions on the scope and availability of legal aid enacted by LASPO should be reversed, in particular the removal of provision for early advice, for example, for welfare benefit and debt cases, which has led to hardship and avoidable litigation.
- Make early legal advice available in all areas of law.
- Restore legal aid to include claims for damages caused by disrepair, with costs to be paid by the landlord.
- Increase legal aid rates (unchanged since 1996 which has led to legal representation and advice deserts across the country).
- In addition, consider the establishment of a National Legal Service.
- Ensure that in the event of litigation, there is 'equality of arms' and resources between landlords, tenants and occupiers.
- Maintain the County Court as the forum for dealing with housing disputes.

2

Rights at work

Grahame Anderson and David Green

Introduction

Labour's New Deal for Working People and the commitment to implement significant changes to employment law show that Labour is committed to making workers' rights work. At present, too often they do not. Many of the statutory protections that the labour movement has won over decades are being left to wither on the vine through a lack of effective enforcement. A right is not worth the paper it is written on if courts and tribunals are too expensive and inefficient to access in time.

To achieve a fair day's work for a fair day's pay, safety in the workplace and protection from discrimination, then the rights on the statute book must be made real and enforceable to all.

This chapter sets out how Labour can achieve this in relation to individual (rather than collective) employment law.

The proposed reforms would help British businesses who wish to obey the law. Currently, legitimate businesses face unfair competition from those who are willing to cut their costs by breaking the law, in the knowledge that being held to account is unlikely. Deliberate lawbreakers can offer services cheaper than legitimate enterprises, for example by falsely designating employees as self-employed and avoiding paying holiday pay.

Individuals who know that their actions, taken for gain, are in breach of the laws passed by Parliament currently face little or no personal jeopardy if the laws they break are statutory employment protections. That should change.

Workers who suffer accidents and diseases through their work are all too often not compensated, or under-compensated, and Conservative governments have put barriers in the way of them achieving just recompense. The law in this area should be simpler and fairer.

This chapter does not seek to set out exactly how every collective and individual employment injustice can be remedied. Significant changes will surely be made to reform trade union laws, allowing electronic balloting. Labour has announced a commitment to give workers statutory rights on day one.

Our recommendations, set out in this chapter, explain how Labour's New Deal for Working People, announced by the Rt Hon. Angela Rayner MP, can be implemented as legislation. The aim is a justice system where compliance with statutory employment protections is incentivised, and ignoring them becomes a risk not worth taking.

Single status employment rights

Employment rights, from maternity leave to holiday pay, to protection from dismissal, depend on employment or worker status. You have one set of rights if you're an employee, a different set if you're a worker, and a different set if you're none of the above. So, determining who is an employee and who is self-employed (and thus outside the ambit of employment protection) is fundamental.

If individuals do not know their status legally speaking, then they cannot know what rights they have.

The current law is diffuse, complex and rife with uncertainty, making it difficult to enforce rights.

Different tests exist for employment status under the Equality Act 2010, and the Employment Rights Act 1996, the two main statutes at the core of employment law.

In the Employment Rights Act 1996 (ERA) an employee means 'an individual who has entered into or works under ... a contract of employment'. The ERA defines a 'worker', however, as an individual who has:

entered into or works under … a contract of employment or; any other contract whether express or implied … whereby the individual undertakes to do or perform personally any work or services for another party to the contract whose status is not by virtue of the contract that of a client or customer of any profession or business undertaking carried on by the individual.

These definitions are present across employment law. However, both the ERA and the Equality Act 2010 have 'extended' definitions for certain purposes (in particular for the whistleblowing provisions in the ERA).

Those who do not fall within any of the legislative categories are lumped together as 'self-employed'.

These definitions are not particularly realistic in the context of modern working practices and the proliferating 'gig economy'.

Flexibility may well have some upsides, but recent years have served to show that sham devices and zero-hour contracts can exacerbate existing disadvantage and have fuelled a 'race to the bottom' for employment rights. Groups particularly affected are often those with one or more protected characteristics: women, disabled people, minority Black and ethnic people, older people, and those in certain categories of economic vulnerability (for example, migrant workers, domestic workers, temporary or fixed-term workers, and so on).

Aside from the economic injustice, the uncertainty in the present law of employment status leads to satellite litigation. Employment tribunals are frequently detained by disputes as to whether or not a given claimant is in fact an 'employee' or a 'worker' or neither. The substantive claim is left in abeyance for months or, more likely, years.

Our view is that a single employment status is needed, simplifying the law. The single status could be defined as follows: 'An "employee" means an individual (A) who is engaged by another person (B) to work for B or on B's behalf, other than where the engagement is genuinely for the purposes of a business operated by A.' This definition would apply to all employment rights, across both the ERA and the Equality Act 2010 (and thus the concept of a 'worker' would become otiose).

This is similar to a definition suggested by the Institute for Employment Rights,[1] who also suggest (and we agree) that there should be a rebuttable presumption that an individual is an employee unless the contrary is proved.

It is to be hoped that the definition provides simplicity and certainty. The use of the term 'engaged' ought to find purchase in all aspects of the labour economy but exclude genuine volunteering. It nevertheless does not rely on there being a contract (express, implied, umbrella or whatever) between A and the person for whom he or she is providing work. Further, the definition of the employer as the entity for whom A is engaged to provide work ought to cut through the usual avoidance devices: personal service companies, agency arrangements, and so on.

The definition may mean, in some circumstances, that there is more than one employer. On the one hand that may be no bad thing (and, for example, companies and employment agencies can come to commercial arrangements between themselves as to indemnities and the like). On the other, if it gives rise to difficulties in specific circumstances, legislation can make accommodations.

His Majesty's Employment Commissioner

The UK is unusual in that it has no labour rights commissioner or central or local regulator tasked with policing employment rights. The enforcement of the rights that successive Labour governments have established, and the wider labour movement has campaigned for, is instead delegated to individuals, who are required to act themselves through the employment tribunal system, bearing their own legal costs for doing so. There are three statutory bodies with roles in enforcing certain employment and allied rights, but each has been hamstrung by political and budgetary decisions.

First, the Health and Safety Executive (HSE) prosecutes companies and individuals for breaches of the Health and Safety at Work Act 1974 or specific workplace regulations made under

---

[1] K. Ewing, J. Hendy and C. Jones (eds), *Rolling out the Manifesto for Labour Law*, IER, September 2018.

it. However, cuts and policy changes directed by successive Conservative governments have turned the HSE into a largely reactive agency, rather than one that can proactively investigate compliance. Second, His Majesty's Revenue and Customs has some role in enforcing the National Minimum Wage (NMW), pursuant to section13 of the National Minimum Wage Act 1998. However, its efficacy is at best patchy, with only 13 per cent of employers paying below the NMW being caught according to research by the Resolution Foundation.[2] Lastly, the Equalities and Human Rights Commission occasionally supports individuals to bring claims in narrow circumstances under powers granted by the Equality Act 2006, but its involvement is limited.

A Labour government should merge the functions of these bodies insofar as they relate to employment rights and health and safety at work into the remit of a new commissioner for work – His Majesty's (HM) Employment Commissioner – responsible for proactively investigating breaches of employment, equality and health and safety laws in the workplace.

The Commissioner could reduce the burden on employment tribunals and reduce legal costs for employees and employers by issuing warning notices, fines and orders for compensation – just as the Pensions Regulator and Pensions Ombudsman does – with employers being given the choice of paying or appealing to the employment tribunal or High Court. We do not propose that the Commissioner would usurp the role of employment tribunals. Individuals would still, of course, be able to bring employment tribunal claims themselves about their own circumstances.

The Commissioner's focus would, instead, be on finding systemic and widespread noncompliance, or on test cases and setting broad principles – rather than intervening in fact-specific disputes about the rights and wrongs of one-off disputes (that is, about conduct dismissals, and so on).

This model is adopted in many developed economies – the booming economy of California is subject to the oversight of such a commissioner, whose stated mission

---

[2]   https://www.resolutionfoundation.org/app/uploads/2020/01/Under-the-wage-floor.pdf.

is to ensure a just day's pay in every workplace in the State and to promote economic justice through robust enforcement of labour laws. By combating wage theft, protecting workers from retaliation, and educating the public, the Commissioner would put earned wages into workers' pockets and help level the playing field for law-abiding employers.[3]

Such a body could be funded from the fines it levies against employers who are in breach of their obligations, just as existing Ombudsmen are now in other sectors. It is important to emphasise that such a commissioner would be to the benefit of legitimate businesses who obey the law and who currently face unfair competition and the prospect of being undercut by competitors who are willing to deprive individuals of key statutory rights on the basis that they are unlikely to face any real jeopardy from doing so due to the hurdles to employment tribunal claims succeeding.

Extended tribunal time limits in parental and maternity discrimination cases

Time limits under the relevant regulations protecting parental leave are extremely tight. New parents must generally bring claims within three months for them to be heard in employment tribunals. This rule undermines parental leave protections, forcing new parents to spend time considering legal action when they should be focusing on parenthood. While there are exceptions, these are narrow and employers and their lawyers will look to take advantage of time limits to defeat parental discrimination claims or dissuade employees from bringing them in the first place.

Our view is that Labour should accept the recommendations of 'Pregnant then Screwed' and extend the tribunal time limit to bring a claim under section 18 of the Equality Act 2010, the Maternity and Parental Leave etc. Regulations 1999, the Paternity and Adoption Leave Regulations 2002 and the Shared Parental Leave Regulations 2014 etc. to six months.

---

[3] https://www.dir.ca.gov/dlse/.

Qualified one-way costs shifting in worker status and pregnancy discrimination cases

In the civil courts, the normal order at the end of the case is that the 'loser' pays the costs of the 'winner'. In major litigation, costs can run into the millions of pounds.

The general rule in employment tribunals, however, is that individuals pay their own legal costs, irrespective of whether they win or lose their case (except in cases of genuinely unreasonable conduct). That principle is generally sound: it allows workers to bring cases with little risk that their employer will be able threaten them with financial ruin if they are unsuccessful.

However, the rule in employment tribunals that each party bears their own costs can make it unviable for individuals to bring complex claims.

Take a new mother who has an arguable case that she has been discriminated against by being made redundant because of her maternity. Her claim may be worth £20,000 and have a 50 per cent chance of success. But her lawyers' fees to fight a case at tribunal are likely to exceed £10,000, money she is unlikely to have. She may well make the understandable decision that litigating is not a financially sensible option. The protections against pregnancy discrimination are empty if they cannot be enforced.

The same dilemma faces a worker who is falsely designated as self-employed. Say a building company fails to pay holiday pay over many years and gives bogus self-employment contracts to individuals who are really employees. Any individual's claim may be worth a fraction of the legal costs required to fight it.

The solution we propose is that the existing system in the civil courts for personal injury claims be adopted in limited classes of employment claims.

If an employment tribunal finds that the employer has broken the law and has falsely designated someone as self-employed or discriminated against them because of their pregnancy, then that employer should be required to pay the employee's legal costs. If the claim is unsuccessful, then the current system of no costs orders would remain.

The benefits would be substantial. Just as in cases involving personal injuries, a conditional fee agreement market would emerge, with lawyers willing to take on the risk of representing pregnant women and falsely self-employed workers against their employers in the expectation that they would be paid if and when (and only if and when) the case succeeded.

This system has the considerable benefit of creating a way of giving individuals access to legal advice they could otherwise not afford. Lawyers would (as they already do in the civil courts) consider the strengths of the claims and be paid out of any costs order that the employment tribunal makes.

For trade unions, who already pay legal costs to support vulnerable workers, they would recover the fees that they expended if cases were successful, making it viable to run more cases.

We recommend limiting this system to specific types of cases to accord with political priorities. It would provide a powerful tool to combat pregnancy discrimination and bogus self-employment.

Unifying the disjointed employment justice system

Employment lawyers often have to break bizarre news to their clients about *where* they can sue. If they want to bring a discrimination or unfair dismissal claim, they must do so in the employment tribunal. If they want to also bring a claim for breach of contract worth over £25,000 they must go to the High Court at the same time, duplicating their legal costs. If they want an injunction to prevent them being dismissed, they must head to the High Court; but if they want an interim order reinstating them, they must head to the employment tribunal. If they have suffered a personal injury as a result of their treatment, they *might* be able to bring that claim, or they might not, depending on the kind of injury and the way it was caused. It is common for individuals to be forced to fight in the civil courts and employment tribunal simultaneously. There is all manner of risk in doing so when issues like *res judicata* (a legal rule that says, broadly, that once a matter has been raised or decided it cannot be reopened) come into play.

This confusing system has few, if any, benefits. It treats employment tribunals as somehow inferior, despite the fact that they are trusted to adjudicate some of the most financially and socially significant cases that come before the court system.

However, pending the adoption of those recommendations, we also recommend that Labour amend the Employment Tribunals Act 1996 and the Employment Tribunals (Constitution and Rules of Procedure) Regulations 2013 to allow High Court judges and section 9 Senior Courts Act 1981 judges to sit in the employment tribunal on the most significant cases, as referred to them by regional employment judges.

A contractual right to holiday pay

The right to holiday pay, found in the Working Time Regulations 1998, is fundamental to allowing workers time to spend recuperating and with friends and family. However, enforcement of holiday pay is patchy because of holes in the employment justice system. For example, if an employee considers that he or she is suffering an underpayment of 20 per cent on holiday pay (perhaps because bonuses and commissions are not being taken into account), then litigating is not an appetising option: the process will take years and legal costs will exhaust any benefit accrued at the end. An employee might be tempted to make such a claim *after* their employment has ended, but the strict three-month limitation provision within Regulation 30 of the Working Time Regulations 1998 often prevents this.

We propose a simple fix. If the right to paid holiday took force as an implied contractual term, rather than a statutory right, it could be enforced by a breach of contract claim on the termination of employment or in the civil courts and subject to the six-year limitation deadline for breach of contract claims. This would stop the effect of the three-month tribunal deadline either dissuading enforcement or forcing workers to go to employment tribunals in undue haste to avoid becoming time-barred.

Funding employment tribunals with statutory penalties

At the heart of the problem with the employment justice system is the catastrophe of under-resourcing employment tribunals – leaving workers waiting many years for their claims to be resolved. Justice delayed is often, quite literally, justice denied. Hearings often take so long to be listed that companies are out of business by the time they are ordered to pay their workers the wages and compensation they owe – meaning the wronged individual will receive nothing (and may have expended many thousands of pounds on legal costs).

Resourcing employment tribunals will cost money. More judges and more tribunal staff are required, urgently. But there will be many demands on taxpayers' money. So, we recommend a scheme to fund employment tribunals – at least partly – from the pockets of those who have been found to be in breach of statutory protections.

It is important to remember that employment rights and cases are not private disputes between two commercial parties. They are the hearings of employers accused of breaking the laws passed by Parliament, often for their own gain. Simultaneously, it is worth noting that a small minority of individuals use the employment tribunal system abusively, making claims that they have no honest belief in the truth of, and acting in such a way that causes the other parties, and the tribunal service, to incur unnecessary costs and expend resources that could have been used on others.

Our experience is that the vast majority of employers wish to follow the law. But some do not. Sometimes it is cheaper not to follow the law, and individuals who are in positions of control in companies may choose to jettison the statutory rights of their employees, safe in the knowledge that any adverse consequences will not fall on them personally, although they may be personally rewarded by the gains that their approach causes the company to accrue.

Our view is that such individuals and employers should no longer be subsidised by the taxpayer. Where an individual has deliberately or recklessly breached the employment rights Parliament has passed, tribunals should have the power to impose financial penalties. Those financial penalties could and should help fund the tribunal system.

A power to award financial penalties already exists under section 12A of the Employment Tribunals Act 1996, but it is circumscribed and underused – with penalties being very rare and low in amount. Labour should change this, creating a duty for the tribunal to consider whether to impose a financial penalty every time it determines that an employer has breached any of the worker's rights.

Further, unlike in cases under the Health and Safety at Work Act 1974, individuals who act through companies are at no risk of incurring financial penalties themselves. Where an individual has caused or induced or instructed another to breach statutory employment rights, and done so deliberately or recklessly, they should be jointly and severally liable for such a penalty.

This reform would likely yield an immediate change of attitude in board rooms. If, for example, the chief executive officer of a large company sought advice about a plan to immediately dismiss their entire workforce and employ agency replacements – deliberately disregarding consultation requirements in the Trade Union and Labour Relations (Consolidation) Act 1992 – their lawyers would inform them that they risked fines personally. Individual company directors and shadow directors can currently be found personally liable for breaches of insolvency, company, tax, and health and safety laws – why should statutory employment protections not have the same status?

Equally, under the Company Directors Disqualification Act 1986, directors of companies can be disqualified for breaches of companies legislation. Labour should consider giving employment tribunals the power to recommend the disqualification of a director where there has been an egregious breach of statutory employment law. This power would, no doubt, be used sparingly, but it would ensure compliance with employment laws was not an afterthought.

Better protection for whistleblowers

When Labour introduced the Public Interest Disclosure Act in 1998, it was supported by employers and employees alike as a way of ensuring that workers did not suffer as a consequence of drawing attention to poor or illegal practices.

The next Labour government should build on this foundation. The list of protected disclosure categories should be extended, because certain disclosures (for example, breaches of important but non-binding industry or regulatory standards) currently do not qualify for protection.

Bizarrely, as the current law stands, workers are only protected if their employer retaliates against them for disclosing information and are *not* protected under the whistleblowing provisions for refusing to do criminal or dangerous acts. This creates a perverse situation, in which employers can argue that it was the workers' refusal that caused the dismissal, not their disclosure of information. This loophole should be closed. Workers need to be protected from detriment and dismissal arising from the surrounding subject matter of the disclosure, and not just the narrow making of the disclosure itself.

Protecting health and safety at work

One of the first workplace reforms introduced by the Cameron–Clegg coalition government was to implement Lord Young's report on health and safety at work. This removed the right for workers to rely on statutory duties in claims for personal injuries at work, a right which had existed since the late 19th century. Now, workers have to prove negligence as well as breach of regulations. This has left workers less well protected at work and has added cost and uncertainty to the process of obtaining compensation for workplace injuries.

Labour should reverse this retrograde step, by repealing section 69 of the Enterprise and Regulatory Reform Act 2013 and providing again for a direct right of civil action for breaches of regulations issued under the Health and Safety at Work etc. Act 1974.

Workers who suffer multiple breaches of their employment rights – say, discrimination, resulting in a psychiatric injury; or a workplace accident for which they are unfairly dismissed – are currently forced to divide their claims between the civil courts and the employment tribunal. But the worker who starts a discrimination or harassment claim in the employment tribunal could find the civil courts barred to them for their personal injury claim, because of the operation of arcane rules about court process. Labour can rationalise this system and make it considerably simpler for individual workers to navigate. First, courts and tribunals should have a statutory discretion to disapply the common law rule in *Henderson v Henderson* where cross-jurisdictional claims arise. Second, there should be a power to transfer claims, or individual components of claims, from one jurisdiction to another, without the worker suffering a limitation penalty from having to start a new claim (or falling foul of rules like issue estoppel and *res judicata*).

Victims of workplace bullying and harassment currently have to show either that (1) their treatment fell within the terms of the Equality Act, (2) it was caused by the employer's negligence or (3) that it met the high threshold set out in the Protection from Harassment Act 1997 (essentially, that the conduct was serious enough to be criminal). This leaves too many workplace victims of non-discriminatory harassment unprotected. Labour should legislate for a new general duty on employers to protect their employees from non-Equality Act harassment at the hands of their bosses and fellow workers.

Workers who do successfully sue their employer for negligence can find themselves denied compensation because of a lack of insurance cover, either because the insurer has withdrawn support for the employer, because the insurer is bankrupt or because the employer never complied with its duty to take out insurance in the first place. Before it lost office, the last Labour government was making plans for an 'insurer of last resort' for employers' liability claims, modelled on the Motor Insurers' Bureau and funded by the insurance industry. The next Labour government should follow through on this reform and establish an Employers' Liability Insurers' Bureau to ensure that victims of workplace accidents and diseases do not go uncompensated.

At present, the justice system for workplace accidents (as for all personal injury claims) is purely compensatory: the victim is paid no less, but no more, than their loss. This fails to recognise that, in certain exceptional cases, the poor conduct of wrongdoers requires appropriate recognition, both for justice to be done to the claimant and for egregious wrongdoing to be penalised and discouraged. Labour should legislate to allow exemplary damages to be awarded in appropriate cases in the torts of negligence and breach of statutory duty.

Justice for victims of industrial diseases

Britain has a tragic and disgraceful record on the most serious industrial diseases, reflecting a history of exposing workers to harmful substances – our death rate from asbestos-related disease, for example, is one of the highest in the developed world.

The current process for compensating victims of the worst industrial diseases does not always work well. Courts can only award compensation either as a lump sum or as a Periodical Payment Order (PPO), but the present structure of PPOs is too inflexible for it to work effectively to pay for expensive treatments for victims of asbestos-related cancers with an uncertain prognosis and life expectancy.

Labour should reform the Damages Act 1996 to allow a more flexible and responsive system for PPOs.

At present, victims in Scotland – but not in England and Wales – can recover damages for 'pleural plaques' (benign thickening of the lung lining caused by asbestos). Labour should permit victims across the UK to obtain just compensation for pleural plaques, with an option to pursue further remedies if their asbestos exposure causes other diseases to develop in the future.

The last Labour government legislated to make sure that victims of one form of asbestos disease – mesothelioma – could recover damages from any one of their former employers, even if they were exposed to asbestos by multiple employers. This was a welcome change but, as medical science in this area has moved on, having a special regime for mesothelioma specifically seems arbitrary when there are so many victims of other occupational diseases. The next Labour government should extend the principle already enshrined for mesothelioma claims in section 3 of the Compensation Act 2006 to all industrial diseases, so that demonstrating a material contribution to the development of the disease is sufficient to recover full damages on a joint and several basis.

Certain occupational diseases arise after many years of exposure to a harmful substance or process. Under the law as it currently stands, a new three-year limitation period begins with each wrongful exposure, meaning that some injured workers have needlessly complex procedural hurdles to cross in order to establish their claims. The formulation currently used in Equality Act protections – that limitation runs from the last in a series of connected wrongs – should be applied to these kinds of cumulative workplace conditions.

Improving the law for workplace accident victims

The Conservative government has consistently followed the desires of the insurance industry to reduce compensation and to increase the difficulty of bringing personal injury claims. But accidents caused by negligence create suffering and cost our economy dear. Labour should recognise the proper place of claims for personal injuries for all victims in both providing fair compensation and in discouraging dangerous and damaging conduct.

Labour should establish a Personal Injury Council (PIC) as a public body drawing in expertise from across the economy, to act as a balanced and permanent guardian of the public interest. The PIC should set the tariff for the recovery of general damages for pain, suffering and loss of amenity (a task currently given to the courts, and crystallised in guidelines issued by the Judicial College), and have a wide remit to review and set these guidelines. They should also be given the statutory power to set the level of the bereavement award in actions under the Fatal Accidents Act 1976, and to expand the list of dependents to whom such awards can be made (which is currently outdated and restrictive). Also, all funeral and memorial costs, which on the current law are arbitrarily divided, should become recoverable in fatal accidents claims.

The law is right to recognise the corrosive effect of dishonest claims on the integrity of the justice system. But, all too often, defendants use speculative or cynical accusations of dishonesty – sometimes on minor or peripheral aspects of a claim – as a way of discouraging claims, or as a naked negotiation tactic in settlements. This can put off honest claimants, worried by the catastrophic effect of costs awards if they are not believed. This is unjust for the vast majority of honest people who bring claims. While the law should still provide for consequences when claimants are found to be dishonest, the playing field needs to be levelled and abuses by defendants prevented. The next Labour government should amend section 57 of the Criminal Justice and Courts Act 2015 to provide costs and other penalties for a defendant who pursues a dishonesty defence which is subsequently dismissed and found to have been unreasonably raised.

Protecting National Health Service resources from negligent employers

The National Health Service (NHS) currently picks up the pieces after accidents and illnesses caused by negligent employers. There is currently a system for NHS charges to be repaid by compensators, but the tariff and cap are too restrictive. The next Labour government should reform the system for the recoupment of NHS costs from compensators so that the taxpayer does not pick up the tab for private negligence.

Conclusion

An incoming Labour government will doubtlessly introduce a variety of new and improved rights for workers. That is welcome. But to be meaningful, rights must be enforceable. As things stand, employment rights on the statute book are too often inaccessible for ordinary workers.

If workers cannot access the statutory rights that the labour movement has worked to legislate for, 'laws are liable to become a dead letter, the work done by Parliament may be rendered nugatory, and the democratic election of Members of Parliament may become a meaningless charade', as Lord Reed said in *R (Unison) v Lord Chancellor* [2017] UKSC 51 at paragraph 68.

Summary of key proposals

- The establishment of HM Employment Commissioner, a consolidated regulator able to directly enforce employment rights.
- Qualified one-way costs shifting in certain employment tribunal cases.
- Extended time limits in maternity discrimination cases.
- Action to protect health and safety at work.

3

Family justice reform

Michael Horton and Hannah Gomersall

Introduction

The family justice system is called upon to provide security and answers at all stages: from the beginnings (via surrogacy and adoption) to children and adults in crisis, to acrimonious family breakdown.

Roughly 270,000 families turn to the family courts each year. That does not include the significant additional number of unmarried couples seeking help from civil courts for resolution of property disputes on breakdown. The system is beset with delays, obstacles to accessing justice and, in places, an inadequate legislative framework.

This chapter sets out how Labour can reform the family justice framework to better serve children and families. This does not address every area but focuses on key proposals covering court practice and required law reform.

First, we suggest that the Family Drug and Alcohol Court (FDAC) be rolled out nationally and comprehensively. We propose this successful and holistic model of supporting families in crisis is expanded to areas beyond substance misuse. We highlight how upfront investment in this model has the potential to save significant sums later down the line, as well as giving children and parents a better chance in life.

We outline the Law Commission's recommendations on surrogacy reform, an area which requires legislative reform.

In light of Labour's announced support to reform laws around cohabitation, we set out proposals and factors to be considered. More and more people live together without choosing to marry or enter into a civil partnership and the number of children brought up in these families continues to grow. Our laws must keep up with the changing shape of families and it must be right that the family court has a role to play in dealing with the financial consequences of relationship breakdowns outside of marriage.

Finally, we propose Labour adopts the recommendations of the Law Commission's 2022 proposals to reform the law around weddings. The proposals would make it easier for couples to get married and to have a greater choice of the form of ceremony. By changing to a system based on approval of officiants, rather than premises, it will also make it easier for couples who have a religious ceremony to have their marriage legally recognised.

Expanding the Family Drug and Alcohol Court

A holistic, hopeful and cost-saving model for family crisis, trauma and domestic abuse

A new Labour government should ensure that the FDAC, currently only available in limited areas in the country, is deployed nationwide and expanded in scope. It saves money and improves outcomes for children and families.

At least 143,469 children in England were subject to family court proceedings in the year 2022–3.[1] Approximately one-third of these cases were public law proceedings where the local authority asserts a child has suffered or is at risk of suffering significant harm and the court is asked to consider removing children from their parents on care plans of adoption, long-term foster care or kinship care. The statutory timetable for proceedings is 26 weeks, although in 2022–3 the average duration was 46 weeks[2] (in large part due to stretched professional and court resources).

---

[1] Cafcass, 'Trends over time', 2022–2023, at www.cafcass.gov.uk/about-us/our-data.

[2] Cafcass, 'Annual data summaries', at www.cafcass.gov.uk/about-us/our-data/.

The concerns presenting to court are overwhelmingly grounded in the 'toxic trio' of domestic abuse, poor mental health and substance misuse. The bleak part: only 12.5 per cent of children in standard care proceedings are likely to be reunified with their primary carer by the conclusion of the case and 54.7 per cent of children will be placed in local authority care. Only 8.1 per cent of parents will have ceased to misuse drugs or alcohol by the end of proceedings.[3]

These poor outcomes are expensive: the emotional cost to these families is profound, as is the financial cost to the state. There are the obvious costs to local authority foster care budgets, to children's services resources, and to courts' and legal aid budgets (including from the inevitable removals of subsequent children). The year 2023 saw the 15th consecutive annual rise in the number of children in care.[4] Four in five local authorities overspent on their children's services budget in 2021–2[5] and the Institute for Fiscal Studies noted that by 2018 English authorities spent nearly half of children's services budgets on the 82,170 children then in care. Less obviously, there are the costs of the fall-out from the cycle of trauma and loss: repeated police and paramedic attendance for parents returning to abusive relationships, alcoholism and substance misuse; the burden on the criminal justice and prison systems of grieving parents (and young people in the flawed unstable care system) turning to criminality; mental health budgets straining at the seams of trying to assist parents and children in crisis. This bleak intergenerational cycle of trauma continues: 40 per cent of mothers in care proceedings had themselves grown up in local authority care.[6]

---

[3] Foundations & National Centre for Social Research, 'Evaluation of Family Drug and Alcohol Courts', 2023, p 9, at https://foundations.org.uk/wp-content/uploads/2024/02/FDAC-report.pdf.

[4] M. Samuel, '15th consecutive rise in care population in England over past year DfE data shows', *Community Care*, 20 November 2023.

[5] County Councils Network, County Spotlight, 'Children's services: putting young people and families at the heart of care', 2023, p 5, at https://www.countycouncilsnetwork.org.uk/wp-content/uploads/Spotlight-Childrens-Services-FINAL.pdf.

[6] K. Broadhurst, J. Harwin and M. Shaw, *Vulnerable Birth Mothers and Recurrent Care Proceedings*, Centre for Child & Family Justice Research, Lancaster University, 2017, p 25, para 3.3.

The good news? There is a demonstrably better way of doing things. The FDAC has been operating since its founding by DJ Crichton in London in 2008 (with three years of pilot funding provided by the then Labour government). It is based on a 'problem-solving' approach which seeks to encourage parents to believe recovery and change are possible. It provides a multidisciplinary team, independent of the local authority. Substance misuse specialists, social workers, psychologists, psychiatrists, domestic abuse specialists and parent mentors provide intensive supports to parents. A specially trained judge facilitates regular fortnightly court reviews to provide structure, authority and motivation (lawyers only attending when there are significant decisions to be made). Parents are offered individual or group therapy, skills development, referrals for appropriate treatment or practical services such as housing.

Study after study has demonstrated this approach to work. The latest August 2023 Foundations report found 52 per cent of children were reunified with a primary carer by the end of proceedings via the FDAC model (as against the pitiful 12.5 per cent in standard proceedings) and 33.6 per cent of parents had ceased to misuse drugs or alcohol by the end of proceedings (versus 8.1 per cent). These results were also demonstrated to be durable over time post-proceedings. FDAC cases were significantly less likely to result in costly final contested hearings and rarely required external expert instructions (unlike most standard cases). Despite some extensions to give parents the opportunity to show sustained abstinence, the average FDAC case still finished three weeks earlier than the average for standard proceedings.

The Centre for Justice Innovation demonstrated that within two years of the start of the case, for each £1 spent on FDAC, £2.30 was saved. Each FDAC team (hearing 30 cases a year and covering three local authorities each) was found to pay back its annual operating cost and generating additional net savings of £271,994 in-year, and, post-proceedings, generating additional savings of £527,222.

Despite this evidenced human and financial success, the uncertain and decentralised funding model has obstructed the roll-out. In 2018 the Conservative government ceased its funding for the FDAC National Unit, despite a Care Crisis Review that same year reporting on a worrying rise in care proceedings and children in care. In 2022–3 just 376 children had their cases diverted to the FDAC, representing a tiny fraction of those subject to care proceedings. Kent, Somerset, and Cardiff and the Vale FDACs have all recently closed due to lack of funding. Given central government has declined to provide the resources required, it is left to individual local authorities to decide whether to buy-in without the upfront resources to do so. Just 38 local authorities in England and Wales presently participate in the FDAC, leaving children and families subject to stark 'postcode lotteries' and areas as notable as Merseyside without any provision. The system is reliant on local champions attempting to persuade a patchwork of public bodies to renew funding every few years. For example, in Bedfordshire, a persuasive case on the cost–benefit analysis has resulted in the police and public health services providing partial funding, for now.

Expansion of the successful FDAC model could be transformative to child protection including in areas beyond substance misuse. A high proportion of parents involved with FDAC proceedings have experienced domestic abuse (with 28 per cent reporting they were still victims of domestic abuse at the start of proceedings). Substance misuse is of course one manifestation of trauma, low self-esteem or adverse childhood experiences in the same way as domestic abuse (both perpetration of and repeated vulnerability to). The FDAC model of providing intensive holistic (and often therapeutic) support for the vulnerable parent at the centre must be a preferential way of working with parents who are in proceedings due to repeated and severe domestic abuse.

Standard care proceedings are rooted in assessment from the outset. A parent who is struggling to protect their children and separate from an abusive partner feels damned either way: does she tell the social worker he turned up on the doorstep and she let him in last night? Or does the fear of her children being removed mean she stays silent only to be later condemned by professionals for dishonesty? This was an issue highlighted by Council of Europe's Committee on Social Affairs as long ago as January 2015, when a report on 'Social services in Europe: legislation and practice of the removal of children from their families in Council of Europe member states' highlighted (para 44):

> There is a particular problem which I was made aware
> of in the United Kingdom, but which may pose a

problem in several other countries, too: many mothers who are victims of domestic violence themselves seem to be re-victimised by the child protection system as the child witnessing such violence (or threats of it) is considered to be subject to emotional abuse and thus significant harm. This means that, if the mother has nowhere to turn to, her child can be taken away from her. This is a problem which should not be underestimated, as the impact of the crisis and the effect of austerity cuts on social services means that more and more mothers are now trapped in abusive relationships (with shelters closing) and afraid to signal domestic violence lest their children be taken away from them.

In standard care proceedings, it is social workers allocated to the *children* that are often required to swiftly assess the capacity of a vulnerable parent to change without having the time, training and resources to work alongside them, to encourage and support that change. Notwithstanding their vulnerabilities, rarely does a parent meet the high threshold for allocation of a social worker from the adult team. The FDAC model might provide the answers to the current challenges for victims (and perpetrators) of domestic abuse in care proceedings. The innovative process is rigorous and demanding but expects and enables honesty around alcohol/drug relapses to prevent the 'shame-spiral'. Self-esteem building, practical support, as well as an element of companionship and motivation through parent mentors are all principles which could transform the standard more punitive approach to victims of domestic abuse in care proceedings.

At a recent Centre for Justice Innovation event at the House of Lords, a mother who had been through the FDAC process spoke frankly about the process which led to her children returning to her care. She noted that "The first thing they said when I came in was 'What can we do for you?' That was huge. I never had someone ask, 'What can I do for you?' What I needed. I was always told what to do."[7] She also credited the FDAC with saving her life.

---

7   M. Fouzder, '"I will never forget my FDAC team": justice minister and Family Division president hear mother's success story', *Law Society Gazette*, 19 October 2023.

In the role of Shadow Health Secretary, Wes Streeting MP has been clear that Labour must put *prevention* at the heart of reshaping the National Health Service. Treating advanced-stage cancers are more costly and result in poor outcomes. Labour has accepted 'firefighting' is not a strategy for health but, instead, front-loaded investment for the right interventions at the right time saves both money and lives in the long run. This thinking must now be applied to the child protection and family justice system.

In 2008 the Labour government put its faith in the innovative pilot of FDAC, a model which has since garnered 15 years of evidence and independent evaluations to prove its human and financial success. At the October 2023 event in the House of Lords, the President of the Family Division, Sir Andrew McFarlane, praised the "life-changing" opportunity of FDAC, adding, "I do not understand why FDAC is not happening in every court. It is left to local courts, local authorities cobbling together money."

We hope the next Labour government will seize the opportunity to finish what it started in 2008: to end the postcode lottery of FDAC, to deploy the success of this model to other topics and areas of the family justice system, to invest in children and parents, and save money and lives in the process.

Surrogacy reform

Lady Hale, the former President of the Supreme Court, described the law in relation to surrogacy as being 'fragmented and in some ways obscure' (*Whittington Hospital NHS Trust v XX* [2020] UKSC 14). This remains the case.

The Law Commission has been reviewing this area of law and possible areas for reform. They published their final report in March 2023: 'Building families through surrogacy: a new law'.

One of the key areas the Law Commission identified as being problematic with the current legal framework for children born via surrogacy is that the intended parents are not recognised as a child's legal parents at birth. As a result, unless and until the intended parents obtain from the Family Court a parental order (the bespoke legal order that recognises the intended parents as parents and extinguishes the surrogate's status as a parent), they have no legal status with the child and are unable to make important decisions (for example, consent to medical treatment). To remedy this, the Law Commission has proposed a new pathway that would enable intended parents to be recognised at birth as a child's legal parents. This would only be available in domestic cases.

In international cases, we would invite the incoming government to consider the creation of a designated list of countries for children born via surrogacy, akin to The Adoption (Recognition of Overseas Adoptions) Order 2013. In such cases there could be automatic recognition of parentage orders obtained overseas in surrogacy cases which would prevent the need for intended parents to apply for family court orders in this jurisdiction.

Cohabitation reform

More and more people live together without choosing to marry or enter into a civil partnership. The number of children brought up in these families continues to grow. On relationship breakdown, the family court has little or no role in dealing with the financial consequences of the relationship breakdown. The Child Maintenance Service may be called upon to deal with financial support for the children. Any dispute about the house must be decided in accordance with the general law of property, which often does not recognise non-financial contributions to the family. The legal system does nothing to improve the lot of women and children when these relationships break down.

The Law Commission proposed back in 2006 that the courts should have the ability to adjust the property rights of such couples on relationship breakdown. The law in Scotland was changed in 2006, and their Law Commission has recently recommended changes to improve their law, reflecting the experience of over 15 years of the law in practice. Yet the Conservative government has tried to kick this issue into the long grass. We welcomed the announcement made by the Shadow Attorney General at the party conference in October 2023 that an incoming Labour government would take action to reform the law in this area.

The question is not, therefore, *whether* there should be reform, but *what* that reform should be. Back in 2015, we argued that an incoming government might wish to consider an opt-in system – similar to the French *PACS* or *pacte civile* system. This has the advantage of giving these couples a real choice – they can get married or have a civil partnership, do nothing, or have a relationship which is legally recognised but does not have the full wide-ranging legal consequences of marriage or civil partnership. It does not impose legal obligations on couples who may have deliberately eschewed the formal commitment of marriage or civil partnership. The introduction of such a system, with the attendant publicity, would be a wake-up call for those who believed themselves to be secure as 'common law' wives – when in fact, of course, no such thing exists.

But there are drawbacks to an opt-in system. It presupposes that both members of the couple will be able to make a free and informed choice as to how their relationship should be governed. If a person through fear or ignorance does not opt in, on relationship breakdown they would still be vulnerable and find themselves in a position where the law does not recognise their non-financial contribution to the relationship. Most commentators now favour an opt-out system. Under this approach, where a couple live together for a qualifying period, say two years, or have a child together, they would automatically be eligible to apply to the court on relationship breakdown. The court would be able to adjust their property rights where these did not reflect the value of a contribution or sacrifice made by one of the parties.

Assuming that an incoming government were to choose an opt-out system (such as that recommended by the Law Commission in 2006 and as has been the law in Scotland since 2006), the real debate therefore centres on the details of such a scheme. We consider there are some difficult issues. We do not consider that a person who is eligible to apply should necessarily lose their right to bring a property law claim (especially if they would receive more under the existing law). We also consider that 'pre-cohabitation contracts' should be legally binding.

Pre-nuptial agreements are no longer a novelty in family law in England and Wales. They are given effect unless they are unfair – and, provided they were entered into of both parties' free will and with a full appreciation of their implications, they will not be unfair unless they leave one party with unmet financial needs. But the rationale for the court making an order between separating cohabitants will not to be to alleviate financial hardship or meet financial dependence. It will be to compensate one party for a non-financial contribution or sacrifice. If both parties sign up to an agreement, with their eyes open, the law ought to respect their autonomy and their decisions.

In relation to child support, we propose:

- couples should be able to make legally binding agreements for child support without having to have a Child Maintenance Service (CMS) calculation imposed on them;
- the family court should be able to make maintenance orders, in addition to child support determined by the CMS, for one parent to contribute towards the childcare costs incurred by the other parent.

Financial remedies

The law which governs how courts should decide on the family finances on the divorce or dissolution of civil partnership was first introduced in 1973. It has been amended several times since then. Some say it is showing its age. The Law Commission is undertaking a review of the law, and we welcome this review. An incoming Labour government should give priority to implementing its proposals.

The recent Nuffield research, *Fair Shares*, published in November 2023, indicates that couples welcome the flexibility of the current law which allows them to tailor a financial solution to their divorce to their individual circumstances. We consider that a more formulaic approach to the resolution of family finance cases, while superficially attractive, is unlikely to do justice in all cases and may end up causing more problems than it is intended to solve.

Marriage

Back in 2015 we proposed making it easier for people to get married, and a relaxation of some of the rules as to where people could have their wedding. We also considered it should be easier for couples who want a religious marriage to have that religious marriage recognised under the law of the land. The case of *Akhter v Khan* in 2020 emphasised these current difficulties where a woman who had an Islamic nikah marriage, and who was promised a civil ceremony to follow, was unable to have that nikah recognised by the legal system. Although married in the eyes of her community and her religion, and under the law of a country in which they lived for several years during their marriage, under the law of England and Wales they were mere cohabitants.

In 2022 the Law Commission published their report, *Celebrating Marriage: A New Weddings Law*. These proposals would make it easier for couples to get married and to have greater choice of the form of ceremony. By changing to a system based on approval of officiants, rather than premises, it will also make it easier for couples who have a religious ceremony to have their marriage legally recognised. We propose that this report be implemented at the earliest possible opportunity.

Conclusion

The family justice system is overwhelmed with backlogs of cases in every area: public and private children cases, financial remedy and family breakdown disputes. The numbers of children in care have risen for the 15th consecutive year and local authority children's services are in financial crisis (in addition to the demands that children and families in crisis are placing on other public services). It is against this backdrop that immediate reform is needed to break the cycle of bleak outcomes. A blueprint is ready to go: the FDAC model having already demonstrated better outcomes for children and families in a cost-effective way, its roll-out having been unnecessarily stifled by a lack of political will and central funding. This is a model whose evidenced successes might also be deployed in other areas of the family justice system, for example, in cases where domestic abuse is raised as an issue. Finally, our proposals to update marriage ceremonies, surrogacy and cohabitation law ensures that statute keeps pace with the changing shape of the family.

Summary of key proposals

- To roll-out the FDAC nationally, ending the postcode lottery and improving outcomes for children and families.
- To explore whether the FDAC model can be successfully deployed in other areas of the family justice system, for example, in cases featuring domestic abuse and mental health difficulties.
- In domestic surrogacy cases, to adopt the Law Commission's proposed pathway that would enable intended parents to be recognised at birth as a child's legal parents. In international surrogacy cases, to explore creating a list of designated countries in respect of which there would be automatic recognition of parentage orders obtained overseas.
- To rapidly implement cohabitation reform to ensure that non-financial contributions to the family (often by women) are recognised. There are benefits and drawbacks to both opt-in and opt-out systems, though we recommend pre-cohabitation contracts should be respected (just as pre-nuptial agreements are increasingly used for couples who choose to marry).
- To consider any proposals made by the Law Commission for reform of financial remedies on divorce, though retaining the existing flexibility for individual circumstances.
- Update marriage law to a system based on approval of officiants, rather than premises.

4

Criminal justice

Laura Janes

Introduction

The criminal justice system is broken. It does not work as intended: it is beset with chaos and delays and creates more harm at every level. With the exception of women and children, the prison population has soared in recent decades, and is projected to increase further. Over a third of those who are incarcerated are convicted of a further offence in a year. The pandemic of violence against women and girls is at an all-time high. The criminal justice system for adults (unlike the system for children which aims to prevent offending) has no clear aim or purpose in statute.

Despite claims by the last government to the contrary, the current criminal justice system side-lines the needs of those affected by it, instead adding on layers of complication to the criminal justice system that prolong the agony of the process.

Restorative justice approaches the system from a completely different perspective, focusing on what harm has been done, and how it can be reduced and prevented in the future. It is not an alternative to punishment (although where appropriate it can be), but actively strives to achieve safer communities.

Something different is required if we are to build safe, respectful communities. Using restorative justice approaches, many of which have been used in educational settings and other jurisdictions to great effect, the system can focus on what really matters. We need to reset the agenda and make it clear that the entire purpose of the criminal justice system is to prevent offending and reduce harm. A new cohort of practitioners, trained in restorative approaches, could transform the experiences of all those affected by crime. This could involve the provision of a mixture of practical, legal and emotional support as well as traditional opportunities for contact between those who have harmed and those who have been harmed.

Given the pandemic of violence against women and girls, the initial roll-out should focus on women affected by crime to ensure that we meaningfully tackle this important issue. This will also ensure that the development of restorative approaches in our criminal justice system is firmly rooted in the need to acknowledge and prevent the scourge of violence against women and girls.

The current system is not fit for purpose

The statutory aim of the youth justice system is to prevent offending. This was provided for by section 37 of the Crime and Disorder Act 1998 as part of the Labour government's commitment to addressing the causes of crime.[1] To facilitate this, the Act also provided for the creation of multi-agency teams including a mixture of law enforcement and specialist workers. The law governing children in conflict with the law allows for a range of outcomes beyond purely punitive ones, including a range of community orders that can also include supportive interventions.

The number of children in custody has dropped in the last 20 years by over 70 per cent.[2] By contrast, the adult justice system has no statutory aim at all. A combination of provisions hints towards specific aspects of the system working towards rehabilitation, but an overall purpose of preventing offending is conspicuously absent. With a few exceptions, the options for adults who break the law are almost entirely punitive. In the last 20 years the number of adults in prison has increased by around

---

[1]   Crime and Disorder Act 1998.
[2]   J. Beard, 'Youth custody', Research Briefing, 2022, at https://researchbriefings. files.parliament.uk/documents/CBP-8557/CBP-8557.pdf.

37 per cent: the overall prison population increased from around 64,000 in 2000[3] to over 87,000 by the end of 2023.[4] Women accounted for around 4 per cent of the prison population (3,529) at the end of 2023[5] and that figure has remained relatively stable for several decades: it was just over 5 per cent in 2020.[6] The vast majority of offending is by adult men and almost all women in the criminal justice system will have suffered physical or sexual violence by men. David Lammy noted in evidence to the Justice Committee in 2019 that the vast majority of women he met in the criminal justice system were 'there because of a man and because of exploitation'.[7]

The pandemic of violence against women

The pandemic of violence against women is now widely recognised but remains rife: As Labour Peer, Baroness Kennedy, has stated 'The truth is that a lot has happened but not enough has changed.'[8]

This sentiment, along with shocking up-to-date statistics, is echoed in a joint manifesto for ending violence against women and girls produced by a coalition of charities with specialisms in supporting women, published in September 2023:

> Whilst the government has repeatedly committed to ending VAWG as a priority, it remains the case that every three days, a woman in the UK is killed by a man and one in four women experience domestic abuse in their lifetimes. In January 2023, the Office for National Statistics (ONS) latest crime figures stated

---

[3]   Home Office, 'Prison statistics, England and Wales 2000', 2001, at https://www.prisonpolicy.org/scans/prisonstats2000.pdf.

[4]   Ministry of Justice, 'Population bulletin: monthly, December 2023', https://www.gov.uk/government/publications/prison-population-figures-2023.

[5]   Ibid.

[6]   Home Office (n 3).

[7]   Justice Committee, 'Oral evidence: progress in the implementation of the Lammy Review's recommendations, HC 2086', 2019, at https://committees.parliament.uk/oralevidence/9156/pdf/.

[8]   H. Kennedy, *Misjustice: How British Law Is Failing Women*, Vintage, 2019.

that sexual offences are at the highest level recorded, whilst police-recorded offences relating to so-called honour-based abuse are also increasing. Overall, 1 in 6 children are estimated to have been subjected to sexual abuse, with girls being three times more likely to experience sexual abuse than boys, and women are 27 times more likely than men to receive online harassment and abuse. Behind the statistics and data, there are adult and child survivors of VAWG, and sometimes bereaved families, dealing with the trauma of these harms.[9]

The charities also recognise that most women in contact with the criminal justice system usually face considerable intersecting disadvantages, noting that 'more than half (57%) of women in prison report having experienced domestic violence, and 53% report having experienced emotional, physical or sexual abuse during childhood'.[10] The charities estimate that, in 2022, the economic and social costs of domestic abuse in England were just under £78 billion and recommend the development of enhanced support services for women to prevent the proliferation of violence against women and girls.[11]

In March 2023, the leader of the Labour Party, Keir Starmer, promised to halve violence against women if he became prime minister.[12] Proposals include the development of specialist 999 operators and the introduction of rape courts. The current data on rape cases shows that less than 5 per cent of rapes reported end up in a prosecution: in the year ending December 2022, less

---

9   End Violence Against Women and others, 'A whole-society approach to ending violence against women and girls: VAWG sector manifesto', 2023, at https://static1.squarespace.com/static/5aa98420f2e6b1ba0c874e42/t/65080f9fd643d63ef7d1ccd1/1695027108908/Full-VAWG-Manifesto-150923.pdf.

10   Ibid.

11   Ibid.

12   J. Elgot, 'Keir Starmer promises to halve violence against women as part of crime "mission"', *The Guardian*, 23 March 2023, at https://www.the guardian.com/politics/2023/mar/23/keir-starmer-promises-to-halve-violence-against-women-as-part-of-labour-crime-mission.

than 3,000 of 67,000 matters reported to the police proceeded to prosecution.[13]

Even the cases that do proceed to prosecution are subject to extensive delays. At the end of 2022, rape cases in the backlog had increased by 80 per cent since the end of 2020.[14] The process of going through the court system as a victim is often traumatic and distressing: in the words of one survivor, 'I spent a long time with him being traumatised yet even longer by the police and CPS being re-traumatised'.[15] It is no wonder then that people, and especially women and girls, are reluctant to report crime and cooperate with prosecutions. A survey by the former Victims' Commissioner, Dame Vera Baird, in 2021 found that just 43 per cent of victims would report a crime again based on their previous experiences of the criminal justice system and just half would attend court again, down from 67 per cent in 2020.[16]

This is not good enough and needs to change but, more than that, the harm needs to be prevented in the first place.

Reoffending rates are too high

To make matters worse, the toughest solution we have to offer, prison, doesn't make us safer or prevent crime once a person has been released. Data published in October 2023 shows that 33 per cent of adults had reoffended within a year of leaving prison or starting an order between October to December 2021.[17] That

---

[13] Centre for Women's Justice, the End Violence Against Women and Coalition, Imkaan and Rape Crisis England and Wales, 'What's changed? Government's "end-to-end" rape review – two years on', 2023, at https://www.endviolence againstwomen.org.uk/wp-content/uploads/2023/06/RapeReview Report-160623FINAL.pdf.

[14] Ibid.

[15] Ibid.

[16] Victims Commissioner, 'Victims' experience: annual survey', 2021, at https:// cloud-platform-e218f50a4812967ba1215eaecede923f.s3.amazonaws.com/ uploads/sites/6/2021/12/VC-2021-survey-of-victims-_amended-27_9_ 21-1.pdf.

[17] Ministry of Justice and National Statistics, 'Proven reoffending statistics quarterly bulletin, October to December 2021', 2023 at https://assets. publishing.service.gov.uk/media/6538e59180884d0013f71a82/PRSQ_ Bulletin_October_to_December_2021.pdf.

figure rose to over 50 per cent in respect of people sentenced to short prison sentences of under 12 months.[18]

While it is true that overall crime has reduced, and in the year ending June 2023, homicides fell by 10 per cent, the high levels of reoffending show a broken system that does not take harm reduction seriously.[19]

The system is not geared to protecting people from harm

The structure of the system is simply not geared towards what most of us need or want: the reduction of harm, including the prevention of offending in the first place and appropriate support for those who have been harmed. There is no overall statutory purpose to the criminal justice system that involves preventing offending or reducing harm as with the youth justice system. This lack of clear statutory purpose underpins the inadequacies of the current system. Rehabilitation of offenders to prevent reoffending appears in various statutes but there is no clear driving force to ensure it happens. For example, it is one purpose of sentencing in section 57 of the Sentencing Act 2020[20] but it is just one of five factors and there is no statutory duty to ensure it happens in practice. Similarly, section 1 of the Offender Management Act 2007 includes as one of six probation purposes 'the supervision and rehabilitation of persons charged with or convicted of offences'.[21] However, this does not apply to people who have not been charged yet, and there is nothing further in the Act to require effective rehabilitation and insufficient resources provided to probation officers to achieve it. It is also interesting that just one of the six probation purposes is geared towards victims and this purpose is just limited to 'giving information' to victims: this may help to explain why victims feel side-lined and insufficiently supported.[22]

---

[18] Ibid.

[19] Office for National Statistics, 'Crime in England and Wales: year ending June 2023', 2023, at https://www.ons.gov.uk/peoplepopulationandcommunity/crimeandjustice/bulletins/crimeinenglandandwales/yearendingjune2023.

[20] Sentencing Act 2020.

[21] Offender Management Act 2007.

[22] Ibid.

Victims are side-lined and their needs, including the need for offenders to be fully rehabilitated, are not met

The system as it currently operates is the state against the perpetrator, a system where society shares the burden of prosecuting offenders on behalf of the victim, acknowledging that a wrong done to any victim is done to the whole community. Attributing blame and dishing out punishment does not necessarily always centre the victim or identify or seek to repair the harm that has been caused. This leaves those affected by crime without the support they need, and offenders without help to live crime-free lives. We have a victims' code and a commissioner (finally again) for victims. But this is still without any proper formal role for victims in the system to have their needs met, beyond giving evidence, being updated and being allowed to make a victim impact statement. Everything designed to put victims at the heart of the system necessarily manifests as an adjunct. Even the Conservative government's attempt at a new 'Victims Bill' in 2023, initially proposed to put right the lack of support for victims, became a 'Victims and Prisoners Bill', with two-thirds of the final Bill, when it was first published, dedicated to changes in the law affecting prisoners.[23] A number of victims' groups complained that they neither asked for nor welcomed the addition of provisions concerning prisoners. Some of the changes concerning prisoners were criticised by campaigners from victims' groups as detracting from the main purpose of the Bill, which received Royal Assent in May 2024.[24]

Headlines focus on heart-breaking individual stories of harm and the indescribable suffering of victims who feel let down and alienated by the system. Much legislative reform in the last decade or so purports to respond to these terrible cases. Yet the system still has very limited space for victim involvement and there is even less space for meaningful support beyond the courtroom. When you have been the victim of a crime, its impact may be all too obvious. It may result in life-long psychiatric injury, such as

---

[23] Victims and Prisoners Bill 2023 (which became the Victims and Prisoners Act 2024).

[24] Victim Support, 'Victim support responds to the Victims and Prisoners Bill', 2023, at https://www.victimsupport.org.uk/victim-support-responds-to-the-victims-and-prisoners-bill/.

trauma, anxiety leaving the house, difficulty sleeping or crushing loneliness. It may affect your relationships, ability to work or study and your very personality. You may find yourself having to deal with complex and alien legal processes such as probate, selling a home you can no longer afford to live in, or participating in the perpetrator's criminal trial, appeal or parole review.

For example, studies have shown that victims of rape are particularly likely to undergo major life changes, such as moving house or changing job, in the aftermath of the offence – in one small study almost half of rape victims had moved home.[25]

You may want to know what your offender looks like now, so you are not constantly looking over your shoulder and wondering if the stranger behind you is the man who raped you. You might just want to know why someone behaved as they did: were they ill, immature or evil, and are they sorry? You might not care what they think but you might want them to know what impact their actions had.

Needs of perpetrators also need to be addressed if they are going to live crime-free lives and avoid future harm. Many perpetrators, especially women, have themselves been victims of crime. Their needs as victims do not disappear because they have transgressed, and sometimes they become harder to deal with. As outlined earlier, many women in prison have been sexually abused. According to His Majesty's Inspectorate of Prisons, self-harm rates for women are, at times, seven times higher than men and surveys from 2022 showed that 82 per cent of women said they had some form of mental health problem, compared with 59 per cent of men.[26] Prison does nothing to treat these and may exacerbate them. If such women are to create crime-free lives for themselves, they too may need help with housing, counselling, breaking addictive habits and crafting a positive new life.

---

[25] J. Dignan, *Understanding Victims and Restorative Justice*, Open University Press, 2005, p 29.

[26] S. Fieldhouse, 'International women's day: have we thought about women in prison?', 2023, at https://www.justiceinspectorates.gov.uk/hmiprisons/2023/03/international-womens-day-have-we-thought-about-women-in-prison/.

Restorative approaches

This is where restorative justice comes in. Restorative justice is not an alternative to the current system, but restorative approaches can be introduced to focus on what harm has been done, who is obliged to put it right and prevent its recurrence. Restorative justice focuses on repairing the harm of crime and engaging individuals and community members in the process.[27]

Restorative justice is sometimes misinterpreted. It is sometimes seen as a soft option, only suitable for minor offences committed by children, retraumatising where it includes direct face-to-face contact with the offender, overly offender focused or something that enables offenders to get away with a lesser penalty. However, as the Restorative Justice Council points out, 'offenders often say they found it much harder to face their victim than to go to court'.[28] A rapid evidence review of restorative justice practices around the world found that while it is predominantly used for children's cases and less serious offences, this does not always need to be the case and evaluations show that it can be effective in reducing reoffending.[29]

Restorative practices can take a range of forms. They fundamentally focus on harm reduction in a way that puts those affected front and centre of the process. In the words of Howard Zehr:

> Are the wrongs being acknowledged? Are the needs of those who were harmed being addressed? Is the one who committed the harm being encouraged to understand the damage and accept his or her obligation to make right the wrong? Are those involved in or affected by this being invited to be part of the 'solution'? Is concern being shown for everyone

---

[27] H. Zehr, 'Restorative justice? What's that?', nd, at https://zehr-institute. org/what-is-rj/.

[28] Restorative Justice Council, 'Restorative justice and policing information pack', 2014, at https://restorativejustice.org.uk/sites/default/files/resources/ files/1z87_info_packs%20(2)%20police.pdf.

[29] The Scottish Government, *Justice in Scotland: Rapid Evidence Review: Uses of Restorative Justice*, 2019.

involved? If the answers to these questions are 'no', then even though it may have restorative elements, it isn't restorative justice.[30]

The one thing that restorative practices have in common is that they formally place the victim front and centre of the process.[31] Nothing can be done to the victim without their agreement, which restores agency to those who have been harmed or violated. This is in stark contrast to the current criminal justice system where, once a matter is reported, the 'case' is owned by the state and may take on a life of its own. The victim may even be compelled to come to court to give evidence against their will if it is considered necessary and appropriate to secure a conviction.

The most commonly understood form of restorative justice takes the form of victim–offender contact, which may involve letters or a physical and virtual meeting.[32] There is no restriction on the types of cases that this may be suitable for. In all these cases, both parties will have to agree to the process and agree the terms on which it is conducted. Generally, each party will be supported in the lead up to the contact by an experienced restorative justice practitioner who will help the parties think through what they want to say or get out of the process, what the other party may want to say or how they might react to the interaction. There can be no expectation that it will go a certain way. Such a conference may result in expressions of remorse or forgiveness or it may just be a cathartic opportunity for the victim to demonstrate the hurt they have felt, ask questions or simply see what the person who harmed them looks like now. It is an entirely individualised process. Many perpetrators of crimes may also have been victims of crimes themselves and may feel aggrieved if they have engaged in the process but the person who harmed them has not. These are all things that need to be considered. People engaging in this direct form of restorative justice will likely need support before, during and after the process.

---

[30] Zehr (n 27).

[31] Victim Support, 'Restorative justice', nd, at https://www.victimsupport. org.uk/help-and-support/your-rights/restorative-justice.

[32] Restorative Justice Council, 'About restorative justice', nd, at https://restorative justice.org.uk/about-restorative-justice.

Of course, there are many instances where the perpetrator has not been caught, may be too ill to participate or may no longer be alive. In these cases, there may be alternative processes that can take place which focus on the harm experienced by the victim.

There may also be cases where victims do not want to participate at all in restorative processes. The Crown Prosecution Service acknowledges that in such cases 'a restorative approach could still be used to deliver the conditional caution, by encouraging the offender to consider what harm their offence may have caused, and how best they might repair it'.[33] However, the House of Commons Justice Committee's 2017 report on the state of restorative justice in England and Wales found 'that restorative justice provision is currently subject to a "postcode lottery" and varying regional buy-in'.[34]

Building a safer future

Restorative approaches can and should be developed beyond the traditional frameworks to provide both practical and emotional support to those affected, including direct and indirect victims, the wider community and, in some cases, the perpetrator, all with a view to limiting the harm, addressing the impact and preventing repeat offences.

The nature of these processes may depend on the victim's needs and the needs of any members of the wider community. For example, a person whose home has been robbed and finds themselves without essential items may have a number of needs: these needs may be practical (to clean or redecorate the home, to increase security measures or restore lost items) and emotional, for example, counselling to overcome anxiety and fear. If a person needs to move home because they no longer feel safe or relaxed in their home, they may need practical and legal support in managing this.

---

[33]   Crown Prosecution Service, 'Restorative justice', nd, at https://www.cps.gov.uk/legal-guidance/restorative-justice.

[34]   https://publications.parliament.uk/pa/cm201617/cmselect/cmjust/164/164.pdf.

Despite many claims by successive governments in recent years to put victims' needs front and centre, there has been very little by way of practical support offered to victims and, when it is on offer, it is often patchy. A report by the Domestic Abuse Commissioner in 2022 found that most victims and survivors sought some form of community-based services, seeking both practical advice as well as support to help them cope and recover from the abuse, but that provision was patchy.[35] The practical support ranged from legal support to counselling.

There may also be educational needs arising from the incident, in terms of ensuring that the wider community is aware of the impact of the offence, and also what is and is not legal. This aspect of restorative approaches, which is concerned with helping communities become less crime-prone, has long been recognised and can involve citizenship programmes and information to children in schools about what is unlawful and why.[36] In relation to some forms of crime such as sexual offending, particularly among young people, this may be the best way forward to prevent future harm. Statistics show that the volume of sexual offences recorded by the police has been increasing over the last decade and figures for the year ending March 2022 show an increase of 31 per cent, compared with the previous year.[37] Mandatory education on sex and relationships now covers telling students that certain behaviours are unlawful.[38] However, there is clearly a need for this aspect of the curriculum to be emphasised in the classroom so children are left in no doubt about what is an offence

---

[35] Domestic Abuse Commissioner, *Patchwork of Provision: How to Meet the Needs of Victims and Survivors across England and Wales*, 2022.

[36] T.F. Marshall, *Restorative Justice: An Overview*, Home Office, Research Development and Statistics Directorate, 1999.

[37] Office for National Statistics, 'Sexual offences in England and Wales overview: year ending March 2022', 2023, at https://www.ons.gov.uk/peoplepopulationandcommunity/crimeandjustice/bulletins/sexualoffencesinenglandandwalesoverview/march2022.

[38] Department for Education/Ministry of Justice, 'Relationships education, relationships and sex education (RSE) and health education: statutory guidance for governing bodies, proprietors, head teachers, principals, senior leadership teams, teachers', 2019, at https://assets.publishing.service.gov.uk/media/62cea352e90e071e789ea9bf/Relationships_Education_RSE_and_Health_Education.pdf.

and the consequences. For example, behaviour such as sexting is so commonplace it is unlikely that children would think much of it. Data about children's online behaviour in England and Wales found that 10 per cent of 13–15-year-olds reported having received a sexual message and girls were significantly more likely to have done so than boys.[39] Children may not consider sexting unlawful, appreciate the harm it can lead to or the consequences of being convicted and labelled as a sex offender as a child, which may include being placed on the sex offenders' register and being barred from certain work, but these are all real risks that such behaviour carries.[40] It is important that children, and society at large, are made aware of the harms and consequences of their behaviours if they are to be prevented.

A truly restorative system focused on harm prevention could look at the whole range of needs and preventative work, but it does need appropriate resources and skills to do so, combined with a willingness to put safety first.

Developing a statutory basis for the adult criminal justice system is essential if the needs of victims and the wider community are to be prioritised. This would mirror the provision for children in section 37 of the Crime and Disorder Act 1998 and could be accompanied by clear statutory duties to work towards this aim.[41]

New multidisciplinary harm reduction practitioners should be trained up to work alongside criminal justice, social, health, education and legal services to roll out restorative approaches to those affected by crime. Separate from the existing organs of the criminal justice system, such as probation, they would be able to

---

[39] Office for National Statistics, 'Children's online behaviour in England and Wales: year ending March 2020', 2021, at https://www.ons.gov.uk/people populationandcommunity/crimeandjustice/bulletins/childrensonline behaviourinenglandandwales/yearendingmarch2020#:~:text=An%20 estimated%20682%2C000%20children%20spoke,19%25%20compared%20 with%2014%25.

[40] Youth Justice Legal Centre, 'Sexting', 2022, at https://yjlc.uk/sites/default/ files/attachments/2022-11/DOWNLOAD%20THE%20CHILDREN%20 FACING%20ALLEGATIONS%20OF%20SEXTING%20LEGAL%20 GUIDE.pdf.

[41] Crime and Disorder Act.

focus on harm reduction in a holistic way, building on best practice and linking in where appropriate with existing statutory services.

The focus should be on making sure everyone understands how the system works, minimising trauma, providing practical support for those affected, whether that is finding new accommodation, helping someone access counselling or a lawyer to handle probate. The priority must be to ensure that victims of crime are able to retain their agency through restorative frameworks to put forward ideas to prevent future harm or, where all parties agree, facilitate offender–victim contact with appropriate support.

Prioritising women and girls

Given the disproportionate harms suffered by women, restorative approaches should be prioritised for women. This should include both women who are victims of crime and women who have been charged or convicted of crime.

Baroness Jean Corston and Baroness Hale have both recognised that the prison system is 'largely designed by men for men' and that women have been marginalised within it.[42] This applies to the criminal justice system at large whose male-centric focus has been damaging to women. To counter this, the development of new resources should be designed with the needs of women and girls in mind. Such a rebalance of the gender perspective is essential to ensuring fairness in the criminal justice system.

Conclusion

It is clear that the current system is failing all involved with it and is doing nothing to prevent crime and keep communities safe. Unless and until the adult criminal justice system has a clear purpose and focus enshrined in statue, there is little hope of creating a system that is geared towards crime-free communities. The first

---

[42] J. Corston, *The Corston Report: A Report by Baroness Jean Corston of a Review of Women with Particular Vulnerabilities in the Criminal Justice System: The Need for a Distinct, Radically Different, Visibly-Led, Strategic, Proportionate, Holistic, Woman-Centred, Integrated Approach* (Home Office 2007); *R (Coll) v Secretary of State for Justice* [2017] UKSC 40, [2017] 1 WLR 2093.

step towards real change and safer futures is to put the prevention of offending on a statutory footing as the purpose of the adult criminal justice system, as is currently the case for children.

Evidence from a number of jurisdictions shows that restorative justice approaches can be effective in reducing harm for both victims and offenders, who are often themselves victims. Restorative approaches should be prioritised within the criminal justice system, especially for women and girls who suffer disproportionately as the pandemic of violence against them continues unabated.

Restorative approaches are not just about interactions to repair harm after the event: they can be central in preventing harm in the first place through the development of public education in communities to prevent crime. Ensuring that children, families and communities generally understand what is against the law and why is essential in preventing future harm and should be prioritised and promoted at every opportunity.

Restorative approaches also include practical and emotional support, such as support with moving home, accessing legal support arising as a result of crime and counselling. At present, too often the focus is on victims having a voice. This is necessary but not sufficient as it leaves many people affected by crime struggling to rebuild their lives. Provision across the country is inconsistent.

Specialist harm reduction practitioners should be created and trained nationally to ensure restorative approaches are prioritised, consistent and effective.

Summary of key proposals

- Put prevention of offending as a statutory purpose of the adult criminal justice system.
- Prioritise restorative justice approaches for both victims and offenders, especially for women and girls.
- Develop public education in communities to prevent crime.
- Ensure restorative approaches include practical and emotional support.
- Create specialist harm reduction practitioners to ensure restorative approaches are prioritised and effective.

5

Access to justice

Grace Cullen

The importance of access to justice

Access to justice is a *basic principle of the rule of law*. In the absence of access to justice, people are unable to exercise their legal rights, challenge discrimination or hold decision-makers to account. Access to justice is part of the foundation of a democratic society and a constitutional right.

For individuals, access to justice can mean being able to claim compensation if dismissed from a job without good reason. It is knowing that their side will be heard in a dispute about where the children live and who they spend time with after a relationship break-up. It means not being unfairly evicted.

However, it is not only the ability *to enforce* these rights that is important. It is the knowledge to both sides in a dispute that these rights are *enforceable*. Put simply, if an employer knows that if they discriminate, they will have to pay compensation, they are less likely to discriminate in the first place. Access to justice therefore provides not just the opportunity to enforce legal rights, but it also protects those rights in everyday life.

A broken system

While most people would agree that access to justice is an important principle, many do not see it as being relevant to their daily lives.

For this reason, access to justice has lost political expediency. For years, legal aid, proper financing of the justice system and advice centres, and access to professional staff and fit-for-purpose court buildings have all been consciously underfunded. The principle of access to justice has been knowingly eroded.

The system is broken. Sadly, it is only when people need it, often at vulnerable moments in their life, that they realise it is not there.

The problems are numerous. There are vast legal aid deserts. Law Centres have closed due to withdrawal of funding. There are huge backlogs in the court system, with delays sometimes of years before a case can be determined. Finally, there is the loss of professionals who can no longer afford to do the job they have trained hard for.

Taken together these problems have profound impacts on society. They entrench inequality and prevent individuals from unlocking their full potential for themselves and their communities. Further, there is a significant impact on the economy, as without the benefit of early professional advice, problems multiply and escalate, ultimately at a higher cost to the taxpayer.

Legal aid deserts

The Law Society has produced several reports from 2019 onwards highlighting the issue of legal aid deserts.[1] Legal aid deserts are areas of the country where people on low incomes facing important legal issues are often unable to get local advice that they are legally entitled to. The number of people who accessed legal aid for cases was over one million in 2009/10 (which was before the Legal Aid, Sentencing and Punishment of Offenders Act 2012 'LASPO'[2]). This fell to 130,000 in 2021/2. However, over the same period of time, the number of people going to court without representation trebled. Reports from the Law Society in February 2024 note the following:

---

[1]   Law Society Futures & Insights Teams, 'Civil legal aid: a review of its sustainability and the challenges to its viability', September 2021, at https:// www.lawsociety.org.uk/topics/research/civil-sustainability-review.

[2]   Legal Aid, Sentencing and Punishment of Offenders Act 2012.

- 53 million people (90 per cent) do not have access to a local education legal aid provider.
- 49 million people (85 per cent) do not have access to a local welfare legal aid provider.
- 42 million people (71 per cent) do not have access to a local community care legal aid provider.
- Around 25 million people (44 per cent) do not have access to a local provider who is able to give legal advice on housing.
- Around 37 million people (63 per cent) do not have access to a local provider of immigration and asylum law.

There is a personal story behind every statistic. For example, legal aid can be the difference between a family staying in a stable home or being made homeless. Loss of a home can mean loss of security, employment, education, friends and family, and professional relationships. It is likely that all this will also come at a greater expense to the public.

How did we get here?

After the Second World War, at a time of societal reform which also saw the introduction of the National Health Service, the Labour government enacted the Legal Aid and Advice Act 1949. For the first time, legislation gave people the right to free legal advice if they could not afford a solicitor. It was means-tested for those of small or moderate means. This meant that almost 80 per cent of people qualified for some form of legal advice in ordinary courts.

More recently, legal aid has become a target for cost-cutting. The Access to Justice Act 1999 put a cap on legal aid spending. In 2011 there was a 10 per cent cut to all civil legal aid fees. Further cuts were made as part of the austerity programme, with a loss of over £950 million[3] to the legal aid budget.

However, the most significant piece of legislation was the Legal Aid Sentencing and Punishment of Offenders Act 2012 (LASPO). Many areas of law were taken out of scope for legal aid, disadvantaging providers and leading to legal aid deserts

---

[3] Law Society Futures & Insights Teams (n 1).

with vast areas of the country losing out on legal aid coverage including housing, family, immigration, employment and welfare benefit payments.

By 2020, only 25 per cent of the population were eligible for civil legal aid.[4] Access to justice in England and Wales could no longer be comprehensively relied upon.

Impact on Law Centres

Law Centres are often the first point of call for people in need of legal advice, who are otherwise unable to afford it. Law Centres are staffed by people who are also experienced in local community issues and can effectively signpost individuals to agencies who are able to help with practical issues.

LASPO specifically reduced funding to legal advice agencies and Law Centres. The number of not-for-profit legal aid providers halved after LASPO, compared to only a 20 per cent reduction in commercial providers. Across Law Centres, legal aid income dropped by 60 per cent. Together with cuts to other public funding, such as local authority support and dedicated casework grants, Law Centres experienced a loss of 40 per cent to their income between 2013 and 2015.[5] This led to the closure of numerous Law Centres, and for those that remained open, legal aid cuts led to a restriction on services they could provide. The constraints to Law Centres' capacity to assist came at a time when demand for Law Centre services has been rising, by as much as 400 per cent in some areas. The Law Centre Network[6] raised concerns in 2018 that LASPO cuts threatened the viability of a range of social welfare law specialisms, both through the loss of experts as well as junior positions that would make up the next generations of social welfare lawyers.

---

4   Ministry of Justice, 'Spending of the Ministry of Justice on legal aid', Briefing Paper, 21 October 2020, at https://commonslibrary.parliament.uk/research-briefings/cdp-2020-0115/.

5   Joint Committee on Human Rights Inquiry, 'Human rights: attitude to enforcement', written evidence submitted by the Law Centres Network, February 2018.

6   Ibid.

Delays to the court system

Anyone using the courts will be aware of the significant and lengthy delays that are crippling some areas of the justice system.

In September 2022, the *Law Gazette*[7] reported that the average time to get to trial in fast-track (medium value cases) and multi-track (high value cases) was 75 weeks. By June 2023,[8] this had risen to 80 weeks. These cases include people who have suffered significant personal injury and loss of earnings and/or employment. The delays are significant and can have a real impact on how the evidence is heard and the outcome of the case.

As with legal aid deserts, it is often a 'postcode' lottery, with vastly different delays across the country. The south-east is the worst performing region with an average wait to trial of 462 days, while the north-east is the best performing region with an average wait of 251 days to get to trial.[9]

The loss of legal aid providers and professionals undertaking legal aid work has also led to a significant increase in litigants in person appearing in courts. Many people now feel they have no choice but to bring their case themselves because they cannot afford or access legal representation.

In 2021, 36 per cent of cases in the family courts were cases where neither party was represented. These cases will usually take more of the court's time and resources and put greater strain on the court system. Litigants in person often do not have the knowledge or experience of how to present their case to address the issues the court needs to decide. Therefore, the judge has a more difficult task trying to make fair and just decisions in cases where parties are wholly unfamiliar with rules of law, evidence and procedure.

---

[7] J. White, 'Delays in our civil courts have now reached crisis point', *Law Gazette*, 15 September 2022, at https://www.lawgazette.co.uk/comment ary-and-opinion/delays-in-our-civil-courts-have-now-reached-crisis-point/ 5113664.article.

[8] C. Moloney, 'Civil court delays the "worst on record"', *Law Gazette*, 1 June 2023, at https://www.lawgazette.co.uk/news/civil-court-delays-the-worst-on-record/5116199.article.

[9] Ibid.

Further, some of these cases may lack merit. Due to lack of appropriate legal advice, cases come before the courts which otherwise would not have been brought or would have settled with the assistance of skilled professionals.

Loss of professionals

The last time that civil legal aid rates were increased for inflation was in 1994.[10] Legal aid rates have been frozen at mid-1990s levels, with a further cut of 10 per cent in 2010. Taken together this represents a real term cut of 49.4 per cent in fees to 2022.

Research from the Law Society[11] demonstrates that there has been a significant decline in the number of civil legal aid providers since legal aid reforms were introduced in 2010. By 2016, there was a loss of 37 per cent of providers undertaking legal aid work after LASPO. This is more than a generational problem. It has become a crisis.

Housing, family and immigration are all areas of law that have been impacted by legal aid cuts. The following sections look at the problems and possible solutions as to how to deal effectively with access to justice issues in these areas.

Spotlight on housing law

Legal aid remains available under LASPO for some areas of housing law, including loss of home, homelessness, claims brought by tenants for damages and injunctions for removal or reduction of serious risk of harm to the individual or their family and some claims of judicial review. [12]

However, advice on welfare benefits and debt was removed from the scope of legal aid, which prevents lawyers from giving

---

[10]   Law Society Futures & Insights Teams (n 1).

[11]   Ibid.

[12]   L. Davies, 'Access to justice: housing legal aid', in Society of Labour Lawyers, *Towards a National Legal Service: New Visions for Access to Justice*, 2023, at https://www.societyoflabourlawyers.org.uk/wp-content/uploads/SLL-Towards-a-National-Legal-Service.pdf.

holistic advice. For example, legal aid covers situations where a tenant is in arrears but does not cover advice about welfare benefits (including housing costs) which may assist the tenant meet the arrears.

Access to early advice and proper legal aid without delays is crucial to any attempt to tackle inequality and poor housing conditions of many of the most vulnerable people in society. The tragic death of Awaab Ishak,[13] a toddler who died in December 2020 due to the extensive mould in his home, highlighted the very serious issues of poor housing conditions experienced in 21st-century England.

There have been some attempts to tackle these problems. In August 2023, the government introduced a new scheme called the Housing Loss Prevention Advice Scheme to fund early legal advice on housing and debt before a court hearing. However, there were difficulties finding firms to bid for these contracts because of the existing damage to the sector. In 12 areas of the country there were no compliant bids.[14] This represents over a tenth of the entire provision, including Liverpool, an urban area with a population of almost half a million people.

Experts in housing law believe that early advice is key to the efficient resolution of problems. The approach should be holistic, covering areas of debt, welfare and housing, and must be properly funded. Early advice can prevent litigation and save public money. The Law Centre Network[15] estimated direct savings of between £212 and £274 million of annual costs associated with debt, temporary accommodation, homelessness, stress, anxiety and ill-health.

The risk of losing your home has a huge impact on a person's mental health and wellbeing, and that of their family and children. Proper advice at an early stage can change lives for the better.

---

[13] P. McCann and L. Horsburgh, 'Awaab Ishak: mould in Rochdale flat caused boy's death, coroner rules', *BBC News*, 15 November 2022, at https://www.bbc.co.uk/news/uk-england-manchester-63635721.

[14] The Law Society (n 2).

[15] Law Centre Network, 'Funding law centres 2014', at https://www.lawcentres.org.uk/policy-and-media/the-case-for-law-centres.

Spotlight on family law

A relationship break-up can be a distressing event, particularly when children are affected. Many families do not need the involvement of the courts, but for others agreement may not be possible. Sometimes disagreements become entrenched. There may be a lack of trust or more specific reasons such as domestic abuse and coercive/controlling behaviour or other safeguarding concerns. These families often need additional support and safe ways to resolve their disputes in the child's best interests. [16]

The Children Act 1989 puts the welfare of the child as the paramount principle. Family judges recognise that delay is not in the best interests of the child. However, delay has now become an unavoidable reality of family litigation. Many private law cases involving decisions about children take over a year to resolve. In more complex cases, including allegations of domestic abuse, which often require separate hearings, the time is far longer.

Without proper legal advice and an early understanding of the problems, disagreements can become long-standing with children caught in the crossfire of parental hostility. The worry over litigation adds to the overall stress of the family. Parents struggle to navigate a family court system that they have no experience of. The impact on children in litigation can be significant, including on their emotional and mental health, their education and relationships with parents and peers. Children often feel their voices are unheard. Sadly, one-third of cases return to the courts after a final Order has been made. This obviously causes greater strain on a system that is already under incredible pressure.

There have been some recent positive developments. A person accused of domestic abuse allegations is no longer allowed to cross-examine the alleged victim of the abuse in court. Instead, the court will appoint an independent advocate to undertake cross-examination to ensure that the case can be heard fairly.

---

[16] JUSTICE, 'Improving access to justice for separating families', in Society of Labour Lawyers (n 13).

Since 2013, there has been a requirement to mediate before a case reaches court. However, many cases are exempt due to issues such as domestic abuse. These cases tend to take most of the court's time and resources, so practical alternatives need to be considered.

Introducing publicly funded early advice for child arrangements would help deal with problems at an early stage. This could help parents understand legal and non-legal issues, manage expectations and promote an understanding about what is in the best interests of the child.

If the case reaches court, there should be a greater emphasis on judicial continuity. Judges do their best in very difficult circumstances, but it is not often possible for the same judge to hear the same case. A 'case progression officer', who is a neutral legally trained court employee, could provide information to litigants in person regarding case management and understanding outcomes. Where cases are complex and/or where parties are particularly vulnerable, the court could make an order that either one or both parties be represented.

There should be further research of the child's role in the proceedings. Children could be given age-appropriate information about the court process, so it is not just left to parents in a dispute to do so. Some children report that they do not feel heard. Consideration should be given to how children can be more involved in proceedings in an age-appropriate way, so that they feel their views have been listened to, acknowledged and understood.

Finally, Cafcass[17] could follow up with the family after a period of time following the conclusion of proceedings, to see how the arrangements for the children which have been made by the court are working in practice. If there are difficulties, the case can be returned to court (before the same judge) for a review. Where arrangements need to be amended, the judge who has heard the case can do so with minimal cost and delay. This would help reduce the number of cases which return to court and prevent families being stuck in patterns of contact which may no longer benefit the child.

---

[17] Cafcass is an organisation of trained professionals who advise the family courts about the welfare of children and what is in their best interests.

Spotlight on immigration law

The system of immigration control caters for people coming to the UK for work and family reasons, as well as those seeking international protection. It is an area of law that has become increasingly complex and one where avenues of appeal and legal challenge have become restricted. At the same time, there is inadequate provision of advice and representation, with significant legal aid deserts across the country. Extensive delays mean people's lives are put on hold. Some people may lack permission to work and may seek support from the state or the informal economy. In such circumstances, they are likely to be more vulnerable and less protected by employment rights. [18]

Not only is the cost of litigation unnecessarily expensive in immigration law, there is a significant overall cost of prolonged asylum support, hotel accommodation and immigration bail support, immigration detention and attempts at enforcement and removal. This has become a significant political issue.

Solutions to the multitude of problems include simplifying the system of administrative decision-making. This could include applying agreed public service standards to enable people to put their case properly and to ensure that high quality decisions are made within a reasonable period. The quality of the decision-making and a fair and just process would reduce the need for legal challenges and judicial review hearings.

Legal dispute resolutions should be increased, with a right of appeal to the First-Tier Tribunal for those seeking to remain in the UK for work in economic or student categories. Presently, there is no right of appeal. People involved in these cases may be professionals who are highly mobile and may choose instead to relocate to other countries in the European Union, United States or Canada. This can lead to a loss of talent for companies seeking to grow their business and can impact the wider economy. The process for those seeking protection as refugees or stateless persons should be simplified, with consideration of the merits

---

[18] S. Naik and A. Berry, 'Legal services in the public law area of immigration and asylum', in Society of Labour Lawyers (n 13).

(or otherwise) of the asylum claim, rather than how a person arrived in the UK.

Finally, means-tested legal aid should be restored for those seeking to join or remain with family members in the UK. British citizens' right to family life is protected under the European Convention on Human Rights and Human Rights Act 1998. The impact of poor decision-making where families have no representation can be devastating.

What are the solutions?

There is a growing consensus including among international bodies, parliamentary committees, professional bodies, charities, law firms and professionals who work in the sector that LASPO is not fit for purpose. The Justice Committee of the House of Commons report, *The Future of Legal Aid*,[19] called for a 'complete overhaul of the civil legal aid system'. The All Party Parliamentary Group on Access to Justice have made various recommendations including legal aid fees should increase with inflation, there should be an independent legal aid fee review panel and return funding for early legal advice to pre-LASPO levels. There are specific recommendations for legal aid funding in housing and family cases and bereaved families in inquests.[20]

The government launched a review of civil legal aid, including means testing.[21] The Ministry of Justice[22] review will consider the civil legal aid system in its entirety; from how services are procured, how well the current system works for users, how civil legal aid impacts the wider justice system and how people access funding and support. Additionally, there will be an external assessment of how such systems work in other comparable countries.

It is essential that the value of legal aid is recognised. Legal aid funding should be increased, and the scope of legal aid widened.

---

[19] The Justice Committee, House of Commons, *Future of Legal Aid*, 27 July 2021.

[20] All Party Parliamentary Group on Access to Justice, 'Recommendations', at https://www.appg-access-to-justice.co.uk/recommendations.

[21] Ministry of Justice, 'Legal aid means test review', 25 May 2023.

[22] Ministry of Justice, 'Review of Civil Legal Aid – call for evidence', 10 January 2024.

Further, there should be specific and targeted investment in areas of legal aid deserts.

Road to a National Legal Service

A radical and innovative proposal is the creation of a National Legal Service[23] with the aim to put the interests of individuals with legal problems first. Such a service would have a mission to improve the ability of people to enforce rights, resolve legal problems and settle disputes.

Unlike the National Health Service, a newly created National Legal Service would not become a state provider of legal services, but would instead provide a holistic framework in which private solicitors, barristers, Law Centres and other professionals could operate.

It could become a trusted network of legal operators providing an integrated service to those who need it. It could range from the basic provision of information online or access to self-help tools, to individualised legal advice and representation.

The National Legal Service would require collaboration with the Ministry of Justice and other government departments including HM Courts and Tribunal Service, as well as the judiciary, and academic institutions and private practitioners, and would require an overall strategic leadership. It would utilise the experience and knowledge of existing practitioners but to be successful it would need to be properly funded. Innovative use of technology could also assist in managing costs, where it is possible to do so.

What about the cost?

The impact of a hollowed-out justice system on individuals, families, businesses and communities is immense. There is a clear legal and moral justification for having a system of civil legal aid that is fit for purpose. However, there are also compelling financial reasons as well.[24]

---

[23]   R. Smith and N. Madge, 'A National Legal Service', in Society of Labour Lawyers (n 13).

[24]   Society of Labour Lawyers (n 13); J. Kelen, 'How to fund it: the economic case for civil legal aid', in Society of Labour Lawyers (n 13).

Other countries have approached the problem of funding legal aid through a number of different initiatives to cover an increase in legal aid rates and to fund a better system of justice. The steps include a minor increase to the cost of court applications for high value claims, additional charges to those who use legal aid funding to gain compensation or require opponents of legal-aid funded cases to pay a small additional cost, and payments from law firms to a centralised civil legal aid fund.[25] Many of these options are established in other common law countries.

Analysis of the current system shows that far from saving costs by cutting legal aid, the state is paying more overall. Citizens Advice[26] found that for every £1 of legal aid housing advice, the state saves up to £2.34. For employment advice £1 saves up to £7 and for benefits advice, the state saves up to £8.80.

These savings are often to the National Health Service, social housing and welfare payments, but also keeping people in their homes and in employment leads to an increase in tax revenues. The benefits of civil legal aid are wide-ranging for the economy.

What are the benefits?

Access to justice for those who need it is a fundamental principle of a democratic state. But as well as a clear valued ideal, there are real practical benefits.

Legal aid is its own economy. Solicitors' firms and Law Centres were a strong presence on the high street, which has diminished in the time since LASPO. As well as providing local jobs they are important assets for the community. Further, there are indirect benefits to the economy. Access to legal advice about housing, employment rights, immigration status and family issues result in more people in work.

The Legal Aid Practitioners Group, who work on the front line of legal aid, stated:[27]

> We don't see legal aid as an end in itself, rather as a mechanism working across government to improve

---

25 Society of Labour Lawyers (n 13).
26 Citizen's Advice, 'Towards a business case for legal aid', 15 December 2015.
27 Proposal for Access to Justice in Civil and Family Law, LAPG (March 2023).

outcomes and reduce inequality'– led by the Ministry of Justice, but acting cohesively with education, housing, local government, health, the Home Office and the DWP to name but a few. We recognise that for those departments to fulfil their obligations to each individual, and for those individuals themselves to fully develop their potential in their communities, they require the tools to do so. The law plays an integral role in unlocking that potential.

The principle of access to justice must mean *effective* access to justice. Without that, it is an empty soundbite, lacking in value and principle.

The goal must therefore be to ensure that when an individual presents with a problem they are able to access legal advice at the right time which addresses all their legal issues and enables them to resolve the problem in a timely manner. LASPO sought to limit state funding to a narrow range of practice areas. This legislative approach was contrary to the accepted understanding of what people need.

It is now time to reframe the argument for legal aid by expanding its scope in ways that reduce poverty and inequality and instead enhance the health, prosperity and opportunities of individuals, families and communities across the country.

Summary of key proposals

- The government must provide proper investment and funding for civil and family legal aid, including an increase in legal aid rates to pre-LASPO levels and in line with inflation.
- Investment should include funding for advice centres and targeted investment in areas of legal aid deserts.
- Consideration of establishing a National Legal Service to provide a co-ordinated system with the aim of providing early, holistic advice and dispute resolution.
- Recognise that investment in legal aid has financial savings in other areas, particularly in areas of housing, welfare and employment.
- Acceptance that access to justice is an important principle in our democracy and that a properly funded system of legal aid has an inherent value to society as a whole.

PART II

Emerging challenges

6

Planning and levelling up

Liz Davies, Rosalee Dorfman Mohajer, Ceri Edmonds, Stephen Hockman, Sally Hughes, Jamie McGowan, Wendy Pettifer, Andrew Pratten and David Watkinson

Introduction

To tackle Britain's housing crisis, we need a commitment to build more than 300,000 new homes a year (the government's current commitment) and at least 150,000 of new homes should be social homes for rent.[1]

The principles underlying Labour's housing policy should be that 'levelling up' means nothing less than demolishing inequality. Residential property and housing development are major economic sectors. Relatively cheap borrowing and house price inflation have been significant drivers of inequality, not only in higher end owner

---

[1] The figure of 150,000 comes from *Building the Social Homes We Need* (New Economics Foundation, 2019, at https://nationwidefoundation.org.uk/wp-content/uploads/2019/11/Building-the-social-homes-we-need_19 1120_150504.pdf). The figure was adopted by Labour Party Conference in September 2021 (L. Heath, 'Labour conference backs pledge to build 150,000 social homes per year', *Inside Housing*, 27 September 2021, at https://www.insidehousing.co.uk/news/labour-conference-backs-pledge-to-build-150 000-social-homes-per-year-72667). However, recent announcements by Labour Party front-bench spokespersons are unclear about whether the Party remains committed to building social housing to this extent. We urge that it retains this commitment.

occupation, but also in the private rented sector, where incentives to private landlords have allowed them to outrun the capacity of ordinary renters to buy in. The private rented sector has also been fuelled by the 'right' to buy council homes with a high proportion no longer in owner occupation long term.

Planning and levelling up

We believe that for too long Labour has failed to recognise that the planning system, and in particular planning policy, provide well-established tools to enable us to fulfil our policy objectives. So long as the National Planning Policy Framework and local development plans contain the right locational social objectives, planning authorities will be able to decide whether a proposal (whether for housing or another form of development) is in conformity with those objectives and make planning decisions accordingly. They will also be able to use planning agreements, not merely to facilitate but also positively to promote socially acceptable development, such as affordable housing.[2] The use of these powers will be critical in enabling authorities to insist on key regional development sites being invested in rather than those where the biggest profits can be made. Labour should review and implement changes to financial viability assessments and appraisals that are currently used to drastically reduce the number of affordable houses being delivered in developments across the country.[3] It has already been noted that changes on viability could increase the numbers of affordable homes.[4]

Labour had rightly pledged to end the inclusion of 'hope value'[5] in the valuation of land being purchased by local authorities under a Compulsory Purchase Order (CPO). This will enable more land to be purchased for socially acceptable development. This proposal was made by the Society of Labour Lawyers in its

---

[2] Achievable under s 106 Town & Country Planning Act 1990.

[3] S. Hill, 'Taking back affordable housing', New Economics Foundation, 22 February 2022, at https://neweconomics.org/2022/02/taking-back-affordable-housing.

[4] *Tackling the Under-supply of Housing in England*, House of Commons Library Research Briefing, 19 May 2023.

[5] 'Hope value' increases the value of land by factoring into the price prospective planning permissions.

Proposals for Housing Law Reform of September 2021, and has now been adopted in the Levelling Up and Regeneration Act 2023.

In addition, Keir Starmer announced at Labour Party Conference 2023 a plan for 'unleashing mayors' by giving them stronger powers over planning and control of housing investment. He also proposed a 'planning passport' for urban brownfield development with fast-track approval and delivery of housing on urban brownfield sites and freeing up appropriate 'greenbelt' land for development, such as wasteland – 'the grey belt'.[6]

Summary of key proposals for planning and levelling up

- Enable national and local planning policy to include locational social objectives with which proposals for development will be required to conform.
- Ensure the use of planning agreements to promote socially acceptable developments, for example, affordable housing.
- End the inclusion of 'hope value' in the valuation of land being purchased by local authorities under a CPO, enabling more land to be purchased.
- Strengthen the powers of mayors over planning and control of investment.
- Speed up the granting of permission for housing development on urban brownfield sites and appropriate low grade 'greenbelt' land, for example, wasteland.

The case for more social and council housing

One and a half million households live in council housing, fewer than in owner-occupied homes, the private rented sector or housing associations.[7] Prior to the introduction of Right to

---

[6] The government is currently consulting on amendments to planning policy to facilitate development on brownfield land: *Strengthening Planning Policy for Brownfield Development*, DLUHC, 13 February 2024, at https://www.gov.uk/government/consultations/strengthening-planning-policy-for-brownfield-development/strengthening-planning-policy-for-brownfield-development.

[7] *English Housing Survey 2022–2023*, 14 December 2023, at https://www.gov.uk/government/collections/english-housing-survey. There are 15.8 million

Buy in 1980, five million households lived in council housing. Right to Buy and stock transfer of council housing has seriously diminished the numbers of council homes. Scandalously, 40 per cent of former council homes in England, bought under Right to Buy, are now let to private tenants by private landlords.[8]

As of March 2022, there were 1.19 million households waiting on local authority waiting lists for council or housing association properties in England. There were 267,000 new social housing lettings in 2021/2, far below the demand for social housing.[9]

Right to Buy was abolished in Scotland in 2016[10] and in Wales in 2018.[11]

Labour should commit to building at least 150,000 new social homes a year, in order to start to meet the demand for social housing. In order to ensure that those social homes remain in the public sector, Labour should abolish Right to Buy in England (together with the government's new proposals of right to shared ownership of council homes and any proposals to introduce Right to Buy in the housing association sector) so that houses that have been built with public money remain in the public sector. Alternatively, Right to Buy should only continue upon strict conditions of one-for-one replacement,[12] with punitive

---

owner-occupied households, representing 65 per cent of all households in 2022–3. The private rented sector makes up 4.6 million or 19 per cent of households. The social rented sector accounts for 4 million or 16 per cent of households in England. Of those, 2.5 million or 10 per cent of the total of households rent from housing associations and just 1.5 million households or 6 per cent rent from councils. We refer to private registered providers as housing associations throughout.

[8] Chartered Institute for Housing, *UK Housing Review 2022*, March 2022, at https://www.ukhousingreview.org.uk/ukhr22/index.html.

[9] 'Social housing lettings in England, tenancies: April 2021 – March 2022', DLUHC, at https://www.gov.uk/government/statistics/social-housing-lettings-in-england-april-2021-to-march-2022.

[10] https://www.gov.scot/policies/social-housing/council-housing/. Housing (Scotland) Act 2014 s 1(1) repealing ss 61–81 Housing (Scotland) Act 1987.

[11] Abolition of the Right to Buy and Associated Rights (Wales) Act 2018, ss 2 and 6, amending Housing Act 1985, Part 5.

[12] We note research for the Local Government Association which found that the current policy of '141 agreements', in operation since 2012, has resulted in no more than 58 per cent of homes replaced and that in the next decade, total replacements are unlikely to be more than 43 per cent, resulting in a

consequences to prevent sale of the property within ten years of purchase and conditions against letting the property.[13]

Local housing authorities are woefully under-resourced and urgently need better funding. While the social rented sector has the lowest numbers of Non-Decent Homes,[14] the Housing Ombudsman reports that the biggest area of complaints received relate to property conditions.[15]

Major estate demolitions have led to a massive loss of council housing stock and disrupted communities. Commitments to rehouse social tenants are not always honoured and the driving up of property prices means that local people are unable to afford to rehouse themselves. Labour committed not to carry out major estate works without a residents' ballot and must retain that commitment. Private development vehicles, set up by local authorities, are inherently risky, do not represent value for money and have the effect of driving up local property prices.[16] Labour should fund local councils to undertake major new building projects and refurbishment projects without having to resort to such financial vehicles.

We support innovative ways of ensuring that public land remains both publicly owned and usefully employed, for housing where possible. Local land commissions can play an important role in slowing privatisation of public land and support community land trusts and other forms of socially conscious land use. So as

---

net loss of around 60,000 from public stock: *HRA Research Right to Buy*, Savills for the Local Government Association, 2023 at https://localgovas soc-newsroom.prgloo.com/news/almost-60-000-homes-sold-through-right-to-buy-will-not-be-replaced-by-2030. It follows that any conditions of one-for-one replacement would have to be a new scheme, much more rigorously enforced by government.

[13] Currently a proportion of the discount has to be repaid if the property is sold within five years of the tenant having bought it under right to buy and, for properties bought after April 2005, if the property is to be sold within ten years of purchase, it must first be offered to the council to buy back at market value (which will be greater than the original purchase price).

[14] Ten per cent: *English Housing Survey 2022–2023* (n 7).

[15] Thirty-seven per cent: Housing Ombudsman Service, *Housing Ombudsman Annual Report 2022–2023*, October 2023, at https://www.housing-ombuds man.org.uk/wp-content/uploads/2024/03/E03040626-HC-627-Housing-Ombudsman-ARA-22-23_Accessible.pdf.

[16] As the history of Croydon Council's Brick By Brick shows.

to allow local authorities to bring empty residential properties into use, the system for Empty Dwelling Management Orders[17] could be reformed, removing the need to apply to a tribunal, so as to make local authority ownership the default position after a defined period. More enforcement action on privately owned empty homes will both increase the stock of publicly owned homes and incentivise private owners to let out properties.

Council tenancies should be a 'home for life', provided that the tenant complies with conditions. Labour should repeal the provisions for fixed term tenancies in Localism Act 2011 and Housing & Planning Act 2016[18] so that all council tenancies are secure after the first introductory year. It should also take steps to buy back former council properties now in private hands, where those properties are rented out.

Summary of key proposals for council housing

- Repeal or severely restrict the availability of the Right to Buy.
- Facilitate the provision of 150,000 social homes for rent each year.
- Ensure ballots are required to be held in respect of estate demolitions.
- Support the establishment of local land commissions.
- Ensure long-term security of tenure.

Home-ownership

Increasing the numbers of home-owners has been government policy since Thatcher. Although ownership is popular and apparently successful, many owners are in severe financial distress through debt (including mortgage debt), disrepair, the cladding crisis, insecure earnings and the cost-of-living crisis. Home-ownership has become increasingly unaffordable and separates the generations. Since 2013–14 there have been more outright owners than owners with mortgages, as the baby boomer generation reaches retirement age and pays off mortgages.[19] The numbers of

---

[17] Sections 132–138, Housing Act 2004.
[18] The latter never brought into force.
[19] *English Housing Survey 2022–2023* (n 7).

owner-occupiers aged 25–34 or 34–45 are gradually decreasing, and a greater proportion of those age groups rent privately.

Many younger people face unaffordable rents and unaffordable house prices. This leaves them without choice and faced with impossible decisions about how and where to live. Uncontrolled and unfulfilled planning decisions (on 'affordables', and social and economic facilities, as well as competition from buy-to-let landlords at home and abroad), have fuelled unaffordable prices, particularly in the south-east. This is reflected by the increase from 5.05 to 8.3 in the ratio of median house price to median gross annual earnings in England and Wales between 2002 and 2023.[20]

These factors drive inequality, leading to extremes of property wealth, with significant variations regionally, and between generations. Huge profits can be derived by house developers, and private wealth is frequently reinvested into residential property.

Further, property poverty does not simply stop at the purchase of the house and there is a risk that the idea of home-ownership simply shifts where the problem lies. For example, a government report estimated that, of the 29 million existing homes in the UK, most of those need upgrades to their heating systems.[21] Similarly, a report published by Green Alliance in 2019 found that UK homes are some of the worst insulated and least energy efficient in Europe, with only 15 per cent of current housing stock having been built after 1990.[22] The ongoing energy crisis exacerbates this continuing problem. A study undertaken by EDF indicated that the insulation installed in the UK's current housing stock is on average at least 46 years old and in need of urgent updating.[23] New

---

[20] Office for National Statistics, *Housing Affordability in England and Wales: 2022*, March 2023, at https://www.ons.gov.uk/peoplepopulationandcommunity/housing/bulletins/housingaffordabilityinenglandandwales/2022.

[21] BEISC, *Decarbonising Heat in Homes: Seventh Report of Session 2021–22*, 3 February 2022, at https://committees.parliament.uk/publications/8742/documents/88647/default/.

[22] Green Alliance, *Reinventing Retrofit: How to Scale Up Home Energy Efficiency in the UK*, February 2019, at https://green-alliance.org.uk/publication/reinventing-retrofit-how-to-scale-up-home-energy-efficiency-in-the-uk/.

[23] EDF, 'Insulation age of homes revealed to be at least 46 years old', EDF Energy, 3 May 2022, at https://www.edfenergy.com/media-centre/news-releases/insulation-age-homes-revealed-be-least-46-years-old.

buyers can encounter significant costs upgrading and maintaining what may be considered dilapidated properties.

Labour should carefully consider the limits of ownership and whether to continue to subsidise a sector that is creating very high profits in property development and the financial sector and at the upper end of personal ownership, while working people are no longer earning enough to participate in the market safely. Some of the properties sold in the leasehold scandal were bought with first-time-buyer subsidy.

The Party should also consider fiscally neutral options, particularly in flat ownership, that would put more power and control in the hands of leaseholders, as well as ensure that onerous and unfair burdens are removed.

During the former Labour government, innovative Commonhold and Right to Manage measures were introduced,[24] but have needed reinforcement and workability. Previous Shadow Housing Ministers have published on the scandal of leasehold and pledged to extend the right to manage.[25] The Conservative government's Leasehold and Freehold Reform Bill is a belated attempt to follow up on the Law Commission's 2020 proposals. There are some welcome measures which should make it cheaper and easier for leaseholders to extend their leases or buy out the freeholds. There are also some further measures to control service charges. However, in many places the Bill does not go far enough. For example, the Bill does little to ensure that leaseholders in blocks of flats will have more control over their future.

Labour should support the reforms in the Bill but should also introduce measures that go further. For example, Labour should ensure that blocks of more than ten flats are either created as commonholds or have tripartite leases in which a lessee-owned management company is responsible for managing the building. Labour should ensure that the requirements of lessee-owned management companies and Right to Manage (RTM) companies are taken into consideration. For example, limiting their ability to

---

[24] Commonhold and Leasehold Reform Act 2002.
[25] J. Healey MP and S. Jones MP, *Ending the Scandal: Labour's New Deal for Leaseholders*, Labour Party, 2019, at https://www.johnhealeymp.co.uk/wp-content/uploads/Labours-New-Deal-for-Leaseholders-document.pdf.

recover legal costs from defaulting lessees may risk the financial sustainability of a lessee-owned company.

These measures are cost-neutral and hold the potential for a long-term reduction in housing costs for lessee flat owners, together with much greater control on management for residents.

Labour should undertake a holistic review of housing costs confronting lower income home-owners, including means-tested financial assistance to keep properties in good condition and to meet the challenges of climate change (insurance, making homes more energy efficient, solar generation, and so on). In addition, Labour must look at area-wide measures to protect existing housing that is vulnerable to extreme weather events. Labour should also consider wealth-based property taxation designed to make local taxation (council tax) more progressive, and to reflect large home-owners' relatively high land use and carbon footprint, penalising properties left empty (in line with local authority power to take those properties into public ownership) and start to tackle the inequalities of wealth distribution caused by house price inflation.

Summary of key proposals for home-ownership

- Home-owners should have more control over how their buildings are run with more opportunities to participate in the management, through commonhold or through lessee-owned management companies
- Legislation needs to take account of the situation of lessee-owned entities, such as RTM companies, to ensure that their financial sustainability is not put at risk
- Property taxes (for example, council tax) should be used to discourage leaving residential property empty.

Building safety and standards

The Building Safety Act received Royal Assent on 28 April 2022. It is an ambitious and wide-reaching piece of legislation which seeks to address all of the recommendations in Dame Judith Hackitt's Independent Review of Building Regulations and Fire Safety. However, as a result of the extensive scope of the Act and the speed with which it was drawn up, there are a lot of inconsistencies and, in some places, mistakes in the Act. For example, the provisions introducing the new right for home-owners to sue the manufacturers of unsafe building products refer variously to buildings with two or more residential units and buildings with one or more residential units. As a result, the extent of this right is unclear.

Much of the detail has been left to regulations. There have so far been more than 20 different sets of regulations dealing with the Act, some of which have already been amended. This makes the legislation confusing and difficult to navigate. More worryingly, many of the necessary regulations have not yet been made. As a result, parts of the Act are not yet in force, and it is not clear how many of the provisions will work in practice.

The Act attempts to give leaseholders some protection from having to pay excessive service charges to cover the costs for remedial works, including removing and replacing unsafe cladding. There is a 'waterfall' system by which a landlord must first seek to recover costs from a developer and cannot charge service charges if their net worth exceeds a certain amount. But the Act does not adequately deal with the very common situation in which the 'landlord' is in fact a lessee-owned entity or where lessees are otherwise responsible for the maintenance of a building. Without adequate central funding for cladding and safety remediation works, there is a real risk of home-owners still facing unaffordable bills to make their homes safe.

Labour should review and build on the Act, correcting the mistakes and bringing all of the provisions into force as quickly as possible. Labour should ensure that no home-owners are faced with excessive bills for remedying defects in their buildings, by closing the loopholes in the Act and ensuring sufficient national funding for building safety works where it is impossible to recover these from developers. Further, Labour should consider clarifying and codifying the tests to be applied under the Building Safety Act. For example, the ability to obtain a Building Liability Order under section 130 is subject to an undefined 'just and equitable' test to be applied by the court. This creates uncertainty as to when it may be appropriate to seek recourse and may lead to leaseholders incurring costs in failed applications. It is of course possible that case law will plug some of these gaps, but this is something Labour should keep under review.

Similarly, prevention is better than cure. While the overhaul of building regulations is welcome, the most cost-effective long-term solution to building safety is to invest in effective oversight and enforcement. This includes local authorities having enough – suitably qualified – building inspectors to ensure that homes are properly and safely built and that breaches of building regulations are remedied before buildings are occupied. Labour should ensure local authorities can recover the costs of this from developers.

Summary of key proposals for building safety

- Review the Building Safety Act 2022 and remedy inconsistencies and mistakes, for example, uncertainty as to the number of residential units in the buildings to which the legislation applies and clarify and provide guidance on when a remedy will be granted.
- Bring the Building Safety Act fully into force as soon as possible and ensure all enabling regulations are clear, transparent and effective.
- Ensure that home-owners are not faced with excessive bills for remedying defects, for example, dangerous cladding, and that there is a national safety net of assistance if it is not possible to recover the costs from developers.
- Take pre-emptive steps to avoid residential buildings under construction being a threat to health and safety and that they are compliant with building regulations by ensuring they are inspected by qualified building inspectors prior to completion. These costs should be borne by the developers.

Costing

So far as the costs to public funds of the proposals set out here and in Chapter 1 are concerned, while the authors are lawyers, not economists, and such assessments would have to be made on Labour coming into office, we make the following points.

It can be assumed that Labour would not be as reckless with public funds as the Conservatives have been. There would be nothing like a VIP lane for government contracts or the scrapping of a part finished HS2 or the continuation of the Rwanda deportation scheme.

A majority of proposals in this chapter do not involve expenditure. In respect of those proposals which do require financial investment, we suggest that what is spent on the one hand can be offset by savings on the other.

The faster processing of homelessness applications would lead to reduction in expenditure on temporary accommodation, an area in which spending has increased by 62 per cent over the past six years.[26] Indeed, early interventions prior to actual homelessness would avoid the costs of dealing with applications and temporary accommodation that would otherwise follow. Security of tenure in the private rented sector would also reduce homelessness, and provide greater stability for tenants, which has economic benefits.

Further, greater provision of local authority housing would reduce both reliance on the high rents charged in the private rented sector and the Housing Benefit/Universal Credit bill, as would the system of rent control by reducing rent. Improving housing standards will also result in significant savings. The medical treatment of people affected by poor quality housing is currently estimated to cost the National Health Service £1.4 billion per year.[27]

The authors question whether the provision of local authority housing is to be regarded as expenditure. It might better be understood as the acquisition of assets that will increase in value. The abolition of 'hope value', which adds to the cost of land, will reduce costs when a local authority acquires it for housing development.

Other proposals, such as the provision of social housing through the revised planning system, would be funded by developers and not public expenditure.

Finally, increasing access to justice would involve expenditure but to a comparatively minor amount and, again, be offset by

---

[26] https://www.gov.uk/government/collections/local-authority-revenue-expenditure-and-financing#2022-to-2023.

[27] https://bregroup.com/news-insights/the-cost-of-poor-housing-to-the-nhs/#:~:text=Key%20findings,the%20housing%20stock%20in%20England.

savings. For example, research referred to in the previous section found that £1 of expenditure on housing advice saved the state £2.34. Advice and representation for tenants and occupiers would result, for example, in early resolution of potential eviction claims, avoiding homelessness or repairs being carried out with consequent results for health and safety.[28]

Conclusion

As is apparent from this chapter and Chapter 1, ensuring accommodation is accessible, affordable, secure and safe involves a raft of measures. This reflects the width of inequality in society, from low or no resources (the homeless), to the better resourced but still pressured leaseholders and home-owners and the different legal regimes affecting them. Much can be achieved by legislation.

While certain, but by no means all, of the recommendations require expenditure, overall, that should be modest and significantly offset by the savings which would be realised elsewhere. Action to overcome the various aspects of the housing crisis – such as ending homelessness and ensuring affordable housing with stability and safety – are long overdue and it is high time it took place.

---

[28] See J. Kelen, 'How to fund it: the economic case for civil legal aid' (in *Towards a National Legal Service*, Society of Labour Lawyers, 2023, pp 27–34) showing that funding civil legal aid in housing cases can reduce the state's resources spent on homelessness by a quarter, prevent reductions in house prices and increase stability in employment, all resulting in significant savings.

7

Constitutional reform: reforming the Lords and upholding standards in public life

Bren Albiston and Jemima Lovatt

Introduction

In this chapter we deal with reforming the House of Lords and reforming the Ministerial Code. The Labour Party has committed to making sweeping reforms to both. Therefore, we have sought to build upon the details provided in respect of these policies and how those policies might best be realised.

Reform of the House of Lords has been the great 'unfinished' work of nearly every radical government for more than 100 years, not because we cannot agree that it should be replaced, rather that we cannot agree what it should be replaced with. However, given the changing nature of the UK's territorial constitution, is an Assembly of the Nations and Regions the answer to that question? We have considered these proposals and attempted to make suggestions as to how best to realise this proposal.

Never before, it seems, have we suffered from such poorly behaved ministers, and prime ministers so willing to let even the most egregious breaches of the Ministerial Code go unpunished. As such, we have considered and sought to build upon the Labour Party's proposals to deal with this lamentable state of affairs.

House of Lords reform

It is currently Labour Party policy to, at some point, abolish the House of Lords and replace it with an elected (to whatever extent) upper house. Labour's vision for a fully reformed upper house has not been set out by the party in any particular detail, however it does appear that is, currently, the Labour Party's intention that the House of Lords should be replaced with what the Commission on the UK's Future called an 'Assembly of the Nations and Regions', which will be given an explicitly territorially representative role. Further, that it will be (at least partially) directly elected. Beyond these two basic points, the Labour Party has not set out any further detail as to the role, powers and structure of the Assembly or how it will be elected, or even if it will be fully elected.

However, the Labour Party's Commission on the Future of the UK led by Gordon Brown (henceforth the Brown Commission), has made a number of recommendations, in its report (henceforth the Report),[1] though it also left a good deal of detail to be worked out by others. We have, therefore, sought to address some of these points of detail.

For the reasons set out here, in our view, if the House of Lords is to be replaced by a directly elected Assembly of the Nations and Regions (henceforth the Assembly), the purpose of the Assembly must be considered with particular care. This first consideration will to a broad extent determine the form and function of the Assembly. We have also described the Brown Commission's recommendations in this regard. While, on balance, we would favour a directly elected "Senate" model upper house (as described in what follows), there are opportunities to incorporate elements of the "Bundesrat" model to create something of a hybrid model upper house.

There are, of course, a number of options which could be pursued in how the Assembly might be structured.

In addressing these points of detail we have made a number of recommendations, in the following categories:

---

[1] *A New Britain: Renewing Our Democracy and Rebuilding Our Economy* (December 2022).

- the role of the Assembly;
- membership; and
- elections.

However, given that the House of Lords will not be abolished in Labour's first term, immediate robust steps must be taken to improve the current arrangements, particularly in respect of appointments to the House of Lords.

In respect of the more immediate reforms to the House of Lords, the Labour Party has indicated that it intends to comprehensively reform the manner in which members are appointed, as well as reduce the number of members and impose a maximum age limit for members. We have, therefore, set out some possible ways that might be done, as well as some further reforms which might be considered.

The role of the Assembly

In reforming the House of Lords, we must be clear what we want that reform to achieve and the role a future upper house should perform. It cannot be the case that reform is led by the feeling that 'something must be done' without having a clear idea of what that something is.

At this stage, it is the Labour Party's intention that the Assembly will take on a territorially representative role. There are broadly two models this could take:

1. The 'Senate' model: This is similar to that of the Australian or Canadian Senates. Both of which, to a greater or lesser extent, were modelled on the House of Lords and therefore take on a similarly revisory role, together with a role in the process for amending their respective constitutions, while also representing and protecting the interests of their respective territories.
2. The 'Bundesrat' model: The German Bundesrat, or the South African National Council of Provinces, typify this model. These bodies also take on something of a revisory function, however their principal function is to protect the position of the various

sub-national units (for example, Lander in Germany), through the requirement that they consent to certain legislation. This includes certain constitutional and non-constitutional matters (such as funding settlements). Put simply, this model would make the upper house the central organ of negotiation between the national government and the devolved institutions. Which is why these types of bodies are not directly elected but are 'indirectly elected'.

The Labour Party has not indicated which of these two models it favours, however, it is apparent from the Report that the Brown Commission favours a hybrid of the two, which leans towards the Senate model, which is reminiscent of the Spanish Senate.

In our view, on balance the Senate model would be preferable, as it would be less constitutionally jarring than the Bundesrat model, we also agree with the Brown Commission that the Assembly should meaningfully represent the interests of the regions and nations. This is not straightforward and requires very careful consideration.

Powers of the Assembly

In order to fulfil this role, the Assembly will necessarily require the powers to do so. The Report recommended that the Assembly largely inherit the same powers and limitations as the House of Lords, save for its ability to delay legislation for a year.[2]

We agree with this, save in respect of the power to delay. It would, in our view, be perverse for the unelected House of Lords to enjoy more powers than an elected Assembly. Further, the power of delay can be an important tool in legislative process, in producing better legislation.

The Brown Commission also recommended that the Assembly should have the power to veto legislation which seeks to repeal or amend certain protected statutes, such as the various devolution

---

[2] Pursuant to s 2(1) of the Parliament Act 1911.

Acts (which it refers to as "Protected Statutes"). The Report refers to this as 'entrenchment'. The Report set out the following mechanism through which the Assembly would exercise its veto power:

1. The Assembly's presiding officer refers a bill to the Supreme Court to determine whether that bill would repeal, replace or amend a Protected Statute.
2. Assuming that the Supreme Court rules that the bill in question would repeal, replace or amend a Protected Statute, then the Assembly can then choose to exercise its veto power or not.

The Report argues that the involvement of the Supreme Court would make this a legal and not a political process. However, recent experience has shown that this is unlikely to be the case. Further, this process also throws up a great many procedural, political and legal questions.

Therefore, while we agree that the Assembly could have a role in securing Protected Statutes, the entrenchment mechanism should be simple. Such as the use of a 75 per cent majority. Entrenchment mechanisms of this kind are straightforward, would not necessarily require the involvement of the Supreme Court and would, in our view, be more effective.

Nevertheless, it should be recognised that this kind of entrenchment will mean that if the correct procedure is not followed to amend, repeal or replace the Protected Statutes, then the Court will be able to strike down that law.

Membership

In our view, there should be no element of appointment in the Assembly. This would fundamentally undermine the legitimacy of the Assembly to take on the role as constitutional guardian, as well as detracting from its territorially representative function.

Nevertheless, if it is decided that some element of the Assembly should be appointed, such members should be entirely appointed by an independent commission, similar to that of the Judicial Appointments Commission, rather than by the UK government as now. Such a commission should be given an express duty to appoint members who are diverse (including geographical diversity) and represent a wide range of expertise. Further, appointed members' involvement should be limited to participating in debates and proposing amendments.

The Report also considers that it may be appropriate for members of devolved governments to participate in the Assembly proceedings. However, while it would be beneficial for the views of devolved leaders to be heard in the deliberations of the Assembly, in our view, these persons should not enjoy an *ex officio* membership of the Assembly. To so otherwise would introduce an unhappy element of the Bundesrat model, which has no real place in an institution which is otherwise consistent with the Senate model.

Elections

In our view, the Assembly should be elected on a regional basis and those regions should be of broadly equal population.[3] In this way, the Assembly will, by design, not simply be representative of the three nations plus the regions of England, but the regions of all of the UK.

We would propose a *degressive* system of allocating seats, which allocates seats on the basis of population size, but which allocates a disproportionate number of seats to less populous regions. The Brown Commission has recommended that the Assembly should have 200 members. No reasoning has been provided for this number. We are concerned that this may be too small a number to carry out the scrutiny function that the Brown Commission envisions the Assembly would retain from the House of Lords. We would therefore suggest a higher number of closer to 250 to 300. This is still significantly smaller than the current membership of the House of Lords and less than half of the number of members of the House of Commons.

On this basis, we have, by way of example, set out Table 7.1. Each region could have a minimum of 14 seats in the Assembly, with a further seat per one million people (rounding up), to

---

[3]   This is a similar proposal to that recommended by the Royal Commission on Reform of the House of Lords in 2000 (the 'Wakeham Report'), see Chapters 11 and 12.

Table 7.1: Example seat allocation

Nation	Number of regions	Minimum seats	Seats based on population	Total
Northern Ireland	1	14	2	16
Wales	2	28	4	32
Scotland	4	56	6	64
England (including London)	9	126	24	150
				262

a maximum of 17 seats per region. Alternatively, top-up seat allocations could be made on the basis of a region's percentage of the UK's population overall.

This, in our view, navigates the difficult line between ensuring that all parts of the UK are properly represented and cannot have change imposed on them, while also not giving the minority an effective veto on change.

Further, in our view, all of the members of the Assembly should be elected using a closed list proportional system, as previously used for electing Members of the European Parliament and used in Wales and Scotland (for those members not elected by individual constituencies), using a 5 per cent threshold. This is because the members of the Assembly are there to represent their regions, rather than individual constituencies, which is properly the role of the members of the House of Commons.

Process of reform

Given that the Assembly will not, on current plans, be created in the first term of the next Labour government, it is necessary, in our view, to make improvements to the current system, about which there is already significant consensus and could, therefore, be achieved almost immediately. Further, these changes could act as a bridge to facilitate the transition from the House of Lords to the Assembly. We would suggest taking the following steps:

• Remove the last of the hereditary peers.
• Remove the Lords Spiritual (that is, the bishops).

- Reform the House of Lords Appointments Commission (HOLAC).
- Fix the number of members of the Lords to match the number of members of the new Assembly.
- Give devolved and local government a role in the appointment of new peers.
- Impose term limits, either in years served or by age.

Removing the remaining hereditary peers seems to us to be an obvious step, given its clear incongruity with a democratic system of government, even one in which members of the national legislature may be appointed for life. The same goes for the Lords Spiritual, who can no longer claim to represent the majority of even those who profess a faith in the UK, not to mention the obviously undemocratic fusion of church and state.

Further, the reform of HOLAC into an entirely independent body with a mandate to ensure that the House of Lords is sufficiently representative, seems to us to be an obvious move in the right direction. The formal inclusion of local and devolved governments in that appointments process seems a logical next step, not just to help ensure a sufficiently diverse and representative membership, but also to help make the transition to a territorially representative chamber. Together with these reforms, life tenure could be abolished, in order to aid better representation and diversity, with the imposition of an upper age limit. For example, in the Canadian Senate, the age is 75. Alternatively, members might have fixed 10- or 15-year terms.

Clearly, limiting the number of members of the House of Lords would address the real issue of there being far too many members, of which there are presently nearly 800. Further, limiting it to the number of members which will make up the proposed Assembly would not only help that transition, but also 'road-test' whether that number would be sufficient to discharge the functions of a second chamber. Limiting the number of members would also act to 'reset' the membership of the house, perhaps in in proportion to the vote achieved by the parties represented in the House of Commons, with a reset following each general election.

Transitional legislation

Whatever reforms are made to the House of Lords, either now or later, will necessarily require legislative machinery to make it happen. There are, broadly, three ways in which this could be achieved, depending on how those reforms are to proceed.

1. If intermediate reforms are to be introduced, of the kind set out earlier, these reforms could be set out in a standalone piece of legislation, to be followed by a second act abolishing the House of Lords and establishing the Assembly. It may be that the first act sets out the process by which the terms of the second will be settled upon, such as a statutory process of consultation, referenda or other mechanism.
2. Alternatively, if intermediate reforms are to be made, followed by the eventual introduction of the Assembly, these could be introduced in the same act.
3. If no intermediate reforms are not to be made, then a single act could be passed, either making the changes immediately, or setting out the mechanisms through which the changes will be made or decided upon, such as through consultation, referenda to other mechanism.

The particulars of the legislative machinery to bring about any such reforms will have to be considered very carefully, and we have not attempted to draft what this may look like (not least because of the uncertainties which still surround exactly what structure the reformed upper house will take). Nevertheless, the Constitutional Reform Group has, in its draft 'Act of Union' bill,[4] set out the kinds of provisions that would be required. In summary, the act establishing the Assembly would, at a minimum, have to do the following:

- Provide for the abolition of the House of Lords.
- Repeal or amend all of the relevant legislation pertaining to the House of Lords.

---

[4] https://www.constitutionreformgroup.co.uk/download/act-of-union-bill-2021/.

- Empower the Secretary of State to make necessary consequential legislative changes.
- Make provision for its membership and manner of appointment or election and any qualifying criteria.
- When the first session of the Assembly will commence (that is, immediately following election of the Assembly or after the abolition of the House of Lords).
- Make provision for legislation that is currently before the House of Lords, but which will not be either enacted or returned to the House of Commons before the abolition of the House of Lords.
- Set out the powers of the Assembly.

If the Labour Party is to pursue a policy of replacing the House of Lords with a directly elected Assembly of the Nations and Regions, it ought to be entirely elected, to do otherwise would undermine the territorial role of the Assembly. Further, that it should be elected on a regional basis using a closed list proportional vote system, so that the members of the Assembly do not cut across the constituent link enjoyed by members of the House of Commons. Furthermore, that the Assembly should take on some role in protecting the constitution, particularly the territorial aspects of the UK's constitution, as well as taking on the powers and responsibilities of House of Lords in scrutinising ordinary legislation. However, these reforms to the upper house should be accompanied with other reforms to protect devolution, through the introduction of an enforceable Sewel Convention, as well as effective entrenchment and consent mechanisms (described in Chapter 10).

However, in circumstances where the House of Lords is not abolished, meaningful and robust reforms to the House should be made, to address its total membership, the nature of that membership, as well as the tenure and appointment of its members.

An Act of Parliament to enshrine the Ministerial Code

The Labour Party has committed to reforming standards in public life and how those standards are maintained and policed. For example, in 2022 Angela Rayner committed to creating an independent Ethics and Integrity Commissioner to stamp out corruption in government, strengthen the rules and ensure they are enforced'.[5] This work is much desired by the electorate; in November 2023, UCL's Constitution Unit published its paper 'The future of democracy in the UK', which revealed that 79 per cent of participants sought reform so that ministers who do not act with integrity are punished and over 50 per cent supported an independent regulator-led investigation, when presented with various breach scenarios. These demands are made for good reason. The frequent stories that those in public office have lied or abused their position have come to be expected by the public. Such that, this kind of behaviour is now 'priced in' by the voters. There are obvious examples; from Partygate to Owen Patterson. Some more subtle examples of how mistruths now pervade the everyday operation of our government and Parliament include: the failure of Lucy Frazer MP to correct the record after misleading Parliament in relation to tax credits, the failure of Penny Mordaunt MP to fulfil her commitment to Parliament, that ministers would be required to declare hospitality they have received within the same timeframes as MPs, amongst others.

There are many challenges and problems in the current system of enforcing and policing standards in public life. Many of these have been explored by Chris Bryant in his book *Code of Conduct*, with admirable clarity. However, here we will concentrate on the codes of conduct that govern the conduct of ministers.

Currently, Members of Parliament must abide by the Code of Conduct for MPs. The Code of Conduct for MPs is a document published with the approval of the House of Commons, it applies to members in all aspects of their public life and incorporates the Seven Principles of Public Life (the 'Nolan Principles'). The Nolan Principles were developed by the Committee on Standards in Public Life in its first report of 1995. They are: Selflessness, Integrity, Objectivity, Accountability, Openness, Honesty and Leadership.

---

[5]   Institute for Government, 'Keynote speech: Angela Rayner MP, Labour's Deputy Leader', Institute for Government website, 13 July 2023, at https://www.instituteforgovernment.org.uk/event/angela-rayner; Commission on the UK's Future (2023).

An alleged breach of the Code is subject to an investigation led by the Parliamentary Commissioner for Standards and, as necessary, referred to the Committee on Standards and the Independent Expert Panel who will test whether the breach has been proven on the balance of probabilities.

Whereas, 'ministers' conduct is also subject to the Ministerial Code. This sets out the standards of conduct expected of ministers and how they should discharge their duties. Ministers are responsible for their conduct and ensuring that their actions meet the standards set by the Code. Where an allegation is made, the prime minister must decide, in consultation with the Cabinet Secretary, whether it warrants further investigation. The prime minister may refer the matter to the Cabinet Office or the Independent Adviser on Ministers' Interests. Ultimately, the prime minister will determine whether a breach of the expected standards has occurred. Where the prime minister decides a breach has occurred, but he retains confidence in the minister, he may require a public apology, remedial action or removal of ministerial salary for a period. Where he does not retain confidence in the minister, then he will be sacked from his ministerial post.

Ministers must also abide by an unwritten system of 'constitutional conventions' and pay heed to the Cabinet Manual. However, enforcement of and adherence to the Ministerial Code is a political/normative, rather than a legal, issue. An example is that ministers are bound by collective responsibility to support government policy, even if privately they disagree. These conventions have proven extremely valuable to the smooth running of government, but recent governments have all but eroded, or bent these conventions into a completely different shape.

The two systems for MPs and ministers are very different. The Code of Conduct for MPs and the Guide to the Rules functions more or less effectively because it involves the independent non-partisan Parliamentary Commissioner for Standards alongside the Committee on Standards which is constituted with cross-parliamentary and democratically elected members. The Ministerial Code and the associated constitutional conventions are implemented entirely at the will of the prime minister. To further undermine this already highly partisan system, it is applied to people he is linked to, and presumably supportive of, by their very appointment to the Cabinet. Thus, the Ministerial Code and constitutional conventions rely heavily on the players in our constitution abiding by unwritten rules, colloquially known as the 'good chaps' theory of government. As recent events have proven, the 'good chaps' cannot be relied upon.

Some will ask: why does this matter? We know politicians are far from perfect, and why should we care if ethical standards are not upheld, if they deliver? However, standards are essential to facilitating the highest quality delivery. Without an ethical environment, those who are primarily self-interested will flourish at the expense of dedicated ministers. The Government's handling of the vaccine roll-out was effective. However, imagine how much better, and less ruinously expensive, the broader pandemic response might have been if procurement for things such as PPE might have been if access to ministers was not such a key factor in determining who was awarded supply contracts. This is a conduct issue, and one which has led to the likes of Lady Mone (a Conservative Peer) accruing vast amounts of public money, for not very much in return.

Putting the Ministerial Code on a statutory footing

Therefore, we propose that the Ministerial Code is placed on a statutory footing by way of an Act of Parliament (henceforth the Act). This will provide clarity to its substance and gives an opportunity to set out a procedure for its management. We would propose that the Code is not simply transposed into law, but subject to a detailed pre-legislative review and consultation process. We, unlike the Brown Commission, do not believe that the Cabinet Manual should be combined with the Code. Instead, we suggest that the Cabinet Manual be updated and then subject to approval at the start of each Parliament, thus allowing it to remain a 'live' handbook to aid ministers, rather than some contested and static document.

We are also of the view that the new statutory code should be protected from repeal or 'wrecked' by amendment of a future government when it becomes inconvenient. As we saw with the Johnson government, prime ministers are not beyond using their majorities to make ill-judged and self-serving changes to the rules. Therefore, and in the interests of constitutional stability, the Act should be entrenched, per the discussion in Chapter 10.

The Act will need to address enforcement. Currently, the prime minister has the final decision which can result in partisan decision-making. Furthermore, there is a direct conflict if the prime minister is the one charged with breaking the Ministers' Code. The role of an Independent Advisor on Ministers' Interests was created in 2006 in response to a recommendation by the Committee on Standards in Public Life.[6] However, the effectiveness of this arrangement has come under scrutiny, following two of Johnson's Independent Advisors resigning after finding themselves in untenable positions. The first advisor, Sir Alex Allan, resigned in 2020 after leading an investigation which found a breach of the Code had been committed by a minister, but this finding was effectively rejected by the prime minister, who instead supported the minister in question.[7] In 2022, the second office holder, Lord Geidt, also resigned after he was asked to advise on a plan to maintain tariffs on Chinese steel that would have broken World Trade Organization rules, through which Johnson had risked a 'deliberate and purposeful breach of the ministerial code'.[8] This arose shortly after Johnson refused to acknowledge the findings of the Gray Report into alleged gatherings on government premises during COVID-19 restrictions and consequently Lord Geidt found his position untenable.[9] Thus, the respect and significance of the so-called independent advisor has been significantly undermined. If the position is to continue, then we support recommendation

---

[6]   https://cspl.blog.gov.uk/2022/06/16/independent-adviser-role-should-be-strengthened/; https://image.guardian.co.uk/sys-files/Politics/documents/2007/03/27/Standardscommittee.pdf, p 7; https://publications.parliament.uk/pa/cm200506/cmselect/cmpubadm/1457/1457.pdf, p 4.

[7]   ' "Bullying" report chief Alex Allan quits after PM backs Priti Patel', *The Times*, 21 November 2020, at https://www.thetimes.co.uk/article/bullying-report-chief-alex-allan-quits-after-pm-backs-priti-patel-5jgtf7fqg.

[8]   Resignation letter from Lord Geidt, 15 June 2022, at https://assets.publishing.service.gov.uk/media/62ab07d28fa8f503b372588f/Lord_Geidt_letter_to_PM.pdf.

[9]   Ibid.

seven made by the Committee on Standards in November 2021,[10] that the appointment of such a role should be through an enhanced version of the current process for significant public appointments.

However, reflecting on the demands of the electorate to restore standards in public life, we are calling for wholesale reform. The system should be fair, equal and clear such that if you are the most popular person in your party, you should still be subject to investigation. Currently, political outsiders are far more likely to be scrutinised and sanctioned than a party's leading lights. The current system is poorly understood, and no wonder given its labyrinthian nature; there are 15 different bodies in place and a total absence of any navigational guide. John Nicholson MP was called before the Privileges Committee in 2023 in relation to alleged breaches of confidence and impartiality, which it argued amounted to a contempt of Parliament. A number of issues arose during this case. First, the allegations included reference to rules of which no MP was aware. Second, the Committee was unable to identify the test for 'breach of confidence' initially claiming that it would use the 'Plain English' version rather than the legal definition, despite it being a term of art and the dictionary definition relying on the legal definition. Nicholson was left not knowing what test he needed to meet. Third, the Committee refused to allow Nicholson's legal adviser, Dr Sam Fowles, to speak on his behalf or to object to the introduction of new evidence which had not been disclosed in advance and which Nicholson was never allowed to see, despite there being no suggestion that it was sensitive or confidential. Fourth, the Committee made the bizarre request that Nicholson rewrite any submissions drafted by Dr Fowles 'in his own words'. A system that is so challenging for an MP and his legal adviser to understand is clearly not accessible to the ordinary citizen who should be able to observe a clear method in upholding the ethical standards of those in public life.

---

[10] The Committee on Standards in Public Life, 'Upholding standards in public life: final report of the standards matter 2 review', November 2021, at https://assets.publishing.service.gov.uk/media/617c02fae90e071983346 52d/Upholding_Standards_in_Public_Life_-_Web_Accessible.pdf, pp 57–8.

We suggest a new system for enforcement should instead rely upon an independent body for Ministers' Conduct; in this we support the Brown Commission's proposal for an Independent Integrity and Ethics Commission (henceforth the Commission) who should have the role of investigating breaches of the Act. While the final determination could be left up to either a special tribunal, a committee of Parliament (made up of members of both Houses) or, as the Brown Commission has suggested, by the upper house.

At the first instance, the Commission would decide whether a minister has broken the Ministers' Code. This would create independence and oversight as well as separating out the judge and jury, currently both held by the sitting prime minister. If a minister is found to have breached the Act, there ought to be scope for requiring them to leave ministerial office and be disqualified from holding such offices for a minimum period of time, similar to that of a disqualified company director. Thus, the Commission would act as a regulator for ministers.

The primary criticism of this proposal is that a single Commission would amass too much power for a body that exists without the same level of accountability as our elected institutions. However, under our proposal, the Commission would exist by virtue of an Act of Parliament and will therefore have been subject to a robust debate in both Houses. Furthermore, its final determination would be subjected to a body constituted of democratically elected members, such as a parliamentary committee. Overall, the benefits of clarity, consistency and consolidation far outweigh the challenges levelled at the proposed Commission.

The formation of the Commission may allay the critics. Its scope and powers must be precisely defined. We favour a sliding scale approach whereby less serious breaches are dealt with on the recommendation of the Commission while more serious punishment is proposed as an advisory recommendation which is then put to a democratic body for a final decision. At a minimum, it is likely that a minister could seek to appeal a decision of the Commission by way of judicial review. Given the sanctions we are suggesting, it is unlikely that a criminal appeals process would be relevant but there could develop a more wide-ranging appeals process through the civil courts.

The process of creating the new Act could either be done by primary legislation alone or with regulations being made by an appropriate select committee. It's likely that a combination will be appropriate with some issues requiring a marked step-change through the immediate tabling of legislation, and some elements needing further discussion and the building of cross-party consensus through a select committee.

Through this process, there is room for some additions to the Act that develop the substance of the Cabinet Manual and Ministers' Code. For example: a prohibition on second jobs; a requirement for all public appointments to be approved by an appointments regulator; a declaration of any private interests to be published on Parliament's website within 24 hours of a ministerial appointment; a prohibition for any paid or unpaid lobbying activities; a 'Transparency Register' to record anyone who meets with a minister available on request to members of the public; and a declaration of all assets and liabilities at the beginning and end of every term of office to be provided to the commission.

It may also be preferable to provide for the continued development of the Act through a special Parliamentary Committee, given a power to compel an Order in Council to give effect to any changes, insofar as any such changes do not erode the standards by which ministers are held to account.

Turning to how better standards can more immediately be implemented by the next government, there are likely to be a large number of new Members in Parliament. They need to understand the ethical frameworks for MPs and for ministers. The Committee for Standards in Public Life has been asked to address all new MPs setting out what standards new MPs are expected to meet, however we would suggest the next Parliament should include a formal induction process to ensure a consistent and fulsome understanding of the rules. Many of the rules that already exist simply need to be followed. For example, the system for correcting the record is in itself effective, yet it is now blatantly ignored by many ministers who don't regard it worth their time. Whilst reform is undertaken, new ministers must understand and uphold the existing rules and should sign a Ministerial Contract through which they sign up to the

Ministerial Code and this should also make binding on them the recommendations of the Advisory Committee on Business Appointments for when they leave office, thus addressing the 'revolving door' problem.

Conclusion

A new Act of Parliament is a significant step towards rebuilding public trust in politics, which has been eroded in recent years, and repairing relations between the nation states of the UK. Currently, the prime minister is law maker, judge and jury. This has allowed for significant breaches of trust in what the public expect of their leaders. The prime minister, as leader of the Cabinet and the Commons can determine the extent to which conventions are satisfied. This system places too much power in one person which can be abused for their own interest. Therefore, a new Act of Parliament is required to codify the Ministerial Code, to place our conventions on a statutory footing and to create an independent commission responsible for enforcement.

Summary of key proposals

House of Lords reform: immediate/transitionary reforms

- Remove the remaining hereditary peers, as well as the bishops.
- Reform HOLAC into a statutory body, with the power to block appointments.
- Fix the number of seats in the House of Lords.
- Give devolved and local government a role in the appointment of new peers.
- Impose term or age limits on membership.

The Assembly of the Nations and Regions

- Give the Assembly a role in protecting the constitution, through the use of super majority voting requirements.
- Transfer all of the powers of the House of Lords to the Assembly, including the power of delay.
- Preserve and transfer the House of Lords revisory role to the Assembly.

- Make the Assembly entirely elected, using a regional proportional representation system.
- Allocate seats on a 'degressive population basis'.

The Ministerial Code

- Create a statutory Independent Ethics and Integrity Commissioner to enforce the Ministerial Code.
- Place a revised and updated Ministerial Code on a statutory footing, which is entrenched.
- Create a new Parliamentary Committee to periodically update the Ministerial Code.
- Make the punishment for breaches of the Ministerial Code more robust, up to and including disqualification from public office.

8

Devolution

Bren Albiston

Introduction

The UK's constitution is beset with problems and is no longer fit for purpose. It is no longer a mechanism for good government, instead it has become an engine of conflict and failure in governance. Recent history has shown us that the constitution is particularly vulnerable to an executive which is uninterested in upholding the basic tenets of our constitutional order, whether that is the proper use of executive powers, undermining devolution or even the rule of law. There is, therefore, a need for fundamental reform in order to preserve, protect and enhance our constitution, to ensure not only good government, but the continued integrity of the UK.

In this chapter we have focused on securing and enhancing the devolution settlement, which is now, so often, a cause of constitutional conflict and uncertainty. The options outlined here will, in our view, go some way to address the constitutional issues faced by an incoming Labour government.

Reforming the UK's devolution settlement

For the reasons set out in this chapter, we are of the view that the UK's devolution legislation should be consolidated and simplified in order to provide certainty and clarity as to the functions and responsibilities of devolved institutions.

Further, that the UK's devolution settlement should be reformed to ensure the constitutional autonomy of devolved institutions, as well as to introduce the principle of subsidiarity and create a clear mechanism for the further devolution of competences. Furthermore, in our view, the manner in which financial resources are shared across the UK should be reformed to facilitate greater autonomy and certainty for devolved institutions.

The UK's devolution settlement is fundamentally unstable, uncertain and unpredictable. This is because the UK Parliament and, in practice, the UK government can exercise power in any area it chooses, without regard to the Devolved Governments and Legislatures, as found by the Supreme Court *R (Miller) v Secretary of State for Exiting the European Union*.[1] This is the case despite the codification of the Sewel Convention in the Scotland Act 2016 and the Wales Act 2017, which recognises that, although 'the Parliament of the United Kingdom will not normally legislate with regard to devolved matters',[2] the UK Parliament can legislate in any area (devolved or otherwise) without the consent of the devolved legislatures. Indeed, as we have seen, the current Conservative government is largely unconcerned with obtaining such consent, with the result that the UK Parliament and government regularly transgress the division between devolved and reserved competences. One need only look to the Internal Market Act 2020 and the Subsidy Control Act 2022, among others.

A further consequence is that the *future* of devolution is also uncertain. This is because, fundamentally, the devolution of any further powers, resources and responsibilities is within the gift of the UK Parliament and, in reality, the UK government. Indeed, it is also within the power of the UK government to take away competences. This lack of a clear roadmap, or mechanism, for greater devolution, and the lack of constitutional protections for those powers already devolved, creates conflict between different

---

[1]   [2017] UKSC 5.

[2]   Section 2 of the Scotland Act 2016, which amended s 28 of the Scotland Act 1998 and s 2 of the Wales Act 2017, which amended s 107 of the Government of Wales Act 2006.

devolved institutions and between those institutions and the UK government, which generates constitutional uncertainty and ultimately undermines the union.

In addressing these issues, we have set out four sections dealing with the following:

1. The principles underpinning future devolution.
2. The mechanics of future devolution.
3. Protecting the devolution settlement and promoting constitutional autonomy.
4. How to ensure devolved institutions have the resources they need.

Principles underpinning future devolution

In our view, the principles which should underpin the future of devolution across the UK are:

1. Subsidiarity and 'double devolution'.
   Subsidiarity is the principle that state action should be taken at the lowest appropriate level of government. Put simply, it is a principle which seeks to push responsibility for taking action down to the most local level of government appropriate in the circumstances. That action could be either passing legislation or enacting policy. It is predicated on the presumption that state action is most successful when taken at the lowest level of governance, consistent with the subject matter and the objective to be attained.
   'Double devolution' connotes the principle that once powers have been passed down to one level of government, that level of government then further passes those powers down to an even more local level of government, if appropriate.
2. Equivalence.
   In our view, the future of devolution must be built on the principle of *equivalence*. That is, every appropriate devolved institution must have a right (subject to appropriate mechanisms) to all the powers enjoyed by an equivalent devolved institution. For example, Wales ought to have a right to the same powers as enjoyed by Scotland, or Greater Manchester the powers of Greater London.

Presently, any powers not already contained within the relevant devolution legislation, must be granted by the UK government. This creates uncertainty and drives asymmetry, as well as creating constitutional and political conflict, which in turn creates resentment towards the UK government and undermines the Union. Therefore, these points of conflict ought to be removed or ameliorated.

3. Coherence.

We must create a framework for devolution which moves away from the asymmetry that currently defines it. That is not to say that flexibility should be abandoned, quite the opposite. Rather, we must ensure that in developing devolution further, it is less complex and easily understood by the peoples of the UK and their respective governments.

4. Constitutional certainty and autonomy.

The competences of the devolved institutions must be constitutionally guaranteed, which will in turn ensure their constitutional autonomy, this should be achieved through a robust system of entrenchment and the strengthening of the Sewel Convention. This will create constitutional and legal certainty, engender the confidence of both citizens and business in the devolved institutions, which will in turn strengthen the union.

Incorporating subsidiarity

In our view, subsidiarity should be incorporated in two forms: first, as an 'interpretative presumption'; and second, as a constitutional duty.

1. An interpretive presumption.

Incorporating the principle of subsidiarity would best take the form of a presumption or interpretative rule that the courts would be instructed to apply when construing the extent of the limitations on the powers of all levels of devolved governments. Such a rule could be drafted as follows:

> So far as it is possible to do so, primary legislation and subordinate legislation which confers powers to

the Devolved Institutions must be construed in such a way as to give effect to the Principle of Subsidiarity. For the purposes of this Act, The Principle of Subsidiarity means: 'action should be taken at the lowest most appropriate level of government or administration consistent with the subject matter and the objective to be attained, as specified in the relevant primary and subordinate legislation'.

2. A constitutional duty.
   It has been shown that where functions are carried out at the most appropriate level of government, outcomes are significantly improved. However, that level is not necessarily the level to which powers have been formally devolved. Consequently, there may be cause for further, or *double*, devolution. As such, in our view, there ought to be a legal duty on devolved governments to seek to further devolve power as far as possible, and retain responsibility for service delivery responsibilities only insofar as it is necessary.
   The duty could be drafted as follows: 'All relevant Devolved Institutions have a continuing duty to take such action as is necessary to give effect to the Principle of Subsidiarity, giving due regard to the proportionality of doing so.' Necessarily, the extent to which this duty has been complied with would ultimately be a question for a court. We would suggest that in adjudicating this question, the test could be as follows:

   With regard to the duty to give effect to the Principle of Subsidiarity and the proportionality of doing so, the extent to which that duty has been complied with will be assessed using the following test : 'can the objective of the proposed action, or any particular activity in relation to such an action, be reasonably and proportionately be achieved by a lower level of government than the Devolved Institution seeking to take that action?'.

If the answer is yes, then the court can then order the higher level of devolved government to make such arrangements as are necessary to give effect to the *principle of subsidiarity*.

Legislative framework for future devolution

In order to deal with the UK's incoherent, ad hoc and insecure devolution settlement, a clearer statutory framework should first consolidate and rationalise the existing devolution statutes, and second set out the mechanisms for future devolution, together with the entrenchment mechanism described earlier.

Broadly, the new framework should enumerate all the competences which currently could be devolved per level or 'tier' of devolved government. The framework would provide that the relevant devolved institutions have a right (without the necessity for further UK legislation) to take up those powers and competences.

In essence, the framework would set out a menu of powers and competences that can be drawn down, as appropriate to that tier of devolved institution, when the relevant devolved institution chooses to do so.

Ensuring devolved institutions have the resources they need

Meaningful devolution of power, across the UK, can only be achieved through a progressive and secure system of resource distribution. Through this we can effectively empower our communities to take the action needed to help create a fairer more equal economy and society, where the accident of geography does not limit opportunity or determine how bright an individual's or their community's future could be.

In our view therefore, concrete constitutional and legal steps must be taken in order to facilitate a more equal economy. As such, we agree with the Brown Commission Report's recommendation that: 'There should be an explicit constitutional requirement to rebalance the UK's economy so that prosperity and investment can be spread more equally between different parts of the UK than it is today, thereby equalising living standards across the country' (henceforth the Duty). However, in our view, the Duty is not enough on its own. It must be accompanied by a legal requirement to *equalise* resources across the UK.

Equalisation is the transfer of financial resources from wealthier regions to poorer ones, within a national territory. Broadly speaking, equalisation can seek to achieve two things, fiscal capacity equalisation and fiscal need equalisation.

Fiscal capacity equalisation seeks to equalise revenues across sub-national units. Whereas, fiscal need equalisation takes into account a number of different factors, such as historic underspending or the need for greater capital expenditure.

It is broadly recognised that without actually transferring funds from the wealthier parts of the UK to less wealthy parts, any obligation to make the economy and opportunity more equal will be meaningless.

The Barnett Formula is well known, therefore we will not spend time here explaining how it functions. Nevertheless, the Barnett Formula does not attempt to achieve either fiscal capacity or fiscal need equalisation, nor is it set out in statute. Further, in relation to England's regions there is no mechanism to ensure any measure of equalisation. This has led to severe regional inequalities.

The Calman Commission recommended[3] that the Barnett Formula should be reformed to take account of need. That is, *fiscal need*. This is a recommendation, which appears to us, would help achieve the Duty. In our view therefore, the Calman Commission's recommendation should be explored by a Labour government.

It follows that the Duty ought to be accompanied with further provisions incorporating a reformed Barnett Formula. Such provisions should address both fiscal need (as recommended by the Calman Commission) and fiscal capacity. Further, that that statute should apply to the English regions and, eventually, to the existing devolved jurisdictions.

---

[3] The Commission on Scottish Devolution, *Serving Scotland Better: Scotland and the United Kingdom in the 21st Century*, Final Report, June 2009, see Recommendation 3.4, p 10.

Certainty and constitutional autonomy

The UK lacks constitutional certainty, which creates conflict between constitutional actors, instability and unpredictability. Constitutional certainty is derived from a clear delineation of powers and responsibilities between constitutional actors and the predictable use of those powers, together with clear mechanisms for resolving conflicts between those actors. In other words, there is a clear and buttressed separation of powers.

Constitutional certainty is fundamental to the proper and effective functioning of the state. Without such certainty, different constitutional actors lack clarity over what actions they can and cannot take. This can, therefore, create conflict between those actors as they do not have a firm basis on which to negotiate and resolve differences between themselves or effectively exercise their powers and discharge their responsibilities. Constitutional uncertainty also fundamentally undermines the relationship between individuals and the state, and ultimately the rule of law by undermining legal certainty.

The UK's lack of constitutional certainty is no more apparent than in respect of devolution. This arises principally as a consequence of the power the UK government can exercise, either on its own through delegated powers, or through its majority in the UK Parliament. Indeed, the actions of the Conservative government vividly demonstrated the ease with which UK ministers can use executive power and the UK Parliament's legislative supremacy to undermine the devolution settlement. This takes, principally two forms: first, the ability to remove or reduce competences; and, second, the ability to legislate in areas of devolved competence without consent of the devolved legislatures.

This issue must be addressed, not just because constitutional uncertainty can critically undermine the state, leading to failures in governance, but also because constitutional uncertainty risks creating broader *legal* uncertainty, which will, in turn, undermine business confidence and damage the economy. All of which goes to erode individuals' confidence in the UK, which will further fuel the nationalist arguments for the break-up of the UK.

Put simply, there is a lack of constitutional protection for the devolved institutions and the competences which have been devolved to them, which the UK government can transgress or change whenever it is politically expedient to do so. As a result, they lack constitutional autonomy. Consequently, we are of the view that existing competences, and the scope of those competences, should be protected through entrenchment, and that the Sewel Convention should be made binding.

Manner and form entrenchment

There are, broadly, two forms of entrenchment, 'substantive' and 'procedural' entrenchment. Substantive entrenchment dictates *what* laws a legislature can make. Whereas procedural entrenchment dictates *how* certain types of laws are made.

An example of substantive entrenchment can be found in the US constitution, where no one constitutional actor has the power to amend the text of the constitution. An example of procedural, or 'manner and form', entrenchment can be found in sections 31 and 31A of the Scotland Act 1998, which set out that the Scottish Parliament can only make certain changes to the way MSPs are elected by way of a two-thirds majority.

In essence, therefore, entrenchment can either determine the kind of laws a constitutional actor can lawfully enact, or the procedure by which it enacts those laws. Some constitutions contain both of course. However, for our purposes we are concerned only with 'manner and form' entrenchment as there is no limit on what laws the UK Parliament can make.

Manner and form entrenchment is commonplace across other 'Westminster style democracies'. In these countries, manner and form entrenchment takes, principally, two procedural forms. Either, requiring some element of consent and/or requiring a super majority in the national legislature.

Consent based entrenchment usually takes two forms: consent by a majority of electors through a referendum and/or consent from the relevant states/provinces.[4] Whereas, super majority

---

[4]   Amendment of the Australian Constitution requires both majorities in referenda and a majority of states voting in the affirmative.

entrenchment, at its simplest, requires that a minimum number of members of the legislature to vote in favour. Some countries' constitutions contain both super majority and consent requirements. For example, the Canadian Constitution Act 1982 requires both the consent of the Provinces and super majorities in the House of Commons and the Senate, to amend certain parts of that act.

Where a law is protected by manner and form entrenchment, of this type, that is, where a law can only be amended by way of the correct procedure, any purported amendment which did not follow that procedure would be disapplied insofar as it did not conform to those requirements. This therefore, protects the entrenched laws from express and implied amendment and repeal, where the correct amendment procedure is not followed.

This kind of mechanism is legally straightforward, as, usually, all it requires a court to do is to determine whether and to what extent a new enactment amends a protected enactment, and if so whether the amending instrument was enacted using the correct procedure. If the correct procedure is not followed, then insofar as the later enactment impermissibly modifies the protected statute, that later enactment will be disapplied.

In our view, the entrenchment of devolved competences ought to involve both consent and super majority requirements, for changes which would reduce competence. This could be by way of a super majority in the House of Commons, together with either a referendum or consent by the relevant devolved legislature.

The Sewel Convention

The Sewel Convention is, in essence, that the UK Parliament will not legislate in an area of devolved competence, without consent of the relevant devolved legislature. The Sewel Convention was, as mentioned earlier, put into statute in the Scotland Act 2016 and the Wales Act 2017, which state: '[I]t is recognised that the Parliament of the United Kingdom will not normally legislate with regard to devolved matters without the consent of the [Scottish Parliament] [Assembly].' However, the Supreme Court has held that the Sewel Convention is, despite being put on a statutory footing, not enforceable.[5] The Commission on the Future of the UK, led by Gordon Brown, in its report, *A New Britain: Renewing our Democracy and Rebuilding our Economy*, recommended that the Sewel Convention should be made legally enforceable,[6] as has the Welsh government in its paper *Reforming our Union*.[7]

It is important to recall that the UK Parliament can legislate in any area it wishes to, and doing so does not necessarily change the competences which have otherwise been devolved. It simply means that UK legislation will trump any contrary laws enacted by a devolved legislature. Consequently, even if, for example, the Scotland Act 1998 was entrenched using the manner and form method set out earlier, it would not stop the UK Parliament from legislating in areas of devolved competence, it would simply protect what had already been devolved. Whereas, making the Sewel Convention justiciable and removing the 'not normally' wording would prevent the UK Parliament from legislating in an area of devolved competence without prior consent from the relevant devolved legislature.

This consent requirement is another type of manner and form entrenchment. Consequently, it does not alter the scope of the type of legislation the UK Parliament can enact, simply the manner in which it does so. As such, the UK Parliament could legislate to remove this procedural requirement. Therefore, such a requirement may need to be 'doubly entrenched', as described in the following section.

It should also be noted that the Brown Report recommended that the Sewel Convention should be extended to secondary legislation as well, which it currently does not. At present, UK government ministers have power to intervene in the creation of primary and secondary legislation created by a devolved government or legislature, as well as being able to make their own regulations in otherwise devolved areas of competence. Consequently, if the Sewel Convention was to extend to secondary legislation as well, UK ministers would

---

[5]   *R (Miller) v Secretary of State for Exiting the European Union* UKSC 5.

[6]   Commission on the UK's Future, *A New Britain*, 2022, p 103.

[7]   Welsh Government, *Reforming our Union: Shared Governance in the UK*, second edition, June 2021, pp 4–5.

be prevented from doing so without consent from the relevant devolved government.

Making the Sewel Convention justiciable in the manner set out here will functionally prevent the UK government trespassing in areas of devolved competence, which would promote constitutional certainty and predictability.

Double entrenchment

A provision incorporating manner and form requirements is itself susceptible to amendment by ordinary legislation, if it is itself not entrenched. This is what is referred to as 'single entrenchment'. Therefore, in order to protect against the danger of circumventing manner and form entrenchment, by way of amending, repealing or the application of 'notwithstanding clauses' to the entrenching provisions, such provisions will need to be 'doubly entrenched'. Simply put, double entrenchment means that the entrenching provision is itself entrenched.

Conclusion

In order to secure the future of a properly functioning devolution settlement, the legislative framework of devolution must be reformed. That framework must rationalise, consolidate and enhance the current devolution settlement. It must set clear and impartial mechanisms for future devolution of competences and what powers are available. This is to clarify the role of each level of government in the UK, to reduce the frequency and intensity of conflict between constitutional actors which will, ultimately, lead to better governance across the UK. Further, the devolution settlement must be entrenched, and the Sewel Convention made binding. Finally, meaningful devolution requires both a duty to rebalance the UK's economy, together with an effective system of equalisation.

Summary of key proposals

- Introduce the principles of subsidiarity and 'double devolution' through the creation of an interpretative presumption of subsidiarity, and the imposition of a duty of subsidiarity.

- Create a consolidated menu of devolved powers and responsibilities which can be drawn down by devolved institutions by right.
- Introduce a system of resource equalisation, based on fiscal need and capacity.
- Entrench the devolution settlement, backed up with double entrenchment.
- Make the Sewel Convention binding.

9

Environmental law

David Wolfe, Bren Albiston and David Drew

Introduction

People are quite properly ever-more outraged by our polluted rivers, the toxic air we breathe, the depleted state of our natural environment and the lack of action both to head off and deal with the emerging consequences of climate change.

It is, for example, a continuing national embarrassment that water companies still routinely discharge untreated sewage into our rivers, destroying their biodiversity and rendering them toxic for swimmers and other users. Even in the last few years, agricultural practices such as excess spreading of manure have left many of our iconic rivers, such as the River Wye, in a highly damaged state. Polluted air is killing children. Climate change is already leading to weather extremes, provoking flooding, challenging farmers, and risking the health of vulnerable people.

Each of us can act to reduce the environmental harm we personally cause. But significant government action is also needed.

That government action could involve major additional government spending or structural steps such as nationalising the water companies. Many would argue that both are necessary, but both could pose big political and fiscal challenges for a Labour government. On the other hand, large amounts of public money could be saved and environmental damage averted by cancelling damaging Conservative plans including around road building.

This chapter is not about those things. It is about existing environmental law.

This chapter proposes bold steps around the operation and application of environmental law which can bring major environmental benefits and which will mark a radical departure from that of recent Conservative governments, and yet which are readily achievable without great public expenditure or new legislation. Most of the proposals merely involve an adjustment in approach taken by government to *existing* environmental law. As we explain, that shift in emphasis can achieve a lot.

The final section of the chapter sets out proposals for new environmental rights, strengthening the duties on the stewards of our natural environment and helping citizens hold them directly to account. They provide some solutions to the growing sense of outrage about the state of the environment which is only likely to grow if the situation does not improve drastically.

The existing legal framework

Membership of the European Union (EU) required the UK to have a strong framework of environmental protections around the natural environment, air pollution, industrial chemicals, waste, industrial activities, and so on. Almost all of that remains in place as 'assimilated law'[1] – UK legal provisions which replicate the EU legal requirements in place at the point of Brexit. Examples in environmental law include the Habitats Regulations which largely continue to secure the nature protection elements of the EU Habitats Directive, the Wildlife and Countryside Act which continues to secure provisions of the EU Birds Directive, and environmental impact assessment regulations which carry on the essence of the EU environmental impact assessment regime. Brexit has (so far at least) brought few significant departures *of substance* from the EU environmental protections. That should not come as a surprise given the UK's strong historic role in inspiring and promoting many of those EU protections and even

---

[1] Department for Business and Trade, 'Retained EU law dashboard', Gov.uk, last updated 22 January 2024, at https://www.gov.uk/government/publications/retained-eu-law-dashboard.

Conservative political commitments not to reduce the substance of environmental protection law following Brexit.

We also still have, thanks to the last Labour government, the Climate Change Act 2008. It provides a powerful framework for securing the action required to help prevent catastrophic climate change and the steps needed to mitigate those changes which are already upon us or will follow soon including more flooding, heat and unpredictable seasons.

The pressing need for action

However, as we explain, despite that relatively optimistic starting point, led by the Conservative government, there have nonetheless been significant legal changes in the *operation and application* (as opposed to the substance) of some areas of environmental law following Brexit.

Without changing the actual environmental laws, the Conservative government took an approach to the operation and application of many of those existing laws which, in practice, significantly undermined our environmental protections and failed properly to tackle the environmental crises we face.

Some of the issues set out here are administered by the Devolved Administrations. The majority of the issues we address however are the responsibility of the UK government (or address the situation in England). Some involve overlap – for example, the Climate Change Act 2008 imposes obligations on the UK government in relation to greenhouse gas emissions from the whole of the UK (and it is those we consider here), but Scotland, Wales and Northern Ireland have also adopted their own legislative provisions which impose additional obligations on their own administration.

We offer the following themes: a different approach to existing legal protections, some areas where additional legal mechanisms will be needed, and thoughts on the legal regime around climate change.

A different approach

An incoming Labour government will be able to behave differently in the operation of existing environmental protections. It should commit to doing so.

That could prevent major environmental harms and bring about major environmental improvements without significant additional public expenditure and without needing legislative change, certainly not to primary legislation (for which precious parliamentary time would be required).

We offer some examples to illustrate the point, relating to enforcement of existing rules, to the use of powers to authorise pollution, to the approach to 'risk' when it comes to industrial chemicals and in the making and amendment of statutory instruments (an administrative rather than parliamentary process), and in the need to face up to (rather than postponing for later) agreed-to-be-necessary action to protect our natural environment.

At the time of writing, there are live challenges to the *legality* of the approach taken by the Conservative government on some of these issues. Even if those court cases fail – and the Conservative government is held to have acted *lawfully* – that does not change the fact that the Conservatives made political choices in each case; choices which have reduced the action taken to tackle the urgent environmental crises we face. A Labour government should make different choices in the types of situation we illustrate here.

Example 1: Sanctioning criminality

The 'Farming Rules for Water' were introduced in 2018 in England as part of the UK's Enforcement of the EU Water Framework Directive.[2] Similar provisions exist in Scotland, Northern Ireland and Wales. Those rules regulate farming activities (mostly the spreading of manure or manufactured fertiliser on fields) which in excess leads to phosphate and nitrate pollution of rivers which significantly harms nature and adversely affects businesses in the tourist and other industries which depend on the health of our rivers. This is an acute problem in areas where a concentration of intensive poultry units or dairy units has created a huge local surplus of hard to transport manure such as in Wales and England along the River Wye or in the south-west.

---

[2]   The Reduction and Prevention of Agricultural Diffuse Pollution (England) Regulations 2018, at https://www.legislation.gov.uk/uksi/2018/151/made.

That should not be happening because that excessive or unseasonal spreading of manure from poultry and livestock (the main cause of the problem) is a criminal offence. But it persists. Why? It persists because enforcement by (in England) the Environment Agency is weakened partly by it having been starved of resources, but more problematically through pressure, arguably verging on an instruction, to the Environment Agency from the Secretary of State[3] to misinterpret and underenforce the rules. This is akin to the Home Secretary telling police forces to turn a blind eye to speeding unless the driver is doing over 100mph. In effect, law breaking is being sanctioned following a political instruction from the Conservative government. So pollution of rivers continues.

A change of approach is desperately needed. A Labour government should not only ensure that the Environment Agency is sufficiently resourced to do its job properly and help farmers change their practices but – crucially – take active and urgent steps to bring about full compliance with the law to help restore our rivers for wildlife and people alike.

Example 2: Authorising harmful pollution

EU Regulation 1107/2009[4] (which now takes effect in the UK as assimilated law) lays down rules for the authorisation of plant protection products in commercial form and for their placing on the market, use and control within Great Britain. It explains that it is 'underpinned by the precautionary principle in order to ensure that active substances or products placed on the market do not adversely affect human or animal health or the environment'.

Neonicotinoids are manufactured chemicals which were historically applied to sugar beet seeds to protect the crop from yellows virus carried by aphids which can reduce yields and thus profits. But – as neurotoxic pesticides – they also affect the nervous

---

[3] DEFRA, statutory guidance, 'Applying the farming rules for water', Gov. uk, last updated 16 June 2022, at https://www.gov.uk/government/publications/applying-the-farming-rules-for-water/applying-the-farming-rules-for-water.

[4] Regulation (EC) No 1107/2009 of the European Parliament and of the Council, at https://www.legislation.gov.uk/eur/2009/1107/contents.

systems of bees (essential as pollinators) and other important insects, resulting in paralysis and eventually death. For that reason, in 2018 (that is, pre-Brexit) the Conservative government of the time supported new EU-wide rules which prohibited the outdoor use of three neonicotinoids – clothianidin, imidacloprid and thiamethoxam.

But, since Brexit (from 2021) Conversative governments specifically allowed 'emergency authorisations' (contrary to the advice of the Health and Safety Executive [HSE] and the independent Expert Committee on Pesticides) permitting neonicotinoids to be used in the UK as a derogation from the general ban. Such derogations are supposed to be only for 'special circumstances … where such a measure appears necessary because of a danger which cannot be contained by any other reasonable means'. The 'danger' said by Conservative governments to justify allowing for this environmental harm is that profits from growing sugar beet might dip. But, of course, growing sugar beet is a choice for farmers. Allowing the use of neonicotinoids was a political choice, not one driven by necessity.

It is quite inconceivable that repeated derogations on this basis would have been contemplated or allowed by the EU pre-Brexit. This is a good example therefore of how the Conservatives claimed not to have reduced environmental protections post-Brexit, while actually doing exactly that in practice by the way it operated within the framework of those rules.

Through changing that approach (and without additional public spending and without needing any legislative change, let alone to primary legislation) a Labour government could and should work with farmers and others to support and improve our food and farming system in a way which does not involve permitting the unnecessary use of dangerous farm chemicals.

Example 3: Slipping behind

The examples so far are of the government taking a different approach to the environmental rules which have been carried over from the time of the UK's membership of the EU.

There is one significant area where Brexit itself brought a substantial change in the legal regime of environmental protections. This is known as REACH (the Registration, Evaluation, Authorisation and Restriction of Chemicals). It sets the rules for the chemicals which can be sold or included in products and includes everything from the insulation in our sofas to the ink used in tattoo parlours, including the 'forever chemicals' now being released into our environment with possible long-term irreversible health and environmental impacts.

As part of Brexit, the Conservative government made significant changes to the regime of protections which had previously applied. UK REACH[5] is no longer the same as EU REACH. The result is both changes to the rules *and* the way that the HSE – under government oversight and also with stretched resources – operates those rules.

The UK is no longer keeping up with the EU in protecting its people and natural environment. Since Brexit, five new chemicals have been added to the list of those needing special authorisation and justification for use in the EU,[6] including products used as fuel additives, in formulation of inks and in lubricants; all of which potentially imperil human health, and a further eight have been banned or restricted. But not in the UK. We are now more exposed to potentially harmful industrial chemicals than are people in the EU. A Labour government should not tolerate that. We should be at least as well protected, not worse off.

Part of the problem is that the HSE – now going it alone (without other agencies across the EU to work with) – does not have the capacity to keep up, but another part is a change of approach.[7]

For example, the HSE is now (through political choices by the Conservative government) setting a higher bar for evidence of harm before taking action and taking a less precautionary approach than the EU. We doubt that the public want those greater risks

---

[5] HSE, 'UK REACH explained', at https://www.hse.gov.uk/reach/about.htm.

[6] European Chemicals Agency, 'Five substances added to REACH Authorisation List', at https://echa.europa.eu/fr/-/five-substances-added-to-reach-authorisation-list.

[7] https://www.gov.uk/government/publications/uk-reach-rationale-for-priorities/rationale-for-prioritising-substances-in-the-uk-reach-work-programme-2023-to-2024.

to be taken with their health. A Labour government should act to ensure that – even within the downgraded rules of the UK REACH legal framework – the HSE properly applies the precautionary principle in cases where the scientific evidence is uncertain, but the risks are high. That is just one example of the kind of change that is needed.

Example 4: Delaying environmental improvements

People imagine that in modern Britain what they flush away will be processed and disposed of in an environmentally safe way. Sadly, that is not the case.

The well-known horrors of sewage treatment works (now run for private profit) routinely discharging untreated sewage into rivers do not need repeating here. The Labour government could take major steps – including through improved operation of the existing regime which regulates those private sewage works – to help bring that to an end.

Less well known though is what happens to the dry material left from the processing of that part of the sewage which does get treated in the sewage works. The 'sludge'. Ninety-six per cent of that sludge (some 3.5 million tonnes per year) is spread on farmland as a natural fertiliser for crops. On the basis of what was known at the time, and on the basis of the kinds of things we flushed down the toilet at the time, the Sludge (Use in Agriculture) Regulations 1989[8] exempted that activity from needing a waste disposal permit even though it is clearly waste disposal. Those 1989 rules remain in place. As a result, sludge spreading is largely uncontrolled, with little monitoring of the content of the sludge.

However, since 1989, people have changed what we flush down the toilet. It now contains greatly increased quantifies of organic and inorganic chemicals and microplastics which are not removed by the waste treatment process in the sewage works. The Environment Agency and even the Conservative government realised that the uncontrolled spreading of sewage sludge on fields

---

[8]   The Sludge (Use in Agriculture) Regulations 1989, SI 1989 No. 1263, at https://www.legislation.gov.uk/uksi/1989/1263/made.

growing crops 'is no longer acceptable'. The food we eat is grown in fields being fertilised with polluted sludge.

Thankfully, in 2020, the Conservative government of the time decided that the 1989 regulations should be changed to remove the regulatory exemption, so that sludge spreading can then be properly regulated with monitoring and controls on what is done to ensure it is safe. However, four years on, that has still not happened. An initial target deadline of the end of 2023 for changing the rules was abandoned simply on the basis that the Environment Agency and the Department for Environment Food & Rural Affairs (DEFRA) had not got round to dealing with the administrative processes of changing a single statutory instrument. This issue was, in effect, politically kicked into the long grass. A practice which everyone accepts is environmentally unacceptable is carrying on, simply through lack of political will.

A Labour government should prioritise the implementation of this and other agreed-to-be-essential regulatory improvements.

Example 5: Putting off the problem

As it happens, the Conservative government introduced some important new environmental rules which could help tackle our environmental problems. The Conservatives government was thus entitled to trumpet its promotion into law of obligations in the Environment Act 2021 which require government to set and then achieve statutory targets for improvements in our natural environment.[9]

But, as the previous examples have already shown, what matters is not just the laws themselves, but how they are operated in practice by government. In that regard, the Conservative government then immediately slipped behind with action on the targets which it set for itself under its own flagship 2021 Act. The statutory Office of Environmental Protection (OEP) – on which we say more further on – advised in March 2024 that 'very substantial challenges remain, and that government is largely off

---

[9] https://www.legislation.gov.uk/ukpga/2021/30/part/1/chapter/1/enacted.

track to meet [its Environmental Improvement Plan] ambitions, Environment Act targets and other commitments'.[10]

However, rather than promptly acknowledge that problem and act swiftly to get back on track, the Conservative government hid behind the fact that the 2021 Act gives it 12 months to comment on what the OEP had advised. The UK's depleted natural environment cannot afford for government to follow the slow path to action. A Labour government needs to be proactive in setting and acting to achieve strong and clear targets under the 2021 Act. A Labour government should not pretend that enacting legislation is a substitute for taking action, in a way which the Conservative government did in the environmental law sphere.

Climate change: the urgent need for action

National and international action is needed to help slow the onset of climate change and avert global catastrophe, and to mitigate the impacts we are already experiencing and which are imminent.

For a while, there seemed a political consensus in the UK that we should play our part. It was the Labour government that introduced the Climate Change Act 2008.[11] Conservative Prime Minister Theresa May tweaked it in 2019,[12] when the global community recognised in the Paris Agreement 2015 that we needed to reach 'Net Zero' by 2050.

Some background is needed. Many human activities lead to the emission of greenhouse gases, particularly carbon dioxide. Burning fossil fuels (such as petrol) is perhaps the most obvious problem, but there are many others. In contrast, there are other things we can do to remove those same emissions from the atmosphere, such as planting trees which suck them up as they grow. 'Net Zero by 2050' means that we have to reduce the things which create emissions and increase those things which suck them up so

---

[10] Office for Environmental Protection, 'Progress in improving the natural environment in England 2022/2023', January 2024, at https://www.theoep. org.uk/sites/default/files/reports-files/E02987560_Progress%20in%20 Improving%20Natural%20Environment_Accessible.pdf.

[11] https://www.legislation.gov.uk/ukpga/2008/27/contents.

[12] https://www.legislation.gov.uk/ukdsi/2019/9780111187654.

that they are at the same level, that is, net zero. The international consensus, as set out in the Paris Agreement, is that this needs to be achieved by 2050 across the world.

The Climate Change Act provides a legal framework for achieving this change though UK action. Within that framework, the government sets targets (based on advice from the Climate Change Committee) – known as 'Carbon Budgets' – for each five-year period (we are currently in CB4). The country is on track to meet CB4 and indeed CB5, but largely because they were set before the Paris Agreement required all countries to move faster. The Conservative government boasted about meeting the easy targets of CB4 and CB5, while not taking the necessary steps to make achieving CB6 realistic.

Tory backsliding

Part of the problem is that the apparent political consensus on the need for action evaporated, with the Sunak government backtracking even on commitments made by previous Conservative Prime Minister Boris Johnson, for example, on electric vehicles and heat pumps.[13] Prime Minister Rishi Sunak justified the backtracking by claiming that the economic impact of those original commitments was not given sufficient scrutiny. But he was the Chancellor – legally responsible for advising on economic impacts – at the time.

So why is that change of approach a legal issue?

Because the Conservative government did its best to get round the legal protections and requirements of the Climate Change Act 2008. For example, the Secretary of State for Energy Security and Net Zero approved a set of policies and proposals which he stated 'will enable' CB6 to be met (as required by section 13 of the Climate Change Act[14]) even though civil servants had warned that they had low, or even very low, confidence that nearly half of what was being contemplated would actually ever happen.

---

[13]   https://www.gov.uk/government/speeches/pm-speech-on-net-zero-20-september-2023.

[14]   https://www.legislation.gov.uk/ukpga/2008/27/section/13.

In a legal challenge brought by environmental non-governmental organisations, the High Court held that the Conservative Secretary of State acted unlawfully in assuming that all the government's policies and proposals for mitigating climate change would deliver hoped-for emissions savings when he should have looked properly at the risks of non-delivery to come up with a properly deliverable package to help achieve Net Zero. That was essentially a political choice about how to interpret and apply the law. A Labour government needs to make different legal choices, consistent with having pioneered the UK's climate change legal framework. That could include giving clarity about the roll-out of electric vehicles while being active (not passive, like the Conservative government) in ensuring that we have the charging point network that every driver will need.

The Labour government's Climate Change Act 2008 also provided a powerful framework for action on what are known as 'adaptations'. In other words, the things we need to do to deal with the impacts of even that amount of climate change (namely, a 1.5 degree global temperature rise) contemplated by the Paris Agreement and Net Zero: the flooding, the sea level rises, the necessary changes to farming practices, and so on. These are things that *will happen*. The law requires government to act on them: section 58(1) of the 2008 Act[15] requires the government to lay programmes before Parliament setting out its objectives in relation to adaptation to climate change, its proposals and policies for meeting those objectives, and the time-scales for introducing those proposals and policies. The Conservative government's published programme treated that as an obligation simply to try and make things a bit better, rather than actually setting clear objectives for what has to be achieved by when to make us all safer in the face of the impending weather and other changes. The independent statutory Committee on Climate Change complained of the lack of 'clear outcomes supported by a delivery programme with measurable goals, and a demonstration of how the outcomes link to the activities in the programme'.[16] Even

---

[15] https://www.legislation.gov.uk/ukpga/2008/27/section/58.

[16] https://www.theccc.org.uk/wp-content/uploads/2024/03/Independent-Assessment-of-the-Third-National-Adaptation-Programme-NAP3.pdf.

if the court accepts that the government acted lawfully in that regard, the Conservative government still made a political choice to take a minimalist approach to the legal framework. Having put in place that framework in the first place, a Labour government should act to ensure that it delivers for us all, not slow peddle now in a way which will lead to crisis later.

So far, what we have discussed would not need primary legislation (when parliamentary time will be precious) or any real public expenditure. What follows needs the former, and a bit (but not much) of the latter. We think it will be worth it.

The Office of Environmental Protection

As we have explained, much of our environmental law has carried over from our years in the EU. During that time, the UK's compliance with those laws (like that of every other member state) was overseen by the EU Commission. Post-Brexit that is no longer the case. Instead, we have the (recently created) OEP.[17] The OEP is clearly much better than nothing and, like our other environmental regulators, it is staffed by people committed to the best outcomes. However, again like our other environmental regulators, it is under-resourced, lacking in independence[18] and constrained by a legal framework which is so cumbersome as to blunt the OEP's teeth, even if not leaving it actually toothless. A Labour government will enthusiastically comply with environmental law and so has nothing to fear from a strong and independent oversight regulator. It should properly resource the OEP and give it proper independence alongside simplifying the rules it must follow to allow for effective environmental oversight.

An Environmental Rights Bill

Wildlife and Countryside Link (a coalition of the UK's main environmental non-governmental organisations) has been

---

[17] https://www.theoep.org.uk/office-environmental-protection.

[18] See, for example, the way in which the OEP board is appointed by the Secretary of State whose actions it oversees: https://www.legislation.gov.uk/ukpga/2021/30/schedule/1/enacted.

developing an Environmental Rights Bill which the next government is being invited to enact.[19] A Labour government should not find this politically difficult. The thrust of the Bill is to give effect in the UK to provisions of the Aarhus Convention 2005, which the then Labour government signed up to as international law, but which the subsequent Conservative governments have only partly implemented in UK law.[20]

The Aarhus Convention, at its core, seeks to confer on citizens certain rights to better understand and influence environmental policy, to better hold governments to account. However, at its core, it recognises that everyone, both present and future generations, has the right to a clean, healthy and sustainable environment. This is a legal right already enjoyed by citizens in 155 of 193 countries.[21] But the UK is not one of them. Yet.

The Environmental Rights Bill, or legislation advancing the Aarhus Convention's core principles, would confer greater weight on environmental factors in decision-making and give people stronger powers to challenge decisions which harm their environment and health. This would advance human rights, boost nature's recovery and improve health outcomes for millions.

Nuisance

What we have said so far relates to government action and the way in which the public can hold the government to account. But environmental law is also about directly protecting us from (and directly allowing us to challenge) the actions of private organisations, such as our neighbours. That bring us to the law of 'nuisance'.

---

[19]   https://www.wcl.org.uk/environmentalrightsbill.asp. Here we must declare an interest. David Wolfe KC, one of the authors of this chapter, is part of the team which has been developing the Environmental Rights Bill.

[20]   The UK operates a 'dualist' system which means that the government can sign up to international agreements without that, in itself, making any difference to law within the UK: https://en.wikipedia.org/wiki/Monism_and_dualism_in_international_law.

[21]   https://www.europarl.europa.eu/RegData/etudes/ATAG/2021/698846/EPRS_ATA(2021)698846_EN.pdf.

There are, broadly, four types of nuisance: *private* nuisance, *public* nuisance, *statutory* nuisance and *criminal* nuisance. However, we are only concerned with public and statutory nuisance.

A public nuisance is an action which endangers life, health, property, morals or comfort of the public, or obstructs the public in the exercise of enjoyment of rights common to all. Statutory nuisances are those listed in Part III of the Environmental Protection Act 1990 (EPA).

Nuisance is a well-developed area of the law and could be a powerful tool in holding those who damage the environment to account. However, there are principally two hurdles to it being so: (1) 'standing'; and (2) 'limitation'. That is, who can bring the claim and how long, after the action causing the nuisance, a claimant can commence their claim.

Put simply, only the state and those with a tangible connection to the public or statutory nuisance can bring an action. Often the state fails to do so and the private individuals lack the resources to do so. This means that the nuisance may continue and the damage goes unpunished. The Labour government could consider widening the scope of those who can take this kind of action, to any legal person who can show that there is a *public interest* in them doing so.

For both types of nuisance, an action can only be brought within six years of the date on which the action or omission giving rise to the nuisance comes to an end.[22] However, the action can come to an end well before the effect of the nuisance ceases, or even discovered. Therefore, imposing time limits of this kind can have particularly unfair consequences in pollution cases.

The Labour government should consider extending or even abolishing these time limits. There are two possible ways of doing so, either by introducing a 'latent' damage period, as already exists for negligence claims, which creates a secondary three-year period from the date the damage was discovered.[23] Alternatively,

---

[22] Sections 2 and 9 of the Limitation Act 1980 respectively and confirmed in relation to public nuisance in *Jalla v Shell International Trading and Shipping Co Ltd* [2023] UKSC 16.

[23] Section 14A of the Limitation Act 1980.

a claimant could be given the ability to bring an action for as long as the effect of the harm caused by the nuisance continues.

The Public Trust Doctrine

Alongside the Environmental Rights Bill already described, the Labour government should consider introducing the 'Public Trust Doctrine' into UK law.

The Public Trust Doctrine (henceforth the Doctrine) is, in essence, the principle that the state holds certain natural assets *on trust* for the benefit of the general public. That is, that the government would owe fiduciary duties, as trustees, to the general public, as a class of beneficiaries. The kinds of assets classically protected by the Doctrine are 'the air, running water, and sea and consequently the shores of the sea'.[24]

While some argue that the Doctrine already forms part of the English common law, a recent High Court decision found it not to be so.[25] Nevertheless, it has been argued that the Doctrine should be introduced into UK law, particularly given that since leaving the EU we are particularly susceptible (as has been shown by the actions of the Conservative government)[26] to the weakening of environmental protections, as described earlier.[27]

The Doctrine protects natural assets: (1) from *alienation* (that is, selling/giving away protected natural assets); (2) from *diversion* (that is, transferring those assets from one part of the state to another and for a different purpose); and (3) from *damage* by human activity.[28] It would enable individuals to claim against the

---

[24] *Institutes of Justinian*, 2.1.5, at 92 (Sandars trans, seventh edition, 1962).

[25] *R (Marine Conservation Society, Richard Haward's Oysters (Mersea) Limited and Hugo Tagholm) v The Environment Agency, The Water Services Regulation Authority.*

[26] See, for example, 'England to diverge from EU water monitoring standards', *The Guardian*, 27 October 2023.

[27] See, for example, M. Willers and E. Shirley, 'The public trust doctrine's role in post Brexit Britain', UKELA e-law newsletter, March/April 2017, issue 99, at https://www.gardencourtchambers.co.uk/news/the-public-trust-doctrines-role-in-post-brexit-britain

[28] C. Redgwell, *Intergenerational Trusts and Environmental Protection*, Manchester University Press, 1999, pp 47–8.

state, individuals and other legal persons who are responsible for protected natural assets, as well as by the state against individuals and other legal persons.

In fulfilling the duties imposed by the Doctrine, ordinary trust principles would apply. Which means that the state (as trustee) would need to undertake the kinds of balancing exercises all trustees undertake. In this case, the balance is between utilising, or exploiting, natural resources, which might cause damage to the environment, for the benefit of the public, against their duty to protect and preserve those natural resources for the use and enjoyment of the public.

However, in undertaking this balancing exercise the state would also need to consider the rights of future generations to enjoy protected natural assets against those alive now. This is what is sometimes referred to as 'intergenerational equity' (something already featuring in legislation to some extent in the form of obligations around 'sustainable development'), and it is an important principle which underpins the Doctrine. This kind of balancing exercise is well known to the courts and they would have a very great deal of trust law to fall back on in carrying out this analysis.

However, if the Doctrine were introduced, it would not replace environmental protection legislation. Instead, it would act as a legal *backstop*, which allows individual citizens to bring actions where those *normal* environmental protections are inadequate or not properly enforced. In this way, the Doctrine can act to buttress existing regulation, as well as broader environmental law principles, such as the polluter pays principle, and encourage the development of greater environmental protections.

It is, however, a reality that many of the natural assets which would be protected by the Doctrine are used by private entities undertaking public functions, such as water companies. Beyond these, there are many other private activities, such as farming, mining and industrial activities, which exploit protected natural assets. As such, in order to protect these natural assets from damage, as described earlier, the Doctrine would need to extend to these private entities.

The Doctrine is a possibly more flexible and less proscriptive measure than the Environmental Rights Bill described earlier.

That being said, it may have a more far-reaching effect, as it would impose legally enforceable duties on non-state actors.

Conclusion

In the past, Britain was rightly recognised as the 'dirty man [*sic*] of Europe'. But, within the EU, the UK gradually turned things round, promoting and adopting high environmental standards across industry, agriculture, water, waste and beyond. It became safe to drink from every water tap – that had not been the case before.

We have already mentioned the way in which a changed approach post-Brexit to the regulation of chemicals leaves Britain lagging behind in keeping pace with new products and new science. But in some areas the problems and the solutions are long-standing and well understood. And while others move forward the UK is standing still. Take lead shot, still used for shooting wild birds despite the well-known problems it causes for wildlife and water. Now banned in the EU[29] but still widely used in the UK. A Labour government should move swiftly to end its use. Just recently, the Conservative government said the UK will not follow the EU's lead in putting place what is known as 'extended producer responsibility', which means cosmetic and pharmaceutical companies will be asked to contribute to the cost of treating wastewaters if they are causing chemical pollution.

The standards set and adopted by the EU before and since Brexit provide a good benchmark against which to assess the performance of the current and future government. We do not believe that people in Britain want lower environmental protections than those in place in France, Germany, Italy or Spain. Moreover, a Labour government should be seeking to make our air cleaner, our wildlife more abundant, our water clearer and more sparkling than that enjoyed in those other countries. An upward not a downward ambition.

Finally, a Labour government should take concrete steps to empower people to hold government and polluters to account for their actions, or lack of action. It must recognise that we, our

---

[29] https://environment.ec.europa.eu/news/new-rules-banning-hunting-birds-lead-shot-wetlands-take-full-effect-2023-02-16_en.

children and all future generations have a right to a clean and sustainable environment that does not do us harm.

The options outlined in this chapter show how – without significant public expenditure and (in many cases) without using any parliamentary time on new legislation – a Labour Government can take immediate and effective action, to protect and enhance our environment, as well as longer-term reforms to lock in and expand upon those actions.

Summary of key proposals

- Ensuring that the Environment Agency is sufficiently resourced to do its job properly or help farmers change their practices.
- Proper resourcing of the OEP and giving it full independence and simplified operating rules.
- Taking active steps to ensure full compliance with environmental protections under the law avoiding the use of derogations where possible.
- Maintain alignment with the EU's higher environmental standards, for example in relation to REACH (the Registration, Evaluation, Authorisation and Restriction of Chemicals).
- Ensuring the HSE properly applies the precautionary principle in cases where the scientific evidence is uncertain, but the risks are high.
- Prioritising the implementation of agreed regulatory improvements such as removing the regulatory exemption for spreading of sewage sludge on agricultural land.
- Proactively set strong and clear targets to implement the Environment Act 2021 in practice.
- Set clear targets and take specific action to deliver net zero under the Climate Change Act 2008, for example in relation to the roll-out of electric vehicles and the necessary EV charging point network.
- Implement an environmental rights bill to ensure the right to a clean, healthy and sustainable environment as contained under the Aarhus Convention.
- Introduce the Public Trust Doctrine to enshrine the principle that the state holds certain natural assets on trust for the general public.

10

Artificial intelligence: professionalising the AI industry – to control technology, we should regulate humans

Jacob Turner and Tristan Goodman

Origins and features of professionalisation

The origin of professionalisation lies in the medieval 'Guilds of Trade', which restricted entry to certain industries in exchange for minimum quality standards imposed on industry entrants. Today, the professions include lawyers, doctors, dentists, accountants and airline pilots.[1] What have remained largely unchanged are four elements: the individuals involved have specialist training and knowledge; their admission to the profession is conditional on upholding minimum standards; their activities are regulated with sanctions for noncompliance; and they are bound by a common set of values.[2]

Professionalisation has therefore been described as a 'grand bargain'.[3] The public accept lower supply and possibly higher costs

---

[1] Although the term 'profession' has a broader colloquial meaning, in this chapter it specifically refers to those industries or trades which exhibit the four characteristics referenced earlier. References to 'professionals' throughout this chapter should be understood as individual members of these professions.

[2] R. Susskind and D. Susskind, *The Future of the Professions*, Oxford University Press, 2015, p 15.

[3] Ibid., p 9.

of professional services due to restrictions on entry, in exchange for what should be guarantees of quality, safety and trustworthiness. For regulated professionals, the bargain often involves undergoing rigorous, time-consuming training and ongoing obligations throughout their careers, in exchange for the prestige of working in an exclusive and trusted profession,[4] and, in many cases, the feeling of personal fulfilment enjoyed by those for whom their work is not merely a job but a vocation.

As a mode of regulation, professionalisation can take different forms. For professions such as law and medicine, professional standards are mandatory and backed by external regulations, such that those practising without a valid licence can face fines and even criminal sanctions. Mandatory legally backed regulation is particularly justified where a trade or occupation exhibits the following two features:

1. *Technical complexity*. The most regulated professionals are often those whose expertise and outputs are particularly difficult for the average person to understand and scrutinise. Patients are often unable to make an informed assessment of the medical opinion provided by their doctor. Consequently, a patient often has little option but to believe the opinion of their doctor or ask another medical professional for a second opinion.
2. *Societal importance*. The more critical a profession is to society and public safety, the greater the need for its regulation. Though watchmakers may have a high level of technical expertise, their role is not so vital as to warrant professional regulation. If a watchmaker creates a defective watch, the customer might be disappointed and request a refund or replacement. In contrast, if a doctor acts negligently, the consequences can be very significant and possibly irreversible for the patient.

---

[4] As a mark of the communal respect accorded to the professions, the list of individuals who are permitted by the UK government to verify the identity of an applicant for a passport is limited to 'recognised professions' or otherwise persons of 'good standing in their community'. HM Government, 'Countersigning passport applications and photos', at https://www.gov.uk/countersigning-passport-applications/accepted-occupations-for-countersign atories.

In this chapter, we suggest that the development of artificial intelligence (AI) systems[5] exhibit both these features and thus argue that the relevant individuals should be subject to mandatory legally backed regulation. We then explain how professionalising AI development could be achieved in practice, and why the UK is well placed to play a leading role in this process.

Reasons for professionalising the artificial intelligence industry

Although access to AI has greatly increased in recent years, the development of AI systems remains a technically complex task. Those involved must decide on aspects such as the 'hyperparameters'[6] and datasets to train the AI model, as well as select the appropriate computing hardware to run and host it. The most sophisticated AI systems will require the input of many highly skilled individuals. The development of AI systems is also typically opaque to outsiders. Even those who have sufficient skill to understand how an AI system functions may not have the access required for evaluation, since the code, datasets and other relevant inputs are often proprietary to the organisation which created the system in question.

In terms of societal importance, AI systems pose many risks, both in daily life as well as more broadly in terms of public safety.[7] These benefits and risks are growing quantitatively and qualitatively as the technology advances and becomes more

---

[5]   As set out in the section on 'A proposed definition of "artificial intelligence professional"', for these purposes we refer to AI systems as those which are adaptable and autonomous – in the sense that they can perform new forms of inference from datasets which are not directly envisioned by their human programmers and make decisions without the express intent or ongoing control of a human.

[6]   In this context, hyperparameters are pre-defined settings that govern the learning process of a machine learning model, influencing its behaviour and performance. These are distinct from model parameters, which are learned during training.

[7]   These risks were acknowledged by 28 countries (including the UK, US and China) and the European Union at the UK AI Safety Summit at Bletchley Park in November 2023. 'The Bletchley Declaration by countries attending the AI

deeply embedded in social practices and decision-making processes, including high-stakes domains such as healthcare, employment and law enforcement. As US Vice President Kamala Harris recently commented, these risks can be 'existential' in nature for the individuals negatively affected by algorithmic decision-making.[8]

AI is a general-purpose technology which can be put to many different uses, some of which are riskier than others. Though not every AI system is necessarily a matter of public importance, the societal importance of AI as a whole is widely acknowledged. Moreover, with the advent of increasingly powerful foundation models – that is, AI models trained on a broad data at scale and which are adaptable to a wide range of downstream tasks, like GPT-4[9] – the distinction between 'safe' and 'non-safe' AI systems is diminishing, since the same underlying architecture and features may be used across multiple domains.

Given the many uses of AI cannot necessarily be predicted at the time of a system's development or even deployment, it will be the guardrails placed on such technologies by those developing them at every stage of their lifecycle which will help to ensure that, whatever the use case, the essential qualities of safety, security and trustworthiness are upheld. By focusing on the people, rather than the stages of the supply chain, ethical and other regulatory standards can be embedded throughout.

Safety Summit, 1–2 November 2023', 1 November 2023, at https://www.gov.uk/government/publications/ai-safety-summit-2023-the-bletchley-declaration/the-bletchley-declaration-by-countries-attending-the-ai-safety-summit-1-2-november-2023.

[8] K. Harris, 'Remarks by Vice President Harris on the future of artificial intelligence', London, United Kingdom, 1 November 2023, at https://www.whitehouse.gov/briefing-room/speeches-remarks/2023/11/01/remarks-by-vice-president-harris-on-the-future-of-artificial-intelligence-london-united-kingdom/.

[9] R. Bommasani, D.A. Hudson, E. Adeli, R. Altman, S. Arora, S. von Arx et al, 'On the opportunities and risks of foundation models', 2021. https://doi.org/10.48550/arXiv.2108.07258

A proposed definition of 'artificial intelligence professional'

In order to regulate, it is important to be clear who is subject to regulation. There are many roles which impact upon the development of AI systems, including engineers, data scientists and product designers. New roles are also emerging as the technology develops, and the labels given to roles often differ from one organisation to the next. AI development is also a field in which individuals come from a variety of different educational and professional backgrounds, where some are 'self-taught'. These features make it challenging to define who is subject to professional regulation.

Nonetheless, the regulation of other industries has successfully navigated similar issues in the past. For example, there is much to be learned from the regulation of the UK financial industry, which regulates individuals by the *function* they carry out, rather than their job title or academic qualifications.

In response to the diverse and continually evolving nature of the workforce in question, any definition of who should be regulated should focus on functionality rather than terminology. We propose the following definition of an 'AI professional': '*an individual who develops AI systems, either solely or partly in the course of business*'. Next, we elaborate further on the components of the definition.

'*AI systems*': This refers to technologies that are autonomous, meaning that they can make decisions without the express intent or ongoing control of a human, and adaptable in the sense that they can develop responses to previously unseen data. This approach is consistent with definitions recently adopted by the UK government[10] and the Organisation for Economic Co-operation and Development,[11] as well as the latest draft of the European

---

[10] Department for Science, Innovation & Technology, 'A pro-innovation approach to AI regulation', updated 3 August 2023, at https://www.gov.uk/government/publications/ai-regulation-a-pro-innovation-approach/white-paper.

[11] OECD, 'Recommendation of the Council on Artificial Intelligence', OECD/LEGAL/0449, at https://legalinstruments.oecd.org/en/instruments/oecd-legal-0449#backgroundInformation.

Union (EU) AI Act.[12] All machine learning systems would fall within this definition. This definition would also be broad enough to cover other autonomous and adaptable technologies which may be developed in the future. It would then be for Parliament and regulators to decide whether to introduce a graduated system of professional regulation, whereby different levels of training and qualification are required for adaptable and autonomous technologies posing different levels of risk (as further discussed in the section on 'Routes to implementation').

'*Develops*': Development involves the training, creation and some aspects of the deployment of AI systems. Relevant functions would include activities throughout the lifecycle of an AI system, for example:

- selecting and preparing the datasets required to train and validate AI systems;
- selecting the appropriate AI model architecture based on the problem type (for example, regression, classification, clustering, and so on), dataset characteristics, and efficiency requirements;
- selecting hyperparameters and using prepared datasets to train the AI model;
- evaluating the performance of an AI system through testing and validation processes pre-deployment;[13]

---

[12] Regulation of the European Parliament and of the Council laying down harmonised rules on artificial intelligence, as approved by the Council of the EU on 21 May 2024 (EU AI Act).

[13] As discussed in the section on 'The professionalisation of artificial intelligence assurance providers', we suggest that there should be a separate regulatory regime for those who provide *external* testing and validation services for AI systems, known as 'AI assurance'. These services use techniques based on those used by the accounting profession (for example, repeatable audits and certification schemes) to enable people to assess the trustworthiness of AI systems. Much like auditors in accountancy firms, AI assurance providers could become professionals, subject to a regulatory regime that is separate to the professionals they are auditing. While such a regime would help indirectly regulate AI professionals, it is not considered further in this chapter, to avoid doubling up on the work of the UK's Centre for Data Ethics and Innovation, which is currently exploring a regulatory regime for AI assurance professionals. Centre for Data Ethics and Innovation, 'Six lessons for an AI assurance profession to learn from other domains – part one: how can

- fine-tuning the model's hyperparameters to optimise its performance for a specific use case;
- preparing the required computing infrastructure to host and run the AI system;
- establishing data pipelines to ensure a continuous flow of data from sources to the AI system;
- creating monitoring tools and processes to track system performance, track anomalies and ensure smooth operation post-deployment.

'*In the course of business*': This qualifier is intended to distinguish between those individuals who develop AI systems with a view to profiting from such activities (for example, through employment) and those who develop AI systems *only* for genuine non-commercial purposes (for example, for personal use and/or that of a limited number friends and family).[14]

Individuals who do develop AI systems for commercial purposes would be regulated in all regulated activities they undertake, even when they are not for profit. For example, if a machine learning engineer employed by an AI lab develops freely accessible AI systems in their spare time, they will remain subject to professional regulation when developing the free AI systems. The extension of regulation to freely provided services is a feature of professional regulation in other fields. For example, lawyers are required to fulfil their regulatory duties even when acting for no remuneration ('pro bono'). Defining the scope of AI professionals in this manner could help ensure that high quality and safe AI systems can be available to anyone, not just those who can afford to pay.

---

certification support trustworthy AI?', 12 July 2023, at https://cdei.blog.gov.uk/2023/07/12/six-lessons-for-an-ai-assurance-profession-to-learn-from-other-domains-part-one-how-can-certification-support-trustworthy-ai/.

[14] Our approach to this test draws heavily from the approach of the UK Financial Conduct Authority (FCA) to the test for 'acting in the course of business' which is used to distinguish between many activities which are regulated and ones which are not. FCA, *FCA Handbook*, PERG 8.5, at https://www.handbook.fca.org.uk/handbook/PERG/8/5.html.

Inevitably, drawing precise boundaries of who is required to be professionally regulated will be challenging in some edge cases. For example, the precise scope of regulated functions may need to evolve and be clarified over time. But that is so with almost all legal definitions that involve a degree of discretion on the part of a decision-maker, particularly where the potential group of regulated professionals is continually evolving. The great majority of situations would likely fall clearly on one side of the line or the other. Edge cases can be addressed through regulatory guidance and where necessary case law.

All regulation must chart a course between the protection of the public and not placing undue burdens on individuals and businesses – the professionalisation of AI is no different. We consider that drawing the line at individuals who develop AI in the course of business is a pragmatic and principled response. It exempts pure hobbyists, who at present are unlikely to have the knowledge and resources to pose significant harm.[15] If the technology develops in a manner which allows such individuals to become a source of danger then the boundary for regulation can of course be revisited.

Proposed elements of professional regulation

Common set of high-level principles and values

For millennia, doctors have sworn to 'do no harm' on their professional qualification. This is known as the 'Hippocratic Oath', and it binds doctors in jurisdictions around the world to a common set of basic norms.[16] Many other professions have adopted similar high-level principles as the starting point for their regulatory systems.

---

[15] In the case of AI development, only well-funded organisations and state-level actors currently have the computational resources to train the most capable AI systems, like GPT-4 and PaLM-2. E. Seger, S. Dreksler, R. Moulange, E. Dardaman, J. Schuett, K. Wei, et al, 'Open-sourcing highly capable foundation models', Centre for the Governance of AI, 2023, at https://www.governance.ai/research-paper/open-sourcing-highly-capable-foundation-models.

[16] US National Institutes of Health, National Library of Medicine, History of Medicine Division, 'Greek medicine', at https://www.nlm.nih.gov/hmd/greek/greek_oath.html.

We suggest AI professionals should be obliged to adhere to a similar common set of high-level principles and values.[17] The content of the principles is outside the scope of this chapter, since the structures of regulation are separate from its content. That said, we consider it sensible that, so far as possible, the high-level principles should comprise those on which there is already broad consensus in the AI community. A consensus-based approach would help facilitate adoption and compliance by a group of individuals as diverse and international as those developing AI systems and, relatedly, would allow for greater regulatory alignment across borders.[18]

Fortunately, international consensus is beginning to settle on a relatively defined set of principles and values. Accountability, fairness, safety, security, transparency and privacy are all principles which have informed the regulatory approaches emerging in key jurisdictions, such as the UK,[19] the US,[20] the EU[21] and China.[22] These are also principles which leading AI powers and many

---

[17] Such principles and values might cover both professional practice and to some degree the individuals' wider personal lives. For example, in many professions, committing criminal dishonesty or violence in non-professional contexts can lead to professional sanctions on the grounds that such actions might bring the profession into disrepute and demonstrate that the individual concerned is unsuitable to be the subject of public trust.

[18] The Association of Computer Machinery, a major global body for IT professionals, has already adopted a code of ethics. However, this is not specifically tailored to AI and is a purely voluntary code which does not create any legally binding obligations. ACM, *ACM Code of Ethics and Professional Conduct*, at https://ethics.acm.org.

[19] Department for Science, Innovation & Technology (n 11).

[20] The White House, *Executive Order on the Safe, Secure, and Trustworthy Development and Use of Artificial Intelligence*, 30 October 2023, at https://www.whitehouse.gov/briefing-room/presidential-actions/2023/10/30/executive-order-on-the-safe-secure-and-trustworthy-development-and-use-of-artificial-intelligence/?utm_source=link.

[21] EU AI Act (n12).

[22] I.F.C. Liu and D. Edmondson, 'China: new interim measures to regulate generative AI', Baker McKenzie, August 2023, at https://insightplus.baker mckenzie.com/bm/data-technology/china-new-interim-measures-to-regulate-generative-ai_2.

countries (from all geographic regions) have endorsed by signing the 2023 Bletchley Park Declaration.[23]

Detailed code of conduct

Guiding principles are a beginning but should not be the end point for AI regulation. To ensure that AI professionals understand how to uphold the relevant principles and values proposed, any statement of principles must be accompanied by a detailed code of conduct that elaborates on how such principles and values are to be implemented in practice.

Professional regulation in many other fields follows this rubric of high-level principles coupled with detailed codes of practice, which may be supplemented further by regulatory guidance. For example, the Solicitors Regulation Authority (SRA) has a set of 'Principles' which 'comprise the fundamental tenets of ethical behaviour that we expect all those that we regulate to uphold'.[24] In addition to these principles, the SRA Code of Conduct describes in more detail the standards of professionalisation required of regulated individuals.[25] The SRA also provides guidance to solicitors via publications on its website and maintains a Professional Ethics Helpline to enable individuals to seek guidance from the regulator on particular issues.[26] In this way, the structures of professionalisation can facilitate the deliberative processes needed to develop the substance of professional regulation.

There are many examples globally of AI ethical principles and best practices. The US Blueprint for an AI Bill of Rights details how high-level principles can be translated into AI safety policies and practices.[27] These policies and practices include

---

[23] 'The Bletchley Declaration by countries attending the AI Safety Summit, 1–2 November 2023' (n 8).

[24] SRA, *SRA Principles*, at https://www.sra.org.uk/solicitors/standards-regulations/principles/.

[25] SRA, *SRA Code of Conduct for Solicitors, RELs and RFLs*, at https://www.sra.org.uk/solicitors/standards-regulations/code-conduct-solicitors/.

[26] SRA, *Your Health, Your Career*, at https://www.sra.org.uk/solicitors/resources/your-health-your-career/.

[27] The White House, *Blueprint for an AI Bill of Rights: Making Automated Systems Work for the American People*, October 2022, at https://www.whitehouse.gov/wp-content/uploads/2022/10/Blueprint-for-an-AI-Bill-of-Rights.pdf.

pre-deployment testing, risk mitigation techniques and the use of privacy preserving technologies. Many of these policies and practices are reflected in the recent discussion paper published by the UK government, which sets out the current suite of 'frontier AI' organisations' safety policies for the public 'to better understand what good policy might look like' for those organisations.[28]

Although the publications mentioned here do not constitute a detailed code of conduct for AI professionals, they provide valuable foundations on which such a code could be developed. For example, the UK government's discussion paper notes that some of the practices it outlines may not be appropriate for less advanced and lower risk AI systems, since its initial focus is on 'frontier AI' comprising some of the most advanced and potentially highest risk AI systems.[29] As discussed further in the section on 'Routes to implementation', the UK government's proposed approach of differentiated obligations based on the riskiness of the particular activity or system concerned might be carried through into professional regulation of developers.

Disciplinary system

Where AI professionals fail to comply with applicable professional standards, they should be held accountable. This should involve a disciplinary system in which there is a regulatory body set up specifically for overseeing AI professionals' conduct, which is empowered to impose a variety of sanctions depending on the severity of the breach and the available evidence. At one end of the spectrum, sanctions could include warnings, reprimands and fines; at the other end, professional licences could be suspended or, in the most serious cases, permanently revoked. These sanctions would help deter other AI professionals from breaching professional standards.

---

[28] Department for Science, Innovation & Technology, *Emerging Processes for Frontier AI Safety*, 27 October 2023, at https://assets.publishing.service.gov. uk/media/653aabbd80884d000df71bdc/emerging-processes-frontier-ai-safety.pdf.

[29] The UK government recently defined 'frontier AI' as 'highly capable general-purpose AI models that can perform a wide variety of tasks and match or exceed the capabilities present in today's most advanced models'. Ibid.

Typically, professional disciplinary matters are considered in the first instance (and perhaps also on the first appeal) by specialised bodies which comprise both experts in the relevant field as well as, in some cases, lay members whose role is to apply the standards which wider society expects of professionals. Examples include the Solicitors Disciplinary Tribunal or the disciplinary procedures of the General Medical Council in the UK. Often, these internal bodies' decisions are then subject to appeal to the general courts. We consider it would be sensible for a similar waterfall of disciplinary adjudication to apply to AI professionals – with disputes in the first instance being subject to specialised tribunals but with the possibility of appeal to the general courts.

Imposing sanctions for breaches of regulatory requirements would provide comfort to AI professionals and their employers that they are only competing for business, or collaborating, with other individuals who will maintain the same professional standards. At the same time, and much as was the case with the original Guilds of Trade, by requiring all participants to be regulated the public would be assured of a minimum level of competence and expertise when they deal with an AI professional or are in some way impacted by AI systems developed by AI professionals. Lawyers may not trust an opposing party, but they will generally trust the opposing party's lawyers to act with integrity, and it is through such mutual trust that the legal system is able to function efficiently.[30]

---

[30] For example, a solicitor's 'undertaking' is a very powerful tool in English law to assure other parties that something has or will happen, without the other side being provided direct evidence. A solicitor might give an 'undertaking' that certain materials will be deployed. Courts will be very slow to interrogate the truthfulness of such undertakings unless there is compelling evidence. If a solicitor is found to have breached an undertaking then extremely serious professional consequences may follow, including fines, public criticism by the regulator and even being 'struck off' the roll of solicitors. P. Ahlquist, 'Solicitors' undertakings: legal and regulatory considerations for solicitors and law firms', *Practical Law*, 25 April 2022, at https://www.fountaincourt.co.uk/wp-content/uploads/2022/06/Solicitors-undertakings-w-034-0597.pdf.

Public register

To enhance assurance for both the public and AI professionals, there should be a freely accessible public register. The register should confirm, for example, whether an AI professional is currently licensed to practise as an AI professional and if there are any disciplinary or regulatory decisions relating to them. This would enable the public (and AI professionals) to confirm those holding themselves out as AI professionals are in fact so, while also enabling the public (and AI professionals) to report those practising without a valid licence. Such public registers already exist, for example, for regulated individuals in the UK financial services industry,[31] as well as doctors[32] and solicitors.[33]

Professionalisation and the wider regulatory ecosystem

A complementary, rather than complete, regulatory response

Professional regulation is not a panacea for regulating AI. The professionalisation of an industry is never the sole mechanism for achieving quality, safety and trust in that industry. Rather, professionalisation is consistent with, and supportive of, a wider regulatory ecosystem. For example, in the UK financial services industry, certain individual functions are professionally regulated by the Senior Managers and Certification Regime.[34] In response to the 2008 global financial crisis, this regime introduced an accountability framework that focuses on individuals in senior management roles at certain UK financial institutions. Its aim is to ensure that senior management is held accountable for serious conduct failings that occur on its watch. A similar regulatory regime could be introduced for the AI industry, where the risks associated with the conduct failings of those developing AI systems is increasing as the technology advances and becomes more embedded in societal practices and decision-making processes.

---

[31] FCA, *The Financial Services Register*, at https://register.fca.org.uk/s/.

[32] GMC, *The Medical Register*, at https://www.gmc-uk.org/registration-and-licensing/the-medical-register.

[33] SRA, *Solicitors Register*, at https://www.sra.org.uk/consumers/register/.

[34] FCA, *Senior Managers and Certification Regime*, updated 30 March 2023, at https://www.fca.org.uk/firms/senior-managers-certification-regime.

In addition, firms in the financial industry are subject to separate regulations administered by the Financial Conduct Authority (FCA) and/or Prudential Regulation Authority. These regulations require regulated organisations to implement and maintain various corporate governance measures to enhance organisational transparency, accountability and resilience.[35] There is also the potential for *ex post facto* liability for individuals and firms who fall below the relevant standards of behaviour (for example, in a negligence claim).

Serious wrongdoing in the financial industry may well lead to legal consequences at all levels. A similar, multi-layered approach to attributing liability would also be desirable for the AI industry.

Regulating individuals developing artificial intelligence systems, as well as organisation providing them

To date, policy makers have predominantly focused on requirements for technology as the object of the regulation, with organisations building, supplying and deploying AI as the subject. Absent has been any direct focus on the individual people who develop the technology. The EU AI Act imposes design requirements on certain high-risk AI systems which must be satisfied for those systems to be made available in the EU's 'Internal Market'.[36] The EU AI Act will apply to providers, users, importers and distributors of certain AI systems, who can demonstrate compliance through a certification scheme which the Act will introduce. The parties covered will typically be legal persons, but those making the underlying decisions will be the individual human officers and employees – who are not directly regulated.

One danger of the current regulatory focus is that regulation might be seen by those working in AI as something which is externally imposed, and which operates predominantly at the corporate level. Although companies will be expected to impose control over their workers through having their own

---

[35] FCA, *Firms*, at https://www.fca.org.uk/firms.
[36] EU AI Act (n12).

corporate governance mechanisms, professionalisation enables the internalisation of ethical principles within a workforce, thereby providing an additional layer of compliance protection for the companies concerned.

Professionalisation empowers and encourages individual workers to hold their employers to account. When even the most junior lawyer at a firm is asked to do something which they believe is contrary to their professional duties, they are obliged to speak out, and their superiors are obliged to listen. From the perspective of regulators, a professionalised workforce is therefore preferable because it adds a layer of crowd-sourced vigilance over the organisations operating in regulated industries. From the perspective of corporate entities, and perhaps counter-intuitively, the professionalisation of a workforce enables employers to be certain that a common baseline applies where ethical standards are to some degree set centrally. The ability to refer to such baseline may in some circumstances provide protection for businesses against the type of *ad hoc* worker objections to certain projects which have in recent years caused friction between the employees and employers at some AI companies.[37]

With respect to the technical standards, many of the design requirements imposed by any comprehensive framework for AI systems will involve some degree of subjective judgement on the part of those developing them.[38] It is not possible for a legislator or regulator to detail, in advance, how inherently amorphous concepts such as 'fairness' and 'transparency' should be applied in every possible application of an AI system. While some level of guidance is certainly possible, the individuals developing AI systems will not be able to escape engaging in some form of value-laden decision-making. Professional regulation could enable these individuals to obtain, from the start of their training, a clear understanding of applicable regulatory principles and to internalise these principles into their practices. One of professionalisation's

---

[37] N. Tiku, 'Why tech worker dissent is going viral', *Wired*, 29 June 2018, at https://www.wired.com/story/why-tech-worker-dissent-is-going-viral/.

[38] T. Goodman, 'Thinking outside the technical standardisation box: the role of standards under the draft EU Artificial Intelligence Act', *LSE Law Review*, 2023, at https://doi.org/10.61315/lselr.579.

major strengths as a regulatory tool is its ability to standardise professionals' judgement in a way which increases the likelihood that their ultimate assessment will be in line with societal and regulatory expectations. Where a professional's assessment deviates significantly from the assessment of other professionals, this would justify an interrogation into the reason for the discrepancy and, in turn, help drive professional consensus.

In addition to professional regulation which focuses on the people, and risk-based regulation which focuses on the technology and the organisations providing it, there may also be sectoral regulation that imposes additional obligations on AI professionals. There is no contradiction between such regulatory systems and professionalisation. Many professionals are subject to overlapping systems of regulation already. A solicitor qualified in England and Wales, who is regulated by the SRA, could work in-house for a company where they are also a Money Laundering Reporting Officer, and so would also be regulated by the FCA.

The professionalisation of artificial intelligence assurance providers

The professionalisation of AI *development* is distinct from the professionalisation of AI *auditing*. The former relates to the building and use of AI systems, whereas the latter relates to their checking and testing on a periodic basis by independent auditors, usually after the systems have been built. The values to be upheld by a developer and auditor will overlap, but their roles are fundamentally different. Distinct regimes of professional regulation are necessary. For example, the financial statements of companies prepared by professional accountants are then assessed by professional auditors who opine on whether the statements provide a true and fair view of the accounts.

The professionalisation of AI auditing has been proposed elsewhere as a means of regulation.[39] We agree this would be

---

[39] Centre for Data Ethics and Innovation, 'Six lessons for an AI assurance profession to learn from other domains – part one: how can certification support trustworthy AI?', 12 July 2023, at https://cdei.blog.gov.uk/2023/07/12/six-lessons-for-an-ai-assurance-profession-to-learn-from-other-domains-part-one-how-can-certification-support-trustworthy-ai/.

sensible. AI auditing is already becoming an established field of services, even where not legally required. In some jurisdictions, AI audits for particular systems and activities are now mandated by law, albeit that the profession of AI auditing is not yet itself regulated.[40] There will always be limits to the impact which auditors can have, since their role is by nature external to and independent of the organisation or process which they are assessing, and it usually takes place to some degree *ex post facto*.[41] Accordingly, the professionalisation of AI auditing is a sensible additional check and balance which could be imposed alongside the professionalisation of developers. Whereas to date most proposals in this area have focussed on professionalising auditors, we suggest that it is the professionalisation of developers which should be the priority.

Routes to implementation

The professionalisation of AI will require a delivery mechanism to facilitate the requisite training and certification being provided both to new workers as well as existing ones. One major argument against professionalisation of the AI workforce is that seeking to impose regulation on such a large and diverse group of individuals would be ineffective, or at least very challenging.[42] We consider that such criticisms can be overcome.

Although the AI talent pool is fast growing, its source remains limited to a relatively small number of organisations, including universities, private sector companies, and for-profit bootcamps.[43]

---

[40] For example, a New York City law, 'NYC Local Law 144', in force from June 2023, already requires annual 'Bias Audits' take place as regards the use of AI decision making technology in hiring decisions. D.A. Zetoony, T. Boiangin and J.F. Goldberg, 'NYC's Local Law 144 and the final regulations: regulation of AI-driven hiring tools in the United States', *The National Law Review*, 30 June 2023, at https://www.natlawreview.com/article/nyc-s-local-law-144-and-final-regulations-regulation-ai-driven-hiring-tools-united.

[41] Even internal auditors will need to exercise a degree of separation and independence from those who they are auditing.

[42] Zetoony et al (n 42).

[43] Some of these organisations also run online courses (known as 'massive open online courses' or 'MOOCs'), alongside other MOOC providers,

Consequently, these organisations act as gateways through which many of those now acting as AI professionals will pass, either in order to gain their initial training or to gain access to the funding and other resources required to progress their projects. A system of professional regulation that can be delivered through one or more of these gateways would provide considerable coverage of the AI professionals envisaged in this chapter.

In any event, if it were to become mandatory for those developing AI systems in the course of business to obtain a practising certificate, objections based on the diversity of routes into the profession become less relevant. It would be a very strong incentive for those practising in the field to continue to do so by obtaining the relevant certification if failure could result in criminal sanctions. The requirements would not need solely to be enforced by regulators. Employers, counterparties and ultimately members of the public would be entitled to require those they deal with to demonstrate their credentials. Just as is the case with unregulated financial services, a contract for the purchase of an AI system made by an unregulated professional could be rendered void – thus removing any financial incentive to continue practising without a licence.

The initial training required to gain a licence to practise as an AI professional could be delivered by universities as well as by government programmes and bootcamps. Ongoing training could then be delivered as part of internal training programmes in workplaces by those with sufficient expertise (who should themselves have undergone further training necessary to train others). Such workplaces could include governmental bodies as well as private sector companies. For instance, the UK government, which is now a major acquirer and user of AI systems, could facilitate the uptake of professional training by requiring that

---

many of which are freely available. See *The Global AI Talent Tracker*, Macro Polo, at https://macropolo.org/digital-projects/the-global-ai-tal ent-tracker/; 'Bloomberg uses glass.ai to write about the AI Armies of the Tech Giants', glass.ai, 27 March 2023, at https://www.glass.ai/glass-news/ code-red-the-ai-armies-of-the-tech-giants; S. Cesareo and J. White, 'The Global AI Index', Tortoise Media, 28 June 2023, at https://www.tortoiseme dia.com/intelligence/global-ai/#further_reading.

relevant individuals within government (both national and local), as well as many of their suppliers, have requisite qualifications.

Regulation cannot be created and enforced overnight. As with all major and systemic changes, there would need to be a reasonably long transposition period to enable individuals and organisations to bring themselves into compliance before any sanctions apply. None of these issues is unique to AI. The advent of the EU's General Data Protection Regulation required organisations around the world, and across all industries, to make major changes to their practices and procedures during the period between its enactment in 2016 and its entry into force in 2018. The EU AI Act will require similarly seismic shifts. The implementation of AI professionalisation may even be relatively simple in comparison.

The level of training required should factor in matters of cost and proportionality. As a general rule, the greater the capacity for harm caused by developing an AI system, the more the cost of training will be justified. Within the class of AI professionals, there might be a system of different classifications for licences. Those who solely develop AI systems which pose negligible risks, such as those used for narrow, low-impact applications (for example, spam filters), might only be required to hold an entry-level qualification; whereas those developing systems which pose higher risks, such as those used for narrow but high-impact applications or more general-purpose systems (for example, Foundation Models) which *can* be used for high-impact applications, might be required to have far more extensive training. One example of such a graduated system is that operated by the FCA, which authorises or approves individuals to carry out certain regulated financial activities. The authorisations and types of training required vary, depending on the activity in question – for example, advising clients or trading derivatives.

It might also be appropriate for professional regulation to be tailored for individuals undertaking different roles in the AI development lifecycle. For example, a data scientist whose role is to collect and prepare data for the purposes of training and validating an AI system might be treated differently from a machine learning engineer whose role is to create and design the models which are trained on that data.

In addition to training, professional regulation should be implemented and enforced by a professional regulatory body. That body should be empowered to carry out a variety of functions, including: setting the minimum training criteria required to qualify as an AI professional and to continue practising as one, as well as monitoring the performance of organisations which provide that training; developing and drafting professional standards together with guidance on how those standards apply in practice; monitoring AI professionals to ensure they are complying with professional standards, and investigating concerns about AI professionals' standards of practice; where justified, imposing sanctions on AI professionals found to have breached professional standards; and administering a public register of AI professionals.

At first, the professional regulatory body could be established at a national level. Over time, however, national regulatory bodies should aspire to set up an international body, which represents and coordinates its members. Doing so could facilitate harmonisation of standards among regulatory bodies in different countries, thereby reducing costly regulatory barriers.

A professional regulatory body (either national or international) could be primarily funded by those who are regulated, through charging practising/membership fees. A self-funding model is already operated by UK national professional regulatory bodies, such the FCA and the SRA.

Conclusion

There will be a significant lacuna in any regulatory regime for AI unless the individuals who build the technology are regulated. We suggest that the UK is ideally placed to fill this gap, and to benefit in the process.

The UK's professional services industries are world-leading. The UK is the second largest services exporter in the world – behind only the US – and the services sector contributes around 80 per cent of the UK's gross domestic product.[44] In fields such as law, finance and accountancy, the UK's economy benefits

---

[44] Department for International Trade, Department for Business and Trade, and The Rt Hon Kemi Badenoch MP, 'Trade Secretary welcomes record year for services exports', 10 February 2023, at https://www.gov.uk/government/news/business-secretary-welcomes-record-year-for-services-exports.

significantly from the country hosting a significant proportion of the world's top firms. It is no coincidence that these are all professionalised industries, overseen by high quality regulators which are empowered by, and operating in, a robust and effective legal system. The UK can therefore leverage its experience and existing regulatory infrastructure to expand its professional services offering to include the AI industry.

Although professionalising the AI industry would require significant resources and impose additional regulatory burdens, these costs would likely be outweighed by its benefits. Individuals who satisfy professional requirements would gain status and potentially greater earning power, as well as obtain a clear and comprehensive ethical foundation that would assist them through their professional lives as they engage with challenging and societally important issues. Firms employing AI professionals would gain an additional source of assurance that their AI systems will function consistently with societal and regulatory expectations, as well as their own, helping to drive adoption of the technology. The UK's economy would benefit from a new, highly skilled and highly paid workforce – either homegrown or drawn from abroad – as well as the profitable firms which employ them.

China was the first country to enact regulations which specifically address AI. The EU has recently agreed upon the world's most detailed AI legislation in the form of the EU AI Act. The US is now fast catching up, most notably with the publication of the Executive Order on Safe, Secure, and Trustworthy Artificial Intelligence. And yet none of these initiatives has sought to address professionalisation. There is thus a major opportunity for the UK (or indeed any other country) to fill this regulatory gap. Unlike most other countries, the UK already has both the relevant regulatory expertise and a flourishing AI ecosystem.

If the UK government becomes a first mover on professionalising the AI industry, other countries may well follow. The AI Safety Summit at Bletchley Park affirmed the foundational principles for AI development and placed the UK at the forefront of global efforts to regulate the technology. It is now essential to build upon these foundational principles with concrete actions. Professionalisation should be one such action, and the UK is well positioned to play a leading role.

Summary of key proposals

- To maintain safe, secure and trustworthy AI, as well as to build on its position as a world-leader in regulated professional services, the UK should professionally regulate any individual who develops AI systems, either solely or partly in the course of business.
- AI professionals should be bound by a common set of high-level ethical principles and values: a 'Hippocratic Oath' for developers.
- Those high-level principles should be supported by a detailed regulatory code, providing clear guidance and allocations of responsibility for those involved in all stages of the AI lifecycle: designing, training and deploying AI.
- Breaches of the code should be enforced by a regulator, with penalties for noncompliance.
- The UK should create a public register of AI professionals, listing details of skills, qualifications and any regulatory issues.

Disclaimer

The views expressed in this chapter are solely those of the authors and do not represent those of their employers or clients, past or present.

PART III

The global context

11

Asylum and irregular migration

Adrian Berry

Introduction

It is a feature of life in the UK that asylum and irregular migration policy occupies an unwarranted place in the national conversation about political priorities. The number of asylum-seekers ebbs and flows, driven mainly by events overseas and hardly at all by UK policy.

In fact, the number of asylum-seekers is not unusual by historical standards. In 2002, under the last Labour government, the number of asylum-seekers reached over 84,000. However, by 2010, it was down to less than 18,000.[1] That development was not on account of UK policy making but due to changes in the international scene.[2]

At present the number is rising back up to the higher level on account of developments in the Middle East, Asia and elsewhere.[3] Asylum and irregular migration policy needs to be made with this in mind. It is better to prioritise good administration than to consider that legislative policy impacts significantly on the number of persons claiming.

---

[1]   House of Commons Library Paper, *Asylum Statistics*, G. Sturge, 12 September 2023, p 11.

[2]   Ibid., p 16.

[3]   Ibid., p 16.

The role of asylum and irregular migration policy

The challenge for an incoming Labour government is to return asylum and irregular migration policy to its proper place in the public realm. A sober, rule-of-law compliant, legal and administrative policy is required, one that respects international law commitments and de-toxifies the national conversation about the allocation of public goods such as healthcare, education and work opportunities.

Under the Conservative governments from 2010 asylum and irregular migration policy became the site for the performance of extraordinary vices; they are extraordinary because the policies advanced seek not only to bear down oppressively on those targeted but also to make the public complicit in the process through inflammatory media strategies.[4]

The first vice of Conservative policy has been deceit: there has been the deceit in the assertion that the scale of migration, both lawful and unlawful, is responsible for scarcity of provision in hospitals, schools, social housing and social welfare benefits. Where the national conversation ought to be focused on the underfunding and degradation of the public realm by the Conservative government, the movement of asylum-seekers and irregular migrants to the UK has been used as a distraction.[5]

Blaming such people for wider failures of government disguises the Conservatives' wider attack on the role of the state. In Conservative thinking, the model of an active state serving to improve the lives of its citizens in an efficient and participatory way is displaced by the idea that the state is best when pared back, that it can only do so much, and that what little it can do is being undermined by the arrival of asylum-seekers and irregular migrants. As part of re-formulating the idea of the use of the state for the public benefit of individuals and communities, as well as the collective improvement of society, Labour needs to move the national conversation away from a blame game and

---

[4] See, for example, Adam Forrest, 'Tories accused of dog-whistle low as minister claims new towns will be "filled with illegal migrants"', *Independent*, 24 October 2023, at https://www.independent.co.uk/news/uk/politics/labour-tories-migrants-new-towns-b2435115.html.

[5] Ibid.

to focus on the things that make a difference to the lives of the country's inhabitants.

Without a shift in the narrative, it will be harder to achieve meaningful change in social policy. By creating a clear understanding of what causes scarcity of public resources, Labour can build support for what needs to be done to fix the damage done by Conservative rule. Asylum-seekers and irregular migrants need to be taken out of the picture.

The second vice demonstrated by Conservative governments in the making of asylum and irregular migration policy is hypocrisy. Paying lip-service to human rights–compliance while actively working to undermine it serves only to debase the national conversation around policy making and, also, leads to the design of legal and administrative policy that locks in failure. Further, it undermines the wider role of human rights protection in society.

For example, it was the Conservative government's position that the measures taken in the Nationality and Borders Act 2022 (henceforth the 2022 Act) were compliant with the UK's international treaty commitments under the 1951 Refugee Convention and the European Convention on Human Rights.[6] Manifestly, this is not the case: the criminalisation of arrival in the UK by crossing the English Channel is a case in point. That measure impedes access to the UK's refugee status determination (RSD) mechanism and consideration of whether to grant asylum. Merely stating the contrary view does not make a debate on the subject and does not make it true or even arguable. The 2022 Act is studded with measures that function to impede the quest for asylum. Yet the UK remains a State Party to the Refugee Convention and is obliged to carry out its obligations under that Convention in good faith.[7]

The high-water mark of the hypocritical approach to compliance with international law is the Safety of Rwanda

---

[6] See Nationality and Borders Act 2022, ss 12–38; see also Explanatory Notes to the Nationality and Borders Bill, as introduced to the House of Commons on 5 July 2021 (Bill 141), at https://publications.parliament.uk/pa/bills/cbill/58-02/0141/en/210141en.pdf.

[7] Vienna Convention on the Law of Treaties, Article 26, Vienna, 23 May 1969, entered into force on 27 January 1980. United Nations, Treaty Series, vol 1155, p 331.

(Asylum and Immigration) Act 2024 that declares Rwanda to be safe.[8] Rwanda is known not to be safe on account of the recent Supreme Court judgment.[9] The Act seeks to wash this away in reliance on a new bilateral treaty.[10] No new treaty between the UK and Rwanda by itself removes the latter's practice of human rights abuses. It is hypocritical to use international law in this way when other international law (the European Convention on Human Rights) applied by the Supreme Court says Rwanda is not safe.

Labour must eschew such hypocritical approaches to policy making in this area. The UK is a party to the Refugee Convention. For so long as that remains the case, the obligations to which such participation gives rise ought to be discharged in a simple and straightforward way. This means simplifying the process for RSD and the decision as to whether to grant asylum, ensuring that asylum-seekers have access to the necessary legal advice to advance their claims, and providing simple and straightforward mechanisms for appeal to first-instance tribunals. The Conservative government has moved away from this approach (see, for example, the appeals provisions in the 2022 Act[11] that lead to added complexity, added costs and inefficiency in administrative decision-making). The challenge for Labour is to restore simple, efficient and sturdy in-country decision-making and in-country appeals to their central place in the system of immigration control.

The third vice demonstrated by Conservative governments in this area of policy making is misanthropy. In fact, and contrary to the way they have been portrayed, asylum-seekers are not suspicious characters whose behaviour is inherently criminal and whose credibility is suspect; to the contrary, they are men, women and children who have made difficult and dangerous journeys out of desperation, where such experience (and that of life in

---

[8] Section 2(1) Every decision-maker must conclusively treat the Republic of Rwanda as a safe country.

[9] *AAA and Others v Secretary of State for the Home Department* [2023] UKSC 42, [2023] 1WLR 4433.

[10] Agreement between the Government of the United Kingdom of Great Britain and Northern Ireland and the Government of the Republic of Rwanda for the provision of an asylum partnership to strengthen shared international commitments on the protection of refugees and migrants.

[11] Sections 18–28.

their home state) has left them vulnerable to the consequences of their suffering. Statutory measures such as the 2022 Act that impugn their credibility by legal fiat add nothing to the judicial task in assessing the merits of an appeal made to an immigration tribunal. To treat such people with dignity and respect is not at all difficult; it is an ethical imperative.

As among any group of people, a few asylum-seekers will display characteristics that may be unsavoury. However, that does not lessen the obligation on the UK as the receiving state to treat them with dignity and respect, to process their claims fairly, and to abide by the international protection standards that the UK has adopted voluntarily.

As regards the making of policy as to the reception of asylum-seekers, the processing of their claims, the standards by which they will be judged as to whether they require protection, the provision made for the integration of successful claimants, and the procedures for those lawfully refused protection, Labour needs to ensure that asylum-seekers are treated with dignity and respect.

To that end, asylum accommodation must be fit for habitation, support for food and essential living needs must be sufficient to permit a dignified mode of existence, permission to work ought to be a possibility, asylum procedures need to allow an asylum claimant to advance their case fully and for a decision to follow without delay thereafter, the standards for qualifying for protection to be applied need to be those provided for in the UK's international treaty commitments, and the procedure for the treatment of refused asylum-seekers needs to be clearly set out.

In answer to the objection that this will lead to additional cost, delay, administrative inefficiency and fault in the control of immigration, the following points are made. Costs are kept down where asylum claims are decided in a simple and straightforward way and legal differences are resolved on the same basis in tribunals. By such methods, the asylum support bill is reduced, as asylum-seekers spend less time in expensive Home Office accommodation or in detention waiting for a decision. Further, as the long-term future of asylum-seekers is decided quickly, those granted asylum can accelerate the process of their integration into UK society thereafter, while those refused asylum or complementary protection, and who are unsuccessful before the immigration tribunals, have their requirement to leave the UK to return home clearly stated. A Labour government can both bring down costs and do better in the administration of asylum policy by recasting the treatment of asylum-seekers in the UK.

The fourth vice demonstrated by Conservative governments in this area of policy making is cruelty. In seeking to interdict asylum-seekers crossing the Channel,[12] in providing asylum support below levels necessary for a dignified existence,[13] in the conditions and overuse of immigration detention,[14] in providing inadequate resources from claims to be determined justly and for legal disputes to be resolved in like manner,[15] in the culture of disbelief,[16] in the failure to grant asylum to meritorious claims thereby leading to overuse of the tribunals to correct error,[17] and most of all, in seeking to export asylum-seekers to another country (presently, Rwanda) so as to wash its hands of the responsibility, the Conservative government has pursued policies and practices that degrade further the lives of asylum-seekers

---

[12] See, for example, P. Walker, 'Two Border Force cutters redeployed to English Channel, says Sajid Javid', *The Guardian*, 31 December 2018, at https://www.the guardian.com/uk-news/2018/dec/31/two-border-force-cutters-redeployed-to-english-channel-says-sajid-javid.

[13] See, for example, E. Birks, 'Locked into poverty – life on asylum support', *Just Fair*, 5 April 2023, at https://justfair.org.uk/locked-into-poverty-life-on-asylum-support.

[14] See, for example, 'Scared, confused, alone: the stark truth behind immigration detention', British Red Cross, last updated 20 September 2023, at https://www.redcross.org.uk/stories/migration-and-displacement/refugees-and-asylum-seekers/scared-confused-alone-the-dark-truths-of-immigration-detention.

[15] See, for example, K. Hudak and E. Marshall, 'The case for broadening the scope of immigration legal aid', *Public Law Project*, April 2021, at https://publiclawproject.org.uk/content/uploads/2021/04/Legal-aid-briefing.pdf.

[16] See, for example, Freedom from Torture, 'Beyond belief: our new report reveals a Home Office culture tainted by prejudice', 16 June 2020, at https://www.freedomfromtorture.org/news/beyond-belief-our-new-report-reveals-a-home-office-culture-tainted-by-prejudice.

[17] See, for example, D. Taylor, 'Home Office loses 75% of its appeals against immigration rulings', *The Guardian*, 3 September 2018, at https://www.the guardian.com/uk-news/2018/sep/03/inhumane-three-quarters-of-home-office-asylum-appeals-fail.

whose lives are already precarious. Such policies are cruel in method and in the result.

An incoming Labour government must pursue public policy free of the taint of cruelty. Many if not most asylum-seekers will end up being granted asylum or some other form of status. To degrade such persons before seeking their integration is not only wrong ethically, it is also sure to arrest the process of integration and impair their long-term wellbeing. Further, all asylum-seekers, as people, deserve to be treated with dignity and respect. A government that can bear down on people without status in a cruel fashion will find it easier to act cruelly towards other vulnerable groups in society.

The Conservative government's track record as regards asylum-seekers is mirrored in its approach to the less well-off and less secure among the settled population. Its attacks on the Social Fund (a form of residual social assistance),[18] its approach to sanctioning benefit claimants,[19] its approach to Romani Gypsy and Traveller rights,[20] and perhaps most of all its policies and practices towards British citizens and settled Commonwealth citizens in the Windrush scandal,[21] demonstrate that in public policy making, cruelty is infectious.

Respect for human dignity is not simply an ethical imperative or a principle of fundamental rights arising out of natural law or human rights legal codes, it is something that should inform policy making for people in all their variety who are subject to the UK government's jurisdiction, and that includes asylum-seekers and irregular migrants. Such an approach is four-square within the religious and secular ethical traditions of the Labour movement as it developed in each of the nations of the UK.

---

[18] Welfare Reform Act 2012, ss 70–73.

[19] See, for example, P. Butler, 'MPs' inquiry: five things we've learned about benefit sanctions', *The Guardian*, 23 January 2015, at https://www.theguard ian.com/society/patrick-butler-cuts-blog/2015/jan/23/mps-inquiry-five-things-weve-learned-about-benefit-sanctions.

[20] See, for example, Police, Crime, Sentencing and Courts Act 2002, ss 83–85.

[21] See 'Windrush Scandal' page in *The Guardian*, at https://www.theguardian.com/uk-news/windrush-scandal.

Policy reform: commitment to international law

Labour must return the UK to performing its international treaty commitments in good faith. In practical terms that means removing the attempts to narrow and reduce the scope of their provisions by cutting down how those commitments are to be applied in UK law. Both the 2022 Act and the Illegal Migration Act 2023 (henceforth the 2023 Act) contain measures that seek to define terms deployed in the 1951 Refugee Convention in narrow or inaccurate ways that reduce the scope of the Convention for conferring protection.[22] This practice must stop and be rolled back. It puts the UK at odds with the way the Convention ought to be applied; a matter that may be ascertained not only from the interpretations offered by the United Nations High Commissioner for Refugees but also from the judgments of the senior courts of the common law world and elsewhere. At present, the UK deviates from its treaty commitments through domestic legislative policy, when on the plane of international law it remains bound by the Convention's commonly understood provisions. That is not applying the treaty in good faith. Prior to interference by the 2022 and 2023 Acts, it was for UK domestic courts to interpret the terms of the Refugee Convention where applicable; that position needs to be restored.

In parallel with the restoration of the Refugee Convention to its hitherto unremarkable place within the UK's legal system, Labour should restore the principled position that immigration legislation does not interfere with the protection afforded by the Human Rights Act 1998. The latter Act was enacted by a Labour government and applies to everyone within UK jurisdiction. It is a code of fundamental rights that applies to the interpretation and application of all legislation and to the actions of public authorities.

For the Conservative government to have carved out exceptions to the application of human rights protection as the 2023 Act[23] and the Safety of Rwanda (Asylum and Immigration) Act 2024[24] do, is not only to undermine fundamental rights protection in the

---

[22] See n 6; see also Illegal Migration Act 2023, s 39.

[23] Section 1.

[24] Section 3.

UK but to leave UK laws vulnerable to challenge internationally before the European Court of Human Rights. Such a result is the opposite of what Labour sought to achieve in *Bringing Rights Home* (the Labour Party consultation document prior to the 1997 general election) and when in government:

> 1.18 We therefore believe that the time has come to enable people to enforce their Convention rights against the State in the British courts, rather than having to incur the delays and expense which are involved in taking a case to the ... Court in Strasbourg and which may altogether deter some people from pursuing their rights. Enabling courts in the United Kingdom to rule on the application of the Convention will also help to influence the development of case law on the Convention by the European Court of Human Rights on the basis of familiarity with our laws and customs and of sensitivity to practices and procedures in the United Kingdom.[25]

The restrictions in immigration legislation on the applicability of the Human Rights Act 1998 should be removed and the temptation to introduce similar ones in future legislation should be resisted.

Policy reform: refugee status determination

Following UK withdrawal from the European Union (EU), the Conservative government introduced Immigration Rules to provide for the transfer of asylum-seekers who had passed through third countries (usually EU member states) on their way to the UK, to be removed to third countries with which they had no previous connection.[26] By this means, asylum claimants whose claims were held to be inadmissible for UK determination and

---

[25] *Rights Brought Home: The Human Rights Bill*, October 1997, CM 3782.

[26] Immigration Rules, paragraphs 345A–345C (HC 395 of 1993–1994); such provision is now found in sections 80B and 80C of the Nationality, Immigration and Asylum Act 2002 (as amended).

protection may be transferred to a third country said to be safe. It is under these rules that the policy of transfer to Rwanda has been advanced.

However, as a matter of principle, the UK as a State Party to the Refugee Convention should determine in-country the claims of asylum-seekers who reach its territory and offer protection to those who fall within the Convention's scope.

Further, the notion that third-country claim processing and/ or protection will deter those persons who make difficult and dangerous journeys to come to the UK is far-fetched and unsupported by evidence. To place yourself and your loved ones in a lorry and travel from Afghanistan or Eritrea, to cross the Mediterranean in an insecure vessel, to trust smugglers to bring you to Calais and, thereafter, to cross the English Channel in an insecure vessel, is to accept a measure of risk of several orders of magnitude greater than the risk of transfer to Rwanda.

Moreover, the transfer of asylum-seekers, even for off-shore processing of asylum claims, prior to return to the UK (note that in the Rwanda transfer scheme, successful asylum claimants remain in Rwanda), is extremely expensive[27] as compared to simple and straightforward UK in-country claim determination and protection. The cost of transferring asylum-seekers at scale to third countries makes such a programme unrealistic. It is not helpful to develop asylum policy as if such proposals were realistic. It is far better to focus on making in-country decisions and implementing them.

To that end, the provisions in the Immigration Rules that permit transfer of asylum-seekers whose claims are held to be inadmissible to third countries with which they have no connection should be removed. It is a foolish idea, the implementation of which can only lead to political ruin, as it cannot be implemented at scale due to cost. Further, the debate around it is a distraction from the improvement of in-country asylum claim processing and

---

[27] A. Macaskill, 'UK estimates cost of deporting each asylum seeker to Rwanda will be 169,000 pounds', *Reuters*, 26 June 2023, at https://www.reuters. com/world/uk/uk-says-cost-deporting-each-asylum-seeker-rwanda-be-169 000-pounds-2023-06-26/#:~:text=In%20an%20economic%20impact%20 assessment,for%20processing%20and%20legal%20costs.

the swift integration of successful claimants. Further, as noted, the national debate about removal of asylum-seekers to third countries functions further to distract people from wider social and economic problems to which Labour has actual solutions. Labour needs to focus on foregrounding its solutions to social and economic problems and to let asylum policy sink down the list of the public's priorities through making it fuss-free, undramatic and, as far as possible, simply an administrative matter.

Policy reform: cooperation with the European Union

On leaving the EU, the UK ceased to participate in the Common European Asylum System (CEAS)[28] and thus ceased to participate in the provision made for return of asylum-seekers to EU states through which they had passed on their way to the UK (the so-called Dublin III Regulation[29]). In the result, the UK has no legal agreement with any EU member state for, in appropriate cases, the return of asylum-seekers to those countries as safe third countries where their asylum claims can be processed and where protection can be provided. The absence of such an arrangement is a key driver of the Conservative government's attempt to find new third countries such as Rwanda, in order to remove those asylum-seekers whose asylum claims are declared inadmissible by virtue of having passed through an EU state on their way to the UK.

Labour's priority is obvious: to come to a new legal agreement with the EU and its member states as to the detail of the shared endeavour of determining asylum claims and deciding whether to offer protection in accordance with the 1951 Refugee Convention commitments by which the UK and all EU member states are bound. Such an arrangement, consistent with human rights obligations, could involve closer cooperation on border security. However, it will require a degree of pragmatic flexibility.

At present the Dublin III Regulation works as part of EU law and the CEAS; the latter provides common standards for the

---

[28] https://home-affairs.ec.europa.eu/policies/migration-and-asylum/common-european-asylum-system_en.
[29] Regulation (EU) 604/2013.

reception of asylum-seekers, the processing of their claims, and the interpretation and application of the Refugee Convention. Further, the CEAS is subject to the surveillance role of the European Commission and the judicial supervision of the Court of Justice of the European Union. The CEAS is a creature of EU law. For the UK and the EU to reach agreement by way of international law on these topics, flexibility will be required as to the content of such measures, how they are to be enforced, which body is to monitor them, and the extent of judicial supervision. Mutually agreeably solutions are possible and the prize of closer cooperation is worth the effort.

Policy reform: additional immigration powers are not needed

There is plenty of immigration statue law. The primary law is the Immigration Act 1971. For 17 years thereafter, no further immigration laws were required: The Heath, Wilson, Callaghan, and Thatcher governments managed very well without further immigration laws until the Immigration Act 1988, itself a slight thing. Thereafter, the frequency and number of immigration statutes has grown. At times, like the present, an immigration Bill seems like an annual event. The introduction of a new immigration Bill satisfies those with an appetite for something to be done about immigration control. However, the experience of the last few years shows that it is not a substitute for better use of existing powers and for wiser rule-making via the Immigration Rules (Home Office statements of executive policy).

There is a strong case for simplifying and consolidating existing immigration laws into one Act. Indeed, there is a case for the removal of particular immigration powers and provisions. However, what is not needed are further laws to add to immigration powers. The Home Office already has a full suite of all that it might ever need to control those arriving in the UK, to regulate those in-country, and to provide for powers of expulsion. No doubt there are civil servants in Marsham Street (where the Home Office is based), who have a folder containing legislative proposals that could be enacted. An incoming Labour administration would be wise to resist such siren calls. They serve only to distract from the more mundane but necessary task of improving the Home Office's administration of asylum and irregular migration policy and the better use of the Immigration Rules.

Further, Labour has numerous legislative priorities in other policy areas that are urgent. Yet another immigration Bill that adds to existing immigration powers create the false impression that new laws will solve perceived problems. The focus should be on better Home Office administration instead. Moreover, such Bills serve to suck oxygen from the public space in which other national priorities are discussed and focus unmerited blame for social policy failings at the door of asylum claimants and the administration of asylum policy. Labour would be poorly served if were seduced into the more-powers-are-needed approach that has served the Conservative government so poorly.

Policy reform: common law remedies

A further unwelcome feature of recent Conservative asylum policy making has been the restriction of judicial common law remedies, interim remedies in particular, in pursuit of substantive policy goals. The courts are to be prevented from stopping removal of asylum-seekers to third countries, even where there is a strong prima facie case that such action is unlawful. Both the 2023 Act and the Safety of Rwanda (Asylum and Immigration) Act 2024 have this feature. To put government policy, decision-making and action beyond the reach of the courts abuses the Constitutional principles of the rule of law and the separation of powers as they apply in the legal traditions applicable throughout the UK. That is so notwithstanding Parliament's power to enact such legislation. Parliament ought to act responsibly, conscious that the courts too sit at the apex of the constitutional settlement.

It is a fundamental feature of the common law that remedies for wrongs are available to all on an equal basis and against all wrong-doers, even public officials. That is the tradition that the UK exported to Commonwealth countries and others. No one is above the law. It is and should be for the courts to decide whether a remedy is warranted in an individual case. Removing judicial supervision to achieve substantive policy goals is authoritarian in character. As an urgent priority Labour should ensure that immigration legislation is freed from such measures and that no further ones are introduced. In so doing Labour will be loyal to the UK's Constitutional traditions.

Conclusion

There is much to be done. First, asylum and irregular migration policy making must cease to be placed in so visible a position that it dominates the national conversation. There are other, urgent, social and economic problems to be solved and Labour's solutions should be the focus. Second, the Conservative government's vices should be avoided. Third, the UK's fidelity to its international law commitments should be restored. Fourth, and consistently with reducing costs and promoting good administration, the primacy of in-country RSD and asylum decision-making should be restored. Fifth, there should be closer cooperation on matters of mutual concern with the EU and its member states. Sixth, the temptation to add to immigration powers through yet another immigration Bill should be resisted. Finally, in defence of our Constitutional traditions, the general, universal availability of common law remedies should be restored.

Summary of key proposals

- Asylum and irregular migration policy should be less of a dominating feature of the national conversation with the focus switching to other, urgent, social and economic problems and their solutions.
- The new government should avoid the previous government's vices of advancing policies that are oppressive in relation to their targets and are based on inflammatory media strategies.
- The UK's fidelity to its international law commitments should be restored in particular as a party to the Refugee Convention and the European Convention on Human Rights.
- Seek to reduce costs and promote good administration, for example by restoring the primacy of in-country Refugee Status Determination and asylum decision-making.

- Seek closer co-operation on matters of mutual concern with the EU and its member states.
- Avoid the temptation of adding further unnecessary immigration powers through yet another immigration Bill.
- In defence of our constitutional traditions, restore the general, universal availability of common law remedies.

12

Immigration and nationality

Thom Brooks

Introduction

The Conservative Party's immigration plans have proven to be headline-grabbing gimmicks that are not delivered. Promises made are too often broken with campaign manifesto pledges to cut net migration to under 100,000 while seeing it soar to over 700,000 one of many such examples. It should be no surprise that Labour continues to hold a consistent lead on immigration with so much going wrong for the government.

If Labour is to maintain or grow its lead, then it must offer a clear alternative. This is made more challenging with public confidence at an all-time low after 13 years of undelivered promises from the Tories. The public is right to want a clear vision for what a Labour government might deliver if elected and why this will lead to welcome changes that can be realised. This chapter considers new ideas for reforming the fees, work visas and family visas. Any immigration strategy needs an integration strategy, too. I will conclude the chapter with ideas on how the integration of immigrants might be improved. This will include reform of the Life in the UK test and the celebration of citizenship in civic ceremonies.

Immigration and nationality reform is vitally important to me. I am an immigrant from the United States who arrived as a student in the UK in 2001 and began work four years later. I have since had the privilege of becoming British. I have experienced the immigration system first-hand albeit from the privileged position of a White American with a PhD. I know well the lack of support, the high fees, the mind-boggling civics test and somewhat surreal citizenship ceremony. These experiences inform my academic study of a system that has become progressively more chaotic and in need of substantive reform that only a Labour government can deliver.

A self-funded, self-sustaining system

Immigration fees can be so high as to seem extortionate. A three-year work visa can cost £1,500. With a unit processing cost of £151 each, the Home Office earns nearly ten times its costs. Even health and social care workers in an occupation where there are shortages can pay £943 for a three-year visa that costs the Home Office only £129 to process. Overseas students can pay £490 for a visa costing £179 to process. While there are a few exceptions, virtually all fixed-term visas charge applicants far more than their unit costs.[1]

The situation is similar with permanent visas. For example, someone applying for permanent residency (or 'Indefinite Leave to Remain') might be charged up to £3,250 for an application with a Home Office unit cost of just £366. Citizenship applicants wanting to become British must pay a registration fee of up to £1,250 for what costs the Home Office £505. This is in addition to a £50 Life in the UK test fee and £80 citizenship ceremony fee.

There is an extra premium added for anyone wishing an expedited decision. The priority visa service can charge applicants £573 on top of the application fee while it costs £25.08 to administer. This is a mark-up of 228 per cent on top of the mark-up on the application made. The super priority visa service can charge £956 for what costs the Home Office £48.80, which is a 195 per cent mark-up.

---

[1]   Home Office, 'Immigration and nationality fees', 4 October 2023, updated 10 April 2024, at https://www.gov.uk/government/publications/visa-regulations-revised-table/home-office-immigration-and-nationality-fees-4-october-2023.

These examples make clear that the Home Office earns *far* more from application fees − from short-term work visas to naturalisation − than it incurs costs processing them. These applications cover virtually all areas except for asylum-seekers. Setting aside asylum, the income earned from various immigration fees does exceed the costs of running the immigration system. This work is, in effect, self-funded and income-generating. Provided fees are not reduced to cost or below, the system will be sustainably self-funded as the Home Office receives in excess of costs excluding asylum.

Some have proposed that immigration services be removed from the Home Office to become a separate department given that immigration services make up a disproportionate size within the Home Office. But it is not obvious that this would lead to any major gains where the accounting, costs and delivery would be unchanged beyond bureaucratic rebranding. Moreover, with the work split between junior ministers − one focused on legal migration, the other on illegal migration − it is unclear how splitting work off further leads to any necessary gains.

It is recommended that any future Labour government consider a commitment to making the Home Office's immigration services formally *self-funded and self-sustaining.*[2] The first reason is because it is already. The Home Office earns more than it requires to run immigration services for work, family, study and other visas and will continue to do so. This will be true even if fees are reduced provided an income remains above costs overall. The accounting is already in place and there would be no need to reorganise the department in any significant way − and so avoid the expensive costs and time in delivering departmental reorganising.

The second reason why this is recommended is because this commitment sends a significant message to voters. There can be public concerns about immigration insofar as it is seen as imposing costs rather than creating benefits. Labour can counter this concern by vowing a self-funded and self-sustaining immigration system on its watch would not, in fact, cost taxpayers one penny

---

[2]   T. Brooks, *New Arrivals: A Fair Immigration Plan for Labour*, Fabian Society, 2022, pp 44–5.

to run. Immigration would not cost anything. Immigrants would pay for the immigration system.

This proposal would mean there would be identifiable income from immigration fees. This can serve two broad purposes. In the short term, immigration fees could be earmarked for asylum support as an incoming Labour government seeks to clear up the massive backlog built up over 13 years of mismanagement. The new government could claim that the cost to taxpayers is reduced, in part, because of immigration-related income.

A second purpose is more ambitious. Additional income received from immigration-related fees might be earmarked for community renewal projects supporting levelling up. For example, the last Labour government introduced a Migration Impacts Fund. This was a £50 surcharge added onto immigration applications that went into a central fund that was worth £35 million annually.[3] Local health authorities, councils and other bodies to support projects aimed at reducing migration-related impact.

This fund should be re-launched as a *Migration Contribution Fund*.[4] The name would emphasise the financial contribution made by immigrants and the different way this scheme would work. Instead of creating a new surcharge adding extra costs on applications, the fund should be a portion of income earned by the Home Office from immigration-related fees after costs. This way the fund only moves forward when there is cash available and the system as self-funded is always prioritised. Charities and public bodies can bid for available funding to reduce migration-related impacts, but with the proviso that they must bring improvements to the overall community. Local people need to see and feel the benefits shared by all. Decision-making on how to allocate funds should be done by local people in their area giving all a voice in supporting their communities. But every project or programme funded would be required to carry a notice that it was, at least partially, supported by the Migration Contribution Fund. The more this is visible delivering wider benefits, the more positively it should be viewed.

---

[3] M. Gower, 'The new Controlling Migration Fund for England', House of Commons Library Briefing Paper 7673, 7 December 2017, pp 11–12.

[4] Brooks (n 2), pp 45–6.

Overseas students attending our universities bring benefits far beyond their financial contribution, or so I like to believe as a former international student myself, proudly graduating from the University of Sheffield in 2004. This is understood well by higher and further education institutions, but could become more visible for the local communities these institutions are based in. A Labour government might consider some portion of a Migration Contribution Fund in proportion to student visa fee income to supporting migration-related impacts in these communities. This will help make clear that overseas students yield more benefits than to their universities and allow local people to prosper in new ways.

In these ways, immigration will be seen more positively. Taxpayers would pay nothing for a self-funded and self-sustaining system paid only by immigrants. And the extra income received could go towards local improvements benefiting local people as decided by them.

Economic migration

Britain must be open for business. It is no surprise that economic migrants make up one of the largest migrant groups. In the year up to September 2022, there were 585,774 work visas granted.[5] Economic migrants bring significant benefits for driving economic growth. It is key that a future Labour government is able to maximise these benefits with some strategically targeted reforms.

Labour has already rightly announced it would scrap a 20 per cent wage reduction relating to minimum income requirements for hiring overseas staff in shortage occupations.[6] This would help create conditions for better wages for British workers without being undercut by paying overseas workers less than the average

---

[5] Home Office, 'Summary of latest statistics', updated 7 December 2023, at https://www.gov.uk/government/statistics/immigration-system-statistics-year-ending-september-2023/summary-of-latest-statistics#:~:text=There%20were%203%2C383%2C446%20visas%20granted,(%2B54%25)%20to%20585%2C774.

[6] See, for example, 'Yvette Cooper comments on MAC backing Labour's proposal to scrap 20% wage discount for shortage occupations', Labour Party Press Release, 3 October 2023.

going rate. Moreover, Labour would create a strategy for getting occupations off the occupation shortage list. This would ensure employers do not become overly reliant on overseas workers as job shortages can be filled domestically.

The first policy Labour should consider is creating work visas that provide greater flexibility and responsiveness to business needs with no reduction in protective standards. There are several examples to draw on from our doorstep. The Republic of Ireland offers a range of work visas including a short stay business visa costing about £50 for 14 days.[7] There are also work visas available in Switzerland available for up to 90 days[8] or for a maximum of six months in Mexico. One of these options can be introduced in the UK. If a fee like £50 was below costs, the government could introduce a plan such as requiring prospective employers to pay a fee to sponsor these more flexible work visas so that the Home Office is never below cost.

Not every business requires overseas staff for one to three years at a time. For some needs in filling specific job shortages, swifter and more agile options can boost businesses when they need it most. Making it easier for businesses to succeed, while maintaining the usual checks, stimulates their ability to compete and support future growth. Labour can burnish its pro-business credentials by adopting a more pro-business approach like this.

A further way to stimulate growth is to launch a British Wealth Creator Visa. Investor visas can be done well where it better secures a contribution to wealth creation and benefiting local communities. The American Immigrant Investor Visa requires investment of US$1 million or more with a reduced rate of at least US$500,000 if investing in a high unemployment or rural area.[9] Moreover, any such investment must evidence full-time jobs for at least ten American citizens or green card holders. With stringent

---

[7] See, for example, https://www.citizensinformation.ie/en/moving-country/ visas-for-ireland/visas-for-business-people-visiting-ireland/#0ad585.

[8] See, for example, 'Travel to Switzerland for work', UK Government Guidance, at https://www.gov.uk/guidance/travel-to-switzerland-for-work.

[9] US Department of State Bureau of Consular Affairs, 'Immigrant Investor Visas', at https://travel.state.gov/content/travel/en/us-visas/immigrate/ immigrant-investor-visas.html.

anti-money laundering checks in place, a similar scheme could be readily introduced here.

A second policy that might be considered is that sponsors need not pay the full fee upfront for work visas of one year or more. Instead, payments might be made monthly. As noted earlier in this chapter, the visa fees can be prohibitively high to the point of being off-putting. Some businesses might be able to better manage these costs if spread out over six months to a year rather than paying it all in a lump sum upfront – alongside other fees like the immigration health surcharge.

A third policy is introducing regional visas. Normally, a work visa might allow someone to work anywhere in a country. A regional visa only allows employment within a particular area. They can be useful in strategically attracting much needed skills to specific regions. Following the model used in Australia or Canada, a future Labour government might cap the number of general longer-term work visas to work anywhere in the country while setting aside a smaller number of work visas tied to working in specific nations or regions outside London and the south-east. This would help distribute skilled overseas labour to the areas needed most across the UK. It could support levelling up left behind areas, promote national renewal and be managed so the benefits and impacts are more evenly shared.

A pro-business Labour government can support economic growth better. This can be achieved, in part, by policies already announced around scrapping a wage reduction on shortage occupations and looking to end the shortages list with a strategy for ending overreliance on overseas labour. But a future government can go further. More flexible and responsive work visas providing greater agility to gain growth, introducing a British Wealth Creator Visa, the option of monthly payments for covering application fees and introducing a regional visa to promote growth in nations and regions is a recipe for economic growth that will boost Britain's competitiveness globally for the best talent.

Family-friendly for British citizens

Britain's family reunion policies are not family-friendly. Many of us may take for granted the ability to live and grow old with those we love. Sadly, this is not a reality for a sizeable minority. The family rules can keep British families separated. There are high income fees that are above what many earn. A British citizen wanting to return with their family might need to come alone if looking for a job, find employment at a sufficient income level and work several months before being able to make an application for sponsoring family to live with them in the UK. And then this process can take six months or longer. All the way, the family is forced to live apart. It is no wonder that some claim the immigration rules put a price on love that is more than can be paid and means that some citizens are unable to live in their country with their family.

The first step is reviewing the system with an eye towards reform. The UK has had a points-based system since Labour introduced it in 2008. However, family visas work more like a tick-box exercise where all criteria must be met rather than a proper points system that has more flexibility. This system should be reviewed to ensure it is fit for purpose and can command public confidence. It is unclear that it always achieves both.

The second step is to review how family visas are managed where relationships break down. There are two issues that should be addressed. One is that when a relationship ends it invalidates the family visa – but only if the Home Office is aware.[10] In order to improve reporting, the Home Office created an appalling form for reporting relationship breakdowns to UK Visas and Immigration. I have long argued this should be scrapped.[11] It can fuel abuse and is generally unworkable. Since its launch in January 2016, there is no record of a single form being submitted nor of anyone removed as a result.

Instead, the rules should be changed. A spousal visa is no longer valid from when a relationship is not genuine and subsisting.[12]

---

[10] Brooks (n 2), p 24.

[11] T. Brooks, *Reforming the UK's Citizenship Test: Building Barriers, Not Bridges*, Bristol University Press, pp 267–9.

[12] Home Office, 'Relationship with a partner: assessing the relationship with a partner based on the immigration rules: appendix relationship with partner', 4 April 2024, p 9, at https://assets.publishing.service.gov.uk/media/65fac e7f703c42001a58f065/Relationship+with+a+partner.pdf.

This includes when couples divorce or where civil partners receive a dissolution order. A helpful change would be where from the confirmation of a decree nisi or dissolution order the Home Office must be notified, in case individuals affected are on family visas. This small, but important, reform would ensure more effective enforcement of valid visas than the current form for reporting relationship breakdown and without leading to the problems such a form could cause.

A second issue is that a spouse living in the UK for five or more years could be entitled to apply for Indefinite Leave to Remain, but avoid doing so because of a lack of funds or controlling partner. However, with divorce or dissolution, the spouse or partner must leave the UK. If they return, the Home Office resets the clock on their qualifying residency to zero. For example, someone who was married for ten or even 20 years and so may be able to become a permanent resident, but failed to apply before they got divorced, would lose credit for all the time lived in the UK.

The rules should be changed allowing a strict timeframe of no more than six months for someone who met eligibility requirements before a divorce or dissolution to make an application. This gives individuals a fair opportunity to apply, if they wish and meet the criteria, on the same terms. Divorce can have unequal impacts on partners. This reform could help support individuals while maintaining the same standards for determining whether they can remain.

The immigration rules can separate British citizens from their families. A review of how best to manage a points-based system that can exercise proper controls in a fair way that maintains public confidence is overdue and should be launched. At the same time, enforcement of the family visa scheme can be improved. The reporting form no one is using should be binned and replaced by the courts directly contacting the Home Office where marriages or civil partnerships formally end. Individuals who were entitled to apply for permanent residency before their relationships ended should have a short window to make an application before the residency periods clocked up are reset to zero. A Labour government can create a more family-friendly system that is better enforced.

Civics tests and celebrating citizenship

Labour introduced the Life in the UK test for citizenship in 2005. While no government has proposed abandoning it, the test has, in my words, become 'unfit for purpose' and 'like a bad pub quiz' after many years of neglect.[13] There are about 3,000 facts, including 278 historical dates, to memorise but much of this does not actually appear on any test. The questions are not merely trivia, but too often trivial. For example, the current test handbook states that all applicants must know the day, month and year that both Boris Johnson and Theresa May became prime minister, but no one else in British history.[14] This makes no sense. There are errors of fact about the largest denomination of notes in circulation, the first Danish king in the UK and more that require correcting. More importantly, it is a test for British citizenship that few British citizens can pass – and does not enjoy sufficient confidence.

A Labour government should seek to refresh the test to better achieve its aims and purpose supporting integration and building public support. Like when the test was first planned in 2004, a new citizenship advisory group should be launched. Its tasks are to engage with the public, consulting widely on shared expectations on new citizens and rewriting the test accordingly. The group should be led by someone who has first-hand experience of naturalisation and the group must consult with others who have, too. My experience after passing the test and later becoming British in 2011 is that for many it fails to bring people together, but rather can push apart as migrants scramble to meet knowledge requirements for being British that few British know themselves or find relevant.[15] Such a gap is unwelcome for building ever more connected communities. A British citizenship test should contain information based on our shared British values that should be

---

[13] T. Brooks, *The Trust Factor: Essays on the Current Political Crisis and Hope for the Future*, Methuen, 2022.

[14] Home Office, *Life in the United Kingdom: A Guide for New Residents*, 2022, p 69.

[15] T. Brooks, *Becoming British: UK Citizenship Examined*, Biteback Publishing, 2016.

known by most citizens. This could be better achieved by teaching its contents in schools so that more are aware.

A second policy for Labour to consider is a new *contribution test*. Integration is not a one-way street. There are responsibilities on both migrants and the wider community where they settle. These can work together as part of a non-mandatory test that could expedite eligibility for applying for British citizenship. While immigration does bring many benefits, critics claim that these are largely enjoyed by the immigrants themselves and their employers with insufficient impact on the wider public. Of course, such criticism should be challenged, but we might do so with a progressive policy.

Migrants bring skills, experience and knowledge that enrich our communities and benefit the economy. A contribution test should be made available for immigrants considering becoming British.[16] The test would require immigrants spending a nominal amount of time, such as 20 hours, volunteering for any registered charity, public body or religious organisation. This could be delivered all at once or over multiple occasions. The host organisation need only confirm online the time spent. There is nothing to study, no additional fees to pay and it could be done flexibly for whenever convenient. Both immigrants and these organisations would be helping each other towards a common good. Immigrants could gain new contacts and support as they integrate into their communities. Local people would derive tangible benefits from the volunteering delivered by immigrants.

Immigrants that acquire Indefinite Leave to Remain must wait a year before applying for British citizenship. But anyone meeting the contribution test might be permitted to apply after three to six months, cutting their wait by contributing their time to supporting their communities. This would change nothing in the high standards that must be met to become British. But it would change how immigrants might engage in local areas for public benefit in a way that they – that people like me – are perceived as providing benefits not costs and delivering positive outcomes that people can see for themselves.

---

[16] Brooks (n 2), pp 31–3.

Labour introduced citizenship ceremonies. They can serve an important symbolic role where individuals become British. The problem is these ceremonies are too often hidden from view in private rooms with little public acknowledgement. They have become less of a celebration and more of an administrative exercise. The experience can be very different elsewhere. For example, in my native United States, it is not uncommon for new citizens to be sworn in at major sporting events in front of tens of thousands – a willing audience happy to applaud the introduction of new Americans.

Labour can promote its patriotic values by making citizenship more of a celebration. Not everyone might want to become British so publicly as in the United States. But many might and should have the opportunity to enjoy an event afterwards as a great way to mark a special occasion.

Finally, this could be promoted through creating a new bank holiday – a special UK Day.[17] Days of great significance bring us all together. One example is Remembrance Sunday. This is held each November on the second Sunday. It is a commemoration of the contributions of British and Commonwealth military and civilians defending our country. It celebrates what others have done in the past.

A UK Day should be held on the Monday after Remembrance Day as we gather to celebrate our Britishness today and into the future. It is inspired by both the Thanksgiving holiday in Canada and the United States as well as Australia Day where Australians can restate their citizenship oaths alongside large citizenship ceremonies.

The UK has fewer bank holidays than most of our friends. There has been none introduced since 1978. After COVID-19, many of us have come to appreciate more the importance of coming together and supporting our communities. A UK Day bank holiday would be a moment to come together to champion becoming British and reflect on our ties while naturally complementing Remembrance Sunday that raises the profile of the weekend in a more meaningful way.

---

[17] Brooks (n 2), pp 33–4.

Conclusion

It is easy to draw attention to the many failings of a Conservative government that has lost all credibility on immigration. We require a new vision of ambitious, but deliverable, policies under a Labour government that can fix what is broken, rebuild trust in the system and deliver progressive policies in a way that meaningfully speaks to the public's priorities.

This chapter has outlined a series of ideas that are aimed at doing just that. A self-funded and self-sustaining system paid entirely by immigration-related fees and which noticeably contributes funding to public community building, work visas that drive growth and better support businesses, a family visa system that helps British citizens build lives in Britain, fairer visa rules with more effective enforcement, a test for citizenship that British citizens can have confidence in again, celebrating our citizenship and introducing a new bank holiday to help do so – these are only a few of the policy ideas that a future Labour government can champion. Together, they can promote security, prosperity and respect in meaningful ways that are credible and deliverable.

I have every confidence that Labour can be the party of fair and controlled immigration that the public believe in. Policies like these can help make it a reality.

Summary of key proposals

- Consider a commitment to making the Home Office's immigration services formally self-funded and self-sustaining.
- Create a Migration Contribution Fund raised from immigration-related fees to support national renewal.
- Make immigration work better for business and the country:
  - create more flexible and responsive temporary work visas, such as in the Republic of Ireland;
  - launch a British Wealth Creator Visa, inspired by the American Immigrant Investor Visa in the United States;
  - consider work visa fees to be paid monthly, as proposed to the Australian government;
  - introduce regional visas to help support levelling up beyond London and the south-east.

- Making immigration work more fairly for families:
  - review how the points-based system applies to family visas;
  - end the unused form for reporting breakdowns to UK Visas and Immigration and require courts to notify the Home Office about divorce or dissolution orders involving non-UK citizens;
  - grant up to six months grace period for those subject to divorce or dissolution to apply for Indefinite Leave to Remain if they otherwise meet all other eligibility criteria.
- Launch an Advisory Group led by a naturalised British citizen to conduct a public consultation on citizenship and produce a new 4th edition of the Life in the UK test.
- Consider a contribution test where voluntary public service may qualify for expedited naturalisation after obtaining Indefinite Leave to Remain.
- Review use of citizenship ceremonies to make them more of a public celebration.
- Launch a new UK Day as a bank holiday immediately following Remembrance Sunday, inspired by Australia Day and America's Thanksgiving.

13

EU and trade law

George Peretz

Introduction

Brexit threw up new barriers between the UK and almost all the rest of Europe. Indeed, it was intended to do, and sometimes sold as doing, precisely that. There is no reasonable doubt that throwing up those barriers has been economically harmful, especially to small UK businesses unable to cope with those barriers when exporting to (or importing the goods they need from) the European Union (EU).

And one reason why so many businesspeople – and ordinary voters – have abandoned the Tories is that they have utterly failed to deal with, and usually do not even admit, the huge problems for UK businesses – and citizens – created by Boris Johnson's thin post-Brexit deal with the EU.

Both to achieve its missions, and to respond to those voters, the next Labour government will need, as the Labour manifesto promised, 'to make Brexit work'.

However, the new Labour government will have to confront the realities of where the UK now is. And those realities start with the legal realities.

Rejoining the European Union?

The legal reality on 'rejoin' is that whether the UK can rejoin the EU is not in the UK's gift, and many EU member states (all of which have a veto) would have to be convinced that UK membership is in their interests and that the UK was not likely to put the EU through a repeat of the Brexit process in the foreseeable future. Further, to rejoin the EU would require a long negotiating process under Article 49 on the Treaty on European Union – a process that would require an intense and detailed focus across all levels of government, inevitably at the expense of other priorities. Further, the EU would be unlikely to permit the UK to rejoin on the favourable terms that it had as a member state in 2016 (for example opt-outs from the euro, Schengen, justice and home affairs) – terms that were widely resented by other member states at that time. The UK would also have to take the EU as it found it – after many years in which the EU will have been moving forward in its legislation and structures without any UK vote.

Joining the customs union or single market?

Nor is 'joining the single market/customs union' a quick and easy alternative. Indeed, either proposal is in many ways more legally complex and difficult than 'rejoin' (for which the EU treaties make detailed provision, and for which there is an established process).

• As for a customs union, which would commit the UK to the common EU external tariff and customs rules, and in practice to common EU trade remedy policies, the only models at all for that are the EU–Turkey customs union (partial and widely accepted to be dysfunctional) and the customs union with Monaco (a microstate which in countless and obvious respects is very different from the UK). Negotiating a customs union that gave the UK a real say in the tariffs and customs and trade remedies policy it would have to adopt would be fraught with difficulty on the EU side: and any arrangement that tied the UK to those policies without any real say in them is unlikely to be workable for, or acceptable to, the UK.
• As for the single market, the single market is not a club with an application form. What advocates of 'joining the single market' tend to mean is an application to join the European Free Trade Area (EFTA) and then the European Economic Area Agreement (EEA) between three EFTA members and

the EU. However, the EEA model would raise profound problems for the UK, and for the existing EFTA/EEA states. Under that model, the EFTA/EEA states essentially accept EU legislation on not just the four freedoms of the single market (ranging from financial and economic regulation and product regulation to social security) but also on issues such as state aid. Though in theory an EFTA/EEA member state can block the addition of a new EU law, the consequence of exercising that power would be that the EU could take remedial action: and, unsurprisingly, that power to block has remained unused. To put it mildly, it is not obvious either that the addition of such a large country with such a wide range of interests as the UK would be workable from the point of view of existing EFTA/EEA members and EU member states (all of whom would have to agree in order to amend the EEA to include the UK) or that such an arrangement would command a wide and sustainable consensus across the UK.

Building on the Trade and Cooperation Agreement

Putting those proposals on one side, therefore, what is left is building upon the existing Trade and Cooperation Agreement (TCA). In principle, that can mean three things (which are not mutually exclusive):

- Using existing TCA mechanisms to improve cooperation and reduce barriers (for one example among many, Articles 103 to 105 contain commitments to work together in the area of customs, and to reduce red tape and customs formalities, and Articles 121 and 122 give joint bodies under the TCA power to make changes to achieve those objectives).
- Amending or adding to the TCA in ways not provided for by the TCA as it currently stands. It is sometimes suggested that such changes could be proposed as part of the review of the TCA which Article 776 requires to be carried out in 2026 (preparatory work on which will need to start in 2025). However, that overstates the importance of the review provision: such review provisions are fairly routine in free

trade agreements, and (at least in public) the current EU Commission has been keen to lower expectations, emphasising that Article 776 provides for a review of implementation, not a review of possible amendments or additions – though the Commission inevitably and understandably focuses on the current UK government rather than on a possible future Labour government with a different approach. But, leaving aside the review provision, it is open to either the UK or EU to propose side agreements to the TCA at any time: indeed, in April 2024 the EU Commission proposed to member states that it be given a mandate to negotiate a youth mobility arrangement with the UK, which would be such a side agreement.[1]

• Moving towards an overarching 'association agreement' under Article 217 of the Treaty on the Functioning of the EU, in which the UK would participate in certain elements of the EU system.

A number of bodies, including the Independent Commission on UK-EU Relations[2] and the UK Trade & Business Commission,[3] have made detailed suggestions as to ways in which, using one or other of those mechanisms, the barriers to trade erected at the end of 2020 could be lowered. Rather than run through those suggestions we aim to draw out some underlying points.

Legal constraints on the European Union

As in any negotiation, it is critical to bear in mind the objectives and constraints of the other side – in this case, the EU. Contrary to what is sometimes suggested, those constraints are not, primarily, legal: the EU treaties allow the EU considerable latitude in making agreements with third countries, though it is important to be aware that adding new provisions to the TCA or entering into an association agreement would almost certainly be a 'mixed

---

[1] https://ec.europa.eu/commission/presscorner/detail/en/IP_24_2105.

[2] https://www.ukeucommission.org/.

[3] https://www.tradeandbusiness.uk/.

agreement' which would require ratification by each member state, with associated possible complications.[4]

In particular, the EU frequently 'splits the single market' or allows 'cherry picking' by allowing third countries to participate in some of its aspects but not others: almost every agreement between the EU and its neighbours, such as (for example) Ukraine, contains examples of that. The real question is, in each case, what the EU – and its member states – consider to be in its and their interests. That in turn means that – to be achievable – UK negotiating objectives need either to be 'sellable' as also being in the EU's interests, or matched by concessions that offer the EU a quid pro quo.

Nonetheless, any strategy has to bear in mind the procedural constraints on the EU: renegotiation of the TCA beyond the possibilities of amendment and elaboration set out in the TCA itself requires that the Commission obtain a negotiating mandate from member states and the European Parliament (EP) (an example being the Commission proposal in relation to youth mobility mentioned earlier). Any formal negotiations could not therefore start quickly, and would need to be preceded by intense engagement by the UK with the Commission, the EP and member states both to persuade them to take that step – perhaps after an initial 'scoping' exercise – and to secure that the mandate adequately covered the key UK 'asks'.

Alignment

A number of suggestions made to reduce regulatory barriers – such as an agreement on sanitary and phytosanitary (SPS) checks on food products – will involve alignment with EU law and acceptance of the Court of Justice of the EU (CJEU) as ultimate interpreter (and potentially of other aspects of enforcement, such as a role for the Commission or power of UK courts to

---

[4] See, for example, the Dutch referendum in 2016 rejecting ratification of the association agreement with Ukraine, and the recent Irish Supreme Court judgment holding that ratification of the EU/Canada trade agreement would be inconsistent with the Constitution of Ireland (*Costello v Ireland* [2022] IESC 44).

make references to the CJEU). That is obviously so in relation to the Resolution Foundation's suggestion of a 'UK Protocol' that would essentially apply the current Windsor Framework governing Northern Ireland to the whole of the UK, with possible additional consultation mechanisms in place of the 'Stormont brake'.[5] But the same point also extends to more ad hoc arrangements, such as an SPS agreement or agreement on reducing value-added tax barriers by setting up frameworks for information sharing and common notifications. It is important to understand why that is so, what that means, and why the next Labour government should be prepared in at least some cases to agree it.

- *Why alignment?* The reason why the EU will insist on alignment as the quid pro quo for removing or reducing regulatory checks is that the central bargain that lies at the core of the single market in goods and services is that member states allow goods and services from other member states to be sold freely and without checks on their territories in return for a guarantee both that those goods and services are subject to a minimum set of requirements and that those requirements are properly enforced and interpreted in a consistent way – that is to say, ultimately by the CJEU and, critically, by national courts of each member state that accept the authority of the CJEU and apply its interpretations to disputes before them. No third country is going to be allowed such access without signing up not just to the same rules, but also to the same (or equivalent) mechanisms to ensure that those rules are enforced and interpreted in the same way.[6] That point applies even more strongly if the UK's 'ask' is for participation in the EU process

5   See https://economy2030.resolutionfoundation.org/wp-content/uploads/2023/06/Trading-Up.pdf. The authors are – for reasons with which we agree – very cautious about the likelihood of the EU accepting such a proposal, at least in the short to medium run.

6   The EU's agreement on SPS standards with New Zealand is sometimes cited as an example where the EU accepts, to some extent, third country standards as equivalent to its own: but New Zealand exports to the EU are minuscule in comparison to the UK's, and (for obvious geographic reasons) do not involve much fresh produce where risks are greater.

in areas such as medicines or chemicals – areas where there is a very strong UK interest in being part of the EU system rather than to attempt to set up parallel and costly systems of regulation in areas where business realities mean that real divergence is impossible.[7] Further, in areas where cooperation is in the form of intense exchanges of information in areas such as tax, regulation or migration, the EU will need to be certain that the UK respects EU standards for the protection of that information.

• *What does alignment mean?* Alignment in the thin sense of simply copying relevant EU rules may be a good idea for purely domestic reasons (to reduce the costs of regulation for businesses that already comply with EU regulation) – though it should be noted that Tory legislation such as the Retained EU Law (Revocation and Reform) Act 2023 has deliberately made it more difficult or impossible to achieve that result (so that legislation to reform that Act must be an early legislative priority). But to be effective in removing or reducing barriers to single market access, it means not just agreeing to follow EU rules but also, as part of that agreement, having domestic legislation that allows for them to be automatically adopted into domestic law as they develop and, at least in the short to

---

[7] It is striking that despite the Tory government having had power for several years under section 2 of the Medicines and Medical Devices Act 2021 to rewrite medicines legislation in Great Britain as it wishes, those powers have scarcely been used, and the UK medicines regime remains almost entirely that inherited from EU membership. Indeed, to date, products with EU marketing authorisations have essentially been 'passported' into a Great British marketing authorisation: an expedient that minimises delay caused by insisting on further Great Britain-specific authorisation (since most pharmaceutical companies prioritise getting access to the far larger EU market over that of Great Britain) at the price of steady damage to the regulatory capacity of the UK Medicines and Healthcare Products Regulatory Agency (as the detailed and skilled work of medicines regulation is essentially delegated to EU bodies). However, despite the similarity of Great British regulation, products manufactured in Great Britain are subject to the full panoply of EU regulatory controls on export (such as batch testing) and Great Britain is also locked out of the EU pharmacovigilance system (which provides extensive real-time data on problems such as side-effects).

medium term,[8] agreeing that the ultimate interpreter of those rules will be the CJEU, that UK courts will follow the CJEU, and that there are mechanisms for dealing with cases where UK courts fail to follow the CJEU: what might be called 'thick alignment'.

- *Why should a Labour government accept thick alignment?* Accepting CJEU (or equivalent) jurisdiction and the importation of EU law into domestic law will doubtless be condemned by those whose attitude to sovereignty is that of the miser's attitude to money – that it is to be hoarded and never used, even for your own benefit. But the reason why the next Labour government should – in at least some sectors – be prepared to concede those things is that in many areas, such as medicines, chemicals, many manufactured goods with complex supply chains, and SPS rules, the Tory government's approach has led to the worst of all worlds: a world in which the UK is forced by business reality (with some insignificant exceptions) to follow EU rules but gets no benefit from doing so in terms of access to the EU market.[9] Even after several years in which the Conservative government, committed to divergence from the EU, had, under domestic legislation, the power to make substantive changes in areas such as SPS standards and (as noted earlier) medicines regulation,[10] it barely did so. And that in turn is:
  - because there is, in fact, little in that regulation that is unsuitable for the UK, and much that is international (for example, the United Nations Economic Commission for Europe);
  - because much UK business in practice has to comply with EU legislation anyway if it wishes to sell to the EU;
  - because extending different domestic regulation to imports from the EU would require checks and controls on EU

---

[8] We say 'at least in the short to medium term' because in the longer term, and particularly if alignment ended up extending across several sectors of the economy, it might be possible to persuade the EU to accept a form of EFTA Court (the Court that acts as the equivalent of the CJEU for the EFTA/EEA states and is therefore already accepted by the EU in relation to those states) – expanded to include a UK-nominated judge – as a satisfactory alternative to the CJEU.

[9] See note 5 in relation to medicines.

[10] In relation to SPS standards, see section 37 of the Agriculture Act 2020.

imports that would both increase costs to UK businesses and consumers; and

- given that Northern Ireland remains essentially in the EU single market for goods (a result that follows from the Windsor Framework agreed by the Tory government in February 2023, despite its attempts to deny that reality[11]) because divergence between rules for the sale and manufacture of goods as between Great Britain and the EU/Northern Ireland increases barriers to trade between Great Britain and Northern Ireland: indeed, the Tory government's commitments to report on and evaluate any measure that could create further barriers to Great Britain/Northern Ireland trade[12] will create further obstacles to divergence.

A further issue – related to alignment – is obtaining 'EU treatment' for the UK in relation to EU legislation that aims to produce extraterritorial effects. One example of that is the Foreign Subsidies Regulation discussed later in this chapter: but other examples are EU regulations on the carbon border adjustment mechanism or deforestation. In each case, the 'price' of treatment of the UK as anything other than a third country will be a form of thick alignment with relevant EU policy.

Finally, it is worth noting that even the Tory government accepted in one area that thick alignment – including acceptance of CJEU as the binding interpreter of the relevant rules – is in the UK national interest. That is the matter of accession to the Lugano Convention, which provides for common rules as to jurisdiction in civil cases and allows for easier enforcement of judgments (an issue of concern to any business trading across Europe or to UK consumers who buy from EU suppliers). The EU is presently

---

[11] See its White Paper, *Safeguarding the Union*, CP 1021, January 2024, at https://www.gov.uk/government/publications/safeguarding-the-union, in which the table at fig.1 on page 4, that purports to show that Northern Ireland is not in the EU single market for goods, conspicuously ignores any reference to the plethora of EU rules relating to the sale and manufacture of goods, as well as value added tax and state aid rules, to which Northern Ireland remains subject under the Windsor Framework.

[12] Ibid., chapter 6.

blocking UK accession: but removing that block is a reasonable negotiating objective, not least because UK accession would be in the interests of EU businesses and citizens who deal with the UK: a particular factor for Ireland, where the complexities of applying general rules of private international law to cases involving the UK are putting a significant extra burden on its courts.

Mobility

Free movement of people is not on the table, not least because it is a concept that carries with it a whole series of complex legal provisions that make sense only as part of a single market. Labour's position of ruling it out is a recognition of that legal reality.

However, mobility provisions falling short of free movement in the full EU sense are common as between neighbouring countries with similar levels of prosperity: examples can be found as between Australia and New Zealand, between Mercosur countries, and (of course) the common travel area between the UK and Ireland (a largely informal arrangement that does not involve, for example, rights of access to social security benefits or housing on the same terms as nationals – a feature of EU free movement law that sparked much controversy in the UK before the 2016 referendum). Those agreements go well beyond anything we suggest here: but they show that there is plenty of room between having no mobility provisions and free movement of people as under the EU treaties.

Despite its willingness to negotiate some youth mobility provisions with Australia and New Zealand (countries on the other side of the world and accessible only via an expensive flight) the Johnson government refused, on wholly dogmatic grounds, to negotiate any mobility provisions at all with the EU, despite having indicated in the 2019 political declaration (on which it fought the 2019 general election) that it would do so. Despite the fact that some Conservative Brexit supporters have supported the idea,[13] it also responded entirely negatively to the Commission's April 2024 proposal on a youth mobility arrangement (though that

---

[13] See, for example, former Cabinet minister George Eustice MP, at https://www.theguardian.com/politics/2023/jul/08/tory-brexiter-george-eustice-visas-young-eu-workers-labour-shortage.

proposal was in part a response to the Conservative government's indication that it would be prepared to negotiate youth mobility schemes with selected EU member states).

That stance was and is a mistake, for three main reasons.

- First, mobility is intricately linked with the ability to supply services, an area where the UK has particular strengths. That is obvious in the case of the cultural industries (musicians and artists), whose difficulties in operating on the continent Labour has rightly indicated that it wishes to address as a policy priority in this area (the fact that those difficulties do not arise when UK musicians and artists travel to Ireland, where mobility is preserved under the common travel area, shows that the key issue is lack of mobility). But the lack of mobility provision for UK citizens also hits UK businesses who need to move staff temporarily to the continent to gain experience or improve their skills, or to serve clients there (who may be EU businesses or, in the case of travel companies engaging seasonal reps, UK tourists).

- Second, lack of mobility is seen by the EU as symbolic of a UK turning its back on Europe (made worse by the refusal of the UK to accept identity cards instead of passports, with well-publicised impacts on school trips and other travel). More practically, it makes life difficult (and given the cost of UK visas, expensive) for the many EU citizens who want to travel to the UK for extended periods, either to improve their language or other skills or because they are relatives of UK citizens or of the three million EU citizens living in the UK. So (as well as its symbolic value) improved mobility directly benefits the EU as well as the UK.

- Third, many UK citizens – particularly young people wanting to improve their language skills or just to experience living in a different culture, but also retired people, people with close relatives living in the EU, or people who can work remotely for UK employers or clients – would like, without having to go through the uncertainty and hassle of applying for visas, to be able to study and work for a while in the EU, or just to spend time there beyond the 90/180 day Schengen visa-free time limit. In relation to young people, the Commission's youth mobility proposal recognises that there is a strong reciprocal EU interest here, and that reciprocal interest cover would also cover wider mobility arrangements (though the UK 180 days a year visa-free limit for non-working visitors is significantly more flexible than the Schengen limit).

In dealing with this issue, the new Labour government will need to bear in mind that the EU may well be suspicious of proposals that seem to be tailored to specific sectors where the UK is strong (such as music and the arts). Labour should therefore leave itself room to make wider proposals for a mobility agreement that confers broader rights on each side's citizens. That could include, as well as proposals designed to help musicians and others in the cultural industries, responding positively to the Commission's proposal on youth mobility to work or study for a period of (say) up to one or two years, even if making it clear that some of the details of that proposal were not acceptable;[14] and, potentially, a proposal for anyone working for an employer on one side of the Channel to have the right to work for that employer for a period on the other; and/or a proposal for visa-free non-work/remote working visits for longer than the current provisions allow. Claims that such proposal would unfairly discriminate in favour of EU citizens as opposed to citizens of other countries can safely be dismissed: such claims ignore the point that mobility to the EU – because it is only 23 miles or a £20 flight away – is of far more value to UK businesses and to far more UK citizens across a far wider income spectrum than equivalent provisions with countries on the other side of the ocean or of the world (and, of course, such an agreement would not prevent the UK reaching similar agreements on some or any of these areas with, for example, Commonwealth countries, if in the UK's interests to do so).

---

[14] Labour might, for example, want to provide for a quota on numbers (given that many more EU young people speak a sufficient level of English to work or study than UK citizens speaking EU languages to that level) and to resist elements of the proposal that would require EU young people to have access to UK universities and training programmes on the same terms as UK citizens.

Level playing field

The EU closely watches UK legislation in the fields of employment and environmental standards, as part of its monitoring of the 'level playing field'. It may well want those positions strengthened as part of the quid pro quo for UK 'asks'.

In those areas, stronger commitments are unlikely to be problematic in principle for the new Labour government. However, the level playing field provisions of the TCA also contain detailed commitments on the more problematic area of subsidy control, which have in the UK been implemented by the Subsidy Control Act 2022.

From the EU perspective, control of the ability of member states to subsidise their businesses is another core element of the bargain by which each state agrees to let goods and services from other member states be supplied freely on its territory: the state aid rules protect against unfairly subsidised businesses from other member states unfairly undercutting their domestic producers. The EU starting point may well be that any third country that wants anything like comparable access for a substantial proportion of its goods or services will need to operate equivalent controls.

Also from the EU perspective, the current UK subsidy control regime, which is a minimalist approach to the UK's obligations under the TCA, suffers significant weaknesses.

- It is entirely dependent for enforcement on third parties challenging subsidy decisions: but quite apart from the fact that in most cases there is no third party with a sufficient interest and commercial incentive to do so, UK case-law to date has taken a very strict view of how quickly third parties need to move (refusing permission in *British Gas Trading v Secretary of State for Energy Security Net Zero* [2023] EWHC 737[15] on grounds of delay where the application was made only a few days after information about the subsidy was provided) and (in the same case) making it clear that the courts will apply only 'light touch' scrutiny to public authorities' justifications for a subsidy.

---

[15] Now on appeal to the Court of Appeal.

- Although the Competition and Markets Authority must be notified of and give advice about most large subsidies, its practice since the Act came into force has been to list various ways in which the decision could have been improved rather than to provide any overall assessment of whether it considers that the justification for the subsidy is soundly based.
- There is little to deter a public authority from incorrectly deciding that what it is doing is not a subsidy at all (for example, because it is said, perhaps implausibly, to be an arm's length commercial transaction) and not declaring it at all on the subsidy database.

As part of the TCA review, and especially if the UK is seeking a closer relationship, the EU may well therefore want to seek a strengthened subsidy control regime.

How the new Labour government responds to that will depend on precisely what is proposed. And we are very conscious that – in order to achieve the mission of making the UK a clean energy superpower – large subsidies are likely to be required. But we think the following factors need to be borne in mind.

- The EU state aid system is a flexible system that allows the EU to approve very large subsidies in support of projects that further Net Zero and other environmental objectives. Given that, the EU is not in a position to demand any regime from the UK that could prevent the UK from making similarly large and ambitions subsidies to the same end.
- The EU is already in a position to take effective action against UK subsidies to which it objects: it can apply World Trade Organization-consistent countervailing measures (tariffs); and it can take action under its Foreign Subsidies Regulation. The EU is also able to authorise very large subsidies aimed at encouraging business location in the EU rather than in the UK. One of the UK's negotiating objectives in this area could be to obtain exemption from the foreign subsidies regime and for both sides to commit not to use subsidies to encourage relocation from each other.
- Any very large tax incentive, investment incentive or other grant is, if it applies in Northern Ireland, already subject to the

EU state aid regime via Article 10 of the Windsor Framework, and has to be approved by the European Commission or compliant with EU exemptions (a point entirely unaffected by the Sunak government's Windsor Framework agreement with the EU in February 2023).

- Subsidies are a key tool in achieving the Labour clean energy mission and the EU's energy transition objectives. It is in neither side's interests to get into subsidy races, and in both sides' interests to ensure that their subsidies complement rather than contradict each other.

There are various options for stronger TCA provisions and stronger domestic law provisions that could be explored. But the key point is to note that this is an area of EU concern, and where UK movement could be entirely consistent with Labour's priorities and the UK national interest.

Energy and Net Zero

The UK has much to offer the EU in terms of energy cooperation, given its strength in renewables and (for the time being) in gas and oil production, as well as its scientific base. The UK will however face significant issues in responding to EU initiatives in the areas of emissions trading schemes and carbon border adjustment mechanisms. Without linking to the EU schemes in those areas, further significant barriers to trade will arise, and the UK could run risks such as being a recipient for non-European steel diverted from the EU.

Defence, foreign policy and security

The Johnson/Frost TCA was striking in its lack of any provision for cooperation in defence and foreign policy – not even making provision for regular bilateral meetings to discuss those issues (apparently, according to David Frost, because he and Johnson objected to any 'rigid' framework and wanted to avoid the UK being '[left] as a planet orbiting the European sun'[16]).

---

[16] https://www.davidfrost.org.uk/news/churchill-lecture-university-zurich.

Developments since then – the Russian invasion of Ukraine, other threats to global supply chains, and the increasingly deranged and isolationist policies of the Republican Party in the United States – have pushed defence, foreign policy and security up the political agenda across Europe. In response to those threats, the UK and its EU neighbours share the same defence and strategic objectives, and the EU is, increasingly, the vehicle through which the UK's neighbours cooperate in achieving those objectives. The Johnson/Frost decision to ignore the EU in these areas was (as Frost's explanation cited earlier shows) blinkered and dogmatic at the time: it has turned out to be obviously foolish and damaging.

Under the Labour government, the UK should propose an ambitious agreement for structured cooperation in the fields of foreign policy and defence – the areas covered by the EU's Common Foreign and Security Policy (CFSP) and Common Security and Defence Policy (CSDP). Structured cooperation would mean:

- A commitment to regular and frequent meetings between the prime minister/UK Cabinet ministers and EU counterparts (Commission and Council Presidents, EU High Representative): far from imposing 'rigidity', the reality is that without such meetings cooperation inevitably atrophies and loses direction.
- Provisions for systematic exchanges of information about policy intentions, consultation before taking important decisions, and cooperation on implementation of common decisions.
- Provisions for the sharing of intelligence on defence, security and crime.
- While respecting each side's sovereignty, a commitment to seek a common position where possible.
- Cooperation and intense information-sharing with and participation in the work of agencies such as EUROPOL (policing), Frontex (border control), ENISA (cybercrime) and Eurojust (prosecution).
- Cooperation in space programmes, including Galileo.
- Observer status at EU CFSP and CDSP meetings both at preparatory/official level and even at Council level.
- Cooperation in response to natural and man-made disasters.

There is broad agreement that such an agreement is needed,[17] and the EU is likely to welcome a UK initiative in this area. Strong and institutionalised cooperation with the UK will be seen as likely to enhance the EU's effectiveness in this area, given the UK's position as a major European defence and intelligence power, a permanent member of the UN Security Council, and a major contributor to the CFSP and CDSP when it was a member of the EU. The UK can also refer to the fact that the Political Declaration agreed along with the Withdrawal Agreement envisaged much more cooperation in this area than was actually agreed.

Further, the CFSP and CSDP are areas where it is relatively easy for the EU to allow the UK a consultative/observer role in EU policy formation. These areas remain ones based on intergovernmental cooperation, with a limited role for EU institutions (in which, absent Treaty amendment, the UK can play no role): the European Parliament's role is only consultative, legislation is made by unanimity, and the Court of Justice has very limited jurisdiction.

An agreement of the kind envisaged here is not incompatible with developing the European Political Community, which consists of almost all European countries apart from Russia, for example by giving that body a permanent secretariat: but the reality is that the European Political Community is too disparate to be a vehicle for intense strategic cooperation. That said, mechanisms to involve Norway, Iceland and Switzerland in CFSP and CSDP cooperation should also be explored, given those countries' geographically and economically strategic role.

One issue that will need to be negotiated in any such agreement is the issue of how the UK is treated in relation to EU security and defence procurement, given the EU policy emphasis on 'strategic autonomy' – an issue particularly emphasised by France. A situation where the UK is otherwise accepted as a close strategic partner but is shut out of such procurement is unlikely to be acceptable. That is an aspect of the fact that security is no longer a policy silo: areas such as trade (resilience of supply chains/ sanctions), mobility (cooperation on refugees and migration,

---

[17] See, in particular, Sir Julian King's proposal for such an agreement, at https:// www.eiag.org.uk/paper/case-ambitious-uk-eu-security-cooperation-pact/.

ability for scientists and technicians to move each way across the Channel) and energy (resilience) are all security issues as well, and the logic of intense security cooperation should extend to those areas.[18]

That raises the broader issue, which requires careful handling, of the relationship between a UK initiative in the areas of CFSP and CSDP and UK initiatives in other areas such as trade, mobility and energy. The UK has to avoid any impression that it views security as a UK 'card' to be traded for other 'cards' (an impression conveyed by the May government during the Brexit process). The message should be that the UK sees security cooperation as a major gain for both sides – a message that has the major advantage of being true. That said, there is no doubt that deep and intense cooperation in those areas will help rebuild the trust destroyed by the Tory governments, particularly under Johnson, and that that will assist UK negotiations in other areas.

Process

So far, we have discussed various issues that need to be thought about in determining negotiating strategy for fixing Brexit. But thought also needs to be given to the process by which the new Labour government will finalise its strategy – and that process should also extend to trade agreements more generally.

Under the Tories, policy towards the EU (and wider UK trade policy) was formed in a silo, often deaf to business and other interests and concerns – and generally deaf to concerns of devolved and local government. The TCA, in common with other trade agreements, was negotiated without any adequate consultation on strategy or detail with Parliament, let alone any representatives of regional or devolved government or unions or businesses. In the case of non-EU agreements, they have been driven by the desire to reach an agreement at all costs

---

[18] Indeed, the Tory government's spectacular failures in the area of illegal migration are largely due to its inability to accept that the UK cannot deal with the issues of migration and asylum on its own: effective action requires intense cooperation with its neighbours, not quack remedies based on rejecting international law and international cooperation.

in order to obtain a photo and a few pages of favourable press coverage (a well-known example being the concessions made by Boris Johnson, apparently over dinner, in order to secure the UK–Australia FTA). When negotiated, those inadequate trade agreements are then subject to wholly ineffective parliamentary scrutiny: in the case of the TCA consisting of a rushed approval of complex provisions and implementing legislation in only a day, but in other cases, often only under the process under section 20 of the Constitutional Reform and Governance Act 2010 which allows (at most) a single vote on ratification. That poor process leads to poor trade agreements: the UK–Australia FTA was described even by George Eustice, one of the ministers most involved, as a poor deal for the UK; and even David Frost, who negotiated the wholly inadequate TCA, has admitted that the absence of mobility provisions was 'too purist' and '[made] life difficult on both sides [for] youth mobility, movement of specialists like musicians and artists'.[19]

Under Labour, trade policy should be driven by a wider strategy determined by an open democratic process and subject to democratic challenge and scrutiny. Such a process would have a number of advantages. It would require not just the Labour government but subsequent governments to develop and defend a trade strategy that consisted of more than making as many free trade agreements as possible (or, in the case of the EU, taking the miser's approach to sovereignty). It would allow those outside the Westminster/Whitehall bubble to have their voices heard and concerns respected, ensuring that trade policy delivered across the UK. It would increase the democratic legitimacy of trade agreements when made. And it would also strengthen the UK's hand in negotiations, as it would be clear to counterparties that UK 'red lines' were genuine and that the UK government could not just drop them over dinner when put under pressure.

Generally, therefore, the new Labour government should therefore legislate to require an open and transparent process, involving regional and devolved governments as well as businesses, unions, non-governmental organisations and the wider public, to

---

[19]   See the lecture cited at n 16.

determine trade strategy and the mandate for trade negotiations, as well as improving parliamentary scrutiny of trade strategy and negotiations to a level equivalent to the way in which the European Parliament or Congress scrutinises EU or US trade policy (for example, by requiring parliamentary approval of trade negotiating mandates as well as keeping the relevant select committees informed as to, and consulting them on, the course of negotiations).

In the case of the EU, it will probably not be possible to find time for such legislation before preparations need to be made for negotiations with the EU. But nothing would prevent the new Labour government from voluntarily adopting a far more open process for preparing its 'ask' than that adopted by the Johnson government in 2020. One approach might to publish a 'Green Paper' on negotiating objectives with the EU within a short period after taking office, followed – after consultation and parliamentary scrutiny and debate, as well as informal discussions with the EU and member state governments – by a White Paper sometime during the second half of 2025. It would also be sensible to publish at least some draft text as it is prepared (a strategy frequently adopted by the EU). Particularly if – for reasons which we well understand – the Labour manifesto does little more than set out a general direction of travel as far as fixing Brexit is concerned, we consider that such an approach will improve both the legitimacy and the content of any eventual deal.

Conclusion

There is no doubt that Brexit has seriously damaged the UK economy and wider UK defence and foreign policy interests. But there is no quick fix that will reverse that damage. What the new Labour government can realistically achieve is:

- to start lowering at least some of the barriers to trade and opportunity that have been thrown up;
- to repair relations between the EU and the UK after the Tories' promise-breaking and abuse, and to open up platforms for cooperation that benefit both sides and enable both sides

to better achieve their objectives, in particular in relation to defence and security against Russia and other threats and the transition to a green and sustainable economy.

Summary of key proposals

- Negotiate an ambitious agreement for structured cooperation in defence, foreign policy and security including regular meetings, exchange of information and cooperation and coordination where possible, potentially extending to observer status at EU meetings in relation to defence and foreign policy issues.
- Accept that in many areas of regulation it is sensible, and may well assist in obtaining better access to EU markets, to align with EU law: legislation should be introduced to make that possible and avoid unintended and harmful divergence by default.
- Negotiate a form of youth mobility scheme with the EU that allows the UK to limit numbers and does not involve increasing public spending, but gives young people in both the UK and EU the real ability to spend time working and studying in each other's countries with minimal expense and bureaucracy; and seek to extend mobility arrangements for UK and EU musicians – and other professionals – working on a self-employed basis or for their existing employer or for a limited period of time in the other jurisdiction, as well as those wanting to reside in the other jurisdiction without working for a medium-term period for family or other reasons.
- Consider whether to offer firmer commitments in the area of state aid/subsidies as part of securing favourable treatment in areas such as EU action against foreign subsidies and in large-scale procurement in areas affected by 'strategic autonomy' concerns.
- Pass legislation to improve parliamentary and wider society scrutiny of, and involvement in, trade and other negotiations with the EU (and other trade partners). Increase the resource and expertise of UK government departments and embassies in Brussels and across the EU in understanding and seeking to influence EU discussions.

- Reject calls to 'join the single market and/or customs union' given that (a) terms for that are not on offer and would be intensely difficult to negotiate and (b) require an intense cross-government focus at the expense of focusing on delivering Labour's missions.

14

International law

Daniel Jones, David Drew and Joseph K

Introduction

There are a number of levers which affect a state's ability to achieve its foreign policy objectives. These include: economic and trade power; defence capability; diplomatic resource and skill; soft power, including cultural clout; and overseas development policy. Any serious foreign policy strategy is informed by an assessment of the state's capacity in these areas and the effective deployment of its comparative strengths. Significantly, each of these tools is reliant, to varying degrees, on a functional system of international law.

While the relative size of its economy and defence capabilities have reduced in the post-Second World War period, the UK has managed to exert an outsized influence through an effective diplomatic service, a seat at key international tables including the United Nations (UN) Security Council, impressive soft power, a commitment to international development and, above all, a significant role in the shaping and reshaping international law.

Indeed, since 1945, the UK has been central to the moulding of institutions, agreements and norms that govern much international activity (often referred to as the 'rules-based international order'). The UK was present at the establishment of many key intra-governmental bodies, including the UN, International Monetary Fund and International Criminal Court, and at the drafting of treaties that have been essential in regulating state conduct, such as the Universal Declaration of Human Rights, the 1951 Refugee Convention or, in a European context, the European Convention on Human Rights.

The UK has been able to maintain an outsized diplomatic role in large part because of its commitment to the rules-based international order (arguably with a few significant lapses). However, at precisely the moment the UK should, once again, be helping to defend and update this framework – which is central to international peace and security and its own interests – the Conservatives are causing significant damage to the country's international reputation. Repeated threats to break international law over immigration policy and the trading arrangements for Northern Ireland have been noticed by our international partners, and our adversaries.

The Conservatives' approach reflects the powerful strain of cynical populism that is spreading across the globe and indeed the impact of populism on international institutions has been profound. The cause of multilateralism and the concept of pooling of sovereignty to tackle challenges which require cooperation are under sustained attack. The dysfunction within the UN Security Council has immediate consequences in relation to Syria, Ukraine and Israel. It is now inconceivable that a major power would seek a UN resolution in support of military action which it considered central to its national security interests. In international trade, the World Trade Organization (WTO) appellate body has essentially collapsed as the global economy further fragments into trading blocs.

The Conservatives' approach is entirely counterproductive. There is no short- or long-term advantage for the UK in undermining a system based on international law that it was so central to creating. In contrast, David Lammy has started to articulate a vision of Britain looking to rebuild its influence by reconnecting with long-standing international partners. This chapter argues that central to the success of such a vision will be a decisive shift in approach on international law: from a decade in which the Conservatives have been content for the UK to be a 'rule breaker' on the global stage to an era in which Labour would show commitment to the UK playing an active and cooperative role as a 'rule shaper' in international law.

This approach requires a deliberate and sustained effort to rebuild Britain's reputation for respecting the rule of law and become a central actor in restoring the authority of multilateral institutions, starting with the UN Security Council. Reshaping the mandates, composition and decision-making processes will be essential if these institutions are to play a meaningful role in international affairs in future. This will require creativity, flexibility and above all political commitment. A Labour government will also need to respond to the challenges of the age, like climate change and artificial intelligence, by pursuing plurilateral initiatives with like-minded states within a rules-based framework to avoid geopolitical competition preventing essential collective action.

Business and international law

International treaties, which are the building blocks of public international law, have historically imposed obligations on states rather than private enterprises. While in domestic law it has long been accepted that legal entities such as corporations have both rights and responsibilities, traditional international law of both treaties and customary practice historically treated states as their exclusive subjects.[1] This formalistic definition of the subjects of international law began to face pressure over the last century as individuals acquired rights under human rights treaties. People gained rights that could be invoked against both their own and foreign states. From the 1990s onwards, the debate as to the rights and responsibilities of transnational corporations under international law intensified.

However, the actions of the largest global companies can be just as significant as sovereign governments. As Douglas Cassel from the University of Notre Dame puts it, '[i]ntellectually, it's becoming harder to claim that businesses are not subject to international public law'.[2] The UN Guiding Principles on

---

[1] J.G. Ku, 'The limits of corporate rights under international law', *Chicago Journal of International Law*, 12: 729–33 (2012), at https://scholarlycommons. law.hofstra.edu/faculty_scholarship/76.

[2] https://www.ibanet.org/From-soft-law-to-the-hard-edge-of-busin ess#:~:text=For%20instance%2C%20the%20Dutch%20model,subject%20 to%20international%20public%20law.

Business and Human Rights, endorsed by the UN Human Rights Council in 2011, were a recognition that large companies which reach beyond national borders in their operations and supply chains have a responsibility to reduce their environmental and human rights harms.[3]

In the decade since, there have been various developments in so-called 'soft law', including voluntary standards and guidelines against which businesses can measure and report on their environmental, social and governance impacts.[4] While such industry-led initiatives, which reflect the growing number of businesses that recognise they have a role beyond maximising shareholder value, are to be commended, only regulators working domestically and in coordination with international partners can ensure consistency and transparency in how these impacts are defined, measured and mitigated. Furthermore, without a clear enforcement framework, these standards cannot be guaranteed to prevent harms or hold companies accountable.

A number of the UK's international allies have already taken action to move from voluntary initiatives to mandatory legislative requirements for their largest businesses. From 2024, the European Union (EU)'s Corporate Sustainability Due Diligence Directive (CSDDD) will come into effect, obliging firms over a certain size with operations in the EU to identify and prevent negative impacts of their activities on the environment and human rights, both in their own operations and within their supply chains.[5] This

---

[3] United Nations, *Guiding Principles on Business and Human Rights: Implementing the United Nations 'Protect, Respect and Remedy' Framework*, 2011, at https:// www.ohchr.org/sites/default/files/Documents/Publications/Guiding PrinciplesBusinessHR_EN.pdf.

[4] K. Guruparan and J. Zerk, 'Influence of soft law grows in international governance', Chatham House, 17 June 2021, at https://www.chatham house.org/2021/06/influence-soft-law-grows-international-governance.

[5] Council of the European Union, 'Corporate sustainability due diligence: Council and Parliament strike deal to protect environment and human rights', 14 December 2023, at https://www.consilium.europa.eu/en/ press/press-releases/2023/12/14/corporate-sustainability-due-diligence-council-and-parliament-strike-deal-to-protect-environment-and-human-rights/.

follows national legislation which is already in force in France and Germany.[6]

In comparison, the current UK regulatory landscape presents a confused picture. There are a myriad of different laws dealing with specific aspects of environmental and human rights policy offer businesses a minefield full of tripwires to navigate. This is not even to consider court jurisprudence, which has simultaneously expanded the geographical scope of who can bring a claim against a UK company for personal wrongdoing, while also encouraging companies to actively avoid looking into their partners' environmental and human rights dealings so that they can rely on a defence that they were unaware.[7]

Businesses themselves recognise the impact of such complexity and support change. Studies of businesses with a total of over 150,000 employees have shown that nearly 80 per cent are dissatisfied with the existing legal landscape and agree a statute codifying corporate obligations would be beneficial to businesses overall.[8] Such legislation would be popular with the public, too. Surveys indicate that 80 per cent of the British population support new laws that would require companies to take steps to avoid environmental damage and the exploitation of persons in their supply chains.[9]

In government, Labour should introduce a new business, human rights and environmental law to create a general civil duty on the largest businesses operating in the UK to ensure that human rights or gross environmental harms do not take place in their operations or supply chains.[10] The most appropriate model would

---

[6]   France: Loi No 2017-399, 27 March 2017, relating to the duty of vigilance of parent companies and ordering companies 28 March 2017; Germany: Law on Corporate Due Diligence in Supply Chains, 11 June 2021.

[7]   *Vedanta Resources Plc & Anor v Lungowe & Ors* [2019] UKSC 20.

[8]   British Institute of International and Comparative Law, 'A UK failure to prevent mechanism for corporate human rights harms', BIICL, 2020, pp 12 and 14, at https://www.biicl.org/documents/84_failure_to_prevent_final_10_feb.pdf.

[9]   Corporate Justice Coalition, 'New poll shows 4 in 5 of the British public want a law to prevent business human rights and environmental harm, and businesses and investors agree', 25 August 2022, at http://tinyurl.com/mr3mwxja.

[10] Non-small and medium sized enterprises are defined under UK company law as any business which has either an annual turnover of £36 million,

be 'failure to prevent' law, which incentivises companies to take action to prevent abuse and hold them accountable where they fail to do so. This would align with existing duties, for example under the Bribery Act 2010, so as to reduce the regulatory burden of compliance for businesses. It would be appropriate to consult on the exact threshold of UK turnover and employees at which these obligations should kick in, but there are clearly merits for multinational businesses of aligning the legislation with the CSDDD so as to provide greater regulatory certainty.

Human rights and gross environmental harms within the meaning of the new legislation should cover at a minimum those standards which the UK government has ratified or incorporated, but also those recommended by the UN Guiding Principles on Business and Human Rights (as endorsed by the UN Human Rights Council).[11]

The duty would require that companies which meet the relevant threshold put in place reasonable procedures to prevent a human rights abuse or gross environmental harm from occurring, with legislation accompanied by guidance outlining what actions would be considered 'reasonable'. Where those procedures are in place, a company could not be held liable, even if a human rights abuse occurred in its supply chain.[12] If however a company had failed to put in place such measures, then the victims of the abuse – or in the

---

a balance sheet of £18 million, or an average number of employees over a financial year of more than 250. Companies House Accounts Guidance, 5 April 2023, at https://www.gov.uk/government/publications/life-of-a-company-annual-requirements/life-of-a-company-part-1-accounts.

[11] UNOHC, *Guiding Principles on Business and Human Rights Implementing the United Nations 'Protect, Respect and Remedy' Framework*, 2011, at https://www.ohchr.org/sites/default/files/documents/publications/guidingprinciples businesshr_en.pdf.

[12] This would be in line with the Criminal Finances Act 2017, 45(2) and 46(3); and Bribery Act, s 7. If, however, a human rights abuse has occurred of which the company is aware, it should nevertheless attempt to take steps to mitigate it, based on its degree of relationship and leverage it has over the abusing company. For example, this include threatening to end the business relationship with the company, or the companies dealing with the human rights abuser. UN, *Commentary to Guiding Principles on Business and Human Rights*, 2011, p 22, at https://www.ohchr.org/sites/default/files/documents/publications/guidingprinciplesbusinesshr_en.pdf.

case of environmental harms a specifically created environmental officer – should be capable of suing the company for damages, with the money given to ameliorate the harm caused.

It has now been over 75 years since Britain helped the world adopt the Universal Declaration of Human Rights, a breakthrough international treaty which helped protect people across the world from state abuse. The declaration was signed when states played an ever-present role in people's lives. In recognition of the important role that large businesses play in the international order, many countries are beginning place clearer expectations on those enterprises to protect against gross human rights and environmental abuses across the globe. A future Labour government should ensure that it a rule shaper, actively contributing to these international developments, by committing to passing a new Business, Human Rights and Environment Act.

Ecocide in international and UK law

Debates in international and domestic criminal law have also turned their attention to environmental crimes, including those which can be committed by companies. The Stop Ecocide Foundation defines the proposed offence as 'unlawful or wanton acts committed with knowledge that there is a substantial likelihood of severe and either widespread or long-term damage to the environment being caused by those acts'.[13] A growing number of states and other stakeholders are supportive of ecocide being ratified as a crime of international law, alongside genocide, crimes against humanity, war crimes and crimes of aggression.

Shadow Foreign Secretary, David Lammy, has long been a supporter of ecocide becoming a fifth international crime in an amended Rome Statute.[14] In government, Labour should work with the broadest possible coalition of states to propose an

---

[13] Stop Ecocide International, 'Legal definition of ecocide drafted by Independent Expert Panel', June 2021, at https://www.stopecocide.earth/legal-definition.

[14] David Lammy, 'A United Kingdom that looks outwards instead of inwards', *LabourList*, 27 September 2022, at https://labourlist.org/2022/09/a-united-kingdom-that-looks-outwards-instead-of-inwards-lammys-speech/.

amendment to the Rome Statute, the government treaty of the International Criminal Court.

But, Labour does not need to wait for international agreement to act. Thirteen countries now have a crime of 'ecocide' on their statutes, from France to Ecuador. At least six others have similar laws proposed, and a joint proposal has been put forward by the EU Council and EU Parliament. Labour has committed to pursuing a foreign policy that reconnects Britain with the world. By adopting legislation to criminalise ecocide, Labour will place the UK at the heart of a global movement that is gaining momentum. If it fails to do so, the UK is at risk at being left isolated on a key progressive issue that has widespread support. The moral, environmental and political arguments are clear as to why such a law should be implemented in the UK. It should prove a threat only to the most culpable individuals or entities. Now is the time for the next Labour government to make it a reality.

There are of course a number of questions about what the scope of the crime of ecocide should be. First, as a preliminary matter, the crime of ecocide should not hinder sustainable economic development. A proportionality test, balancing the level of environmental damage an act will cause with the public good that it generates, should therefore be included in any legislation. While this will inevitably be a relatively subjective exercise, given how difficult it is to compare the value of the environment to the economy, it also provides a degree of discretion which will allow the vast majority of economic activity to take place, so long as there is at least an attempt to mitigate any potential environmental harm.

In reality, the criminalisation of environmental harms which are 'severe', and 'widespread' or 'long-term', will also mean that only the worst environmental damage is prosecuted. The aim is to cover situations like the intentional mass dumping of waste, or the removal of vast areas of woodland without clear economic or social rationale. Other environmental harms should not be ignored, but instead face either regulatory or civil action, rather than criminal enforcement.

Second, there is the question of how much culpability a company or individual should have before they are prosecuted. While intentional damage should be included, this will often be very difficult to prove in the case of companies, where there may be no clear 'smoking gun' of an overarching order to cause environmental destruction, but instead a number of fragmented decisions each contributing to the company's damaging act. Therefore, a broader test should be adopted, including where either a company knows, or clearly should have known (the notion of 'objective recklessness') that an environmental harm was very likely to be committed by its actions. This will mean that the criminalisation of ecocide will not simply be a token gesture.

Finally, as with environmental and human rights due diligence, a defence should be available where a company tried to prevent or mitigate any environmental damage that resulted. This provides three benefits. First, it means that companies which have put in place adequate measures and procedures should not have to fear prosecution, providing a significant safeguard to companies fearful of the law's scope. Second, it will lead to a reduction in environmental harm, as companies take significant efforts to reduce whatever damage has arisen to reduce their likelihood of prosecution. Third, it will save taxpayers money, as companies would have an incentive to introduce measures which otherwise the government would have to pay for.

Economic resilience, friend-shoring and international law

In her May 2023 Labour Together paper, 'A new business model for Britain', Shadow Chancellor Rachel Reeves gave one of her fullest articulations of Labour's economic strategy for prosperity in an age of insecurity. Reeves invoked US Treasury Secretary Janet Yellen's vision of 'modern supply side economics', in which a more active state works in partnership with the private sector to invest in building domestic economic capacity. The answer to this age of insecurity is 'improving the resilience of an economy to external shocks'.[15]

---

[15] Labour Together, 'A new business model for Britain', 24 May 2023, p 19, at https://www.labourtogether.uk/all-reports/a-new-business-model-for-britain.

In part, the success of Labour's industrial strategy will be measured by how effectively it reduces the country's dependence on fragile international supply chains. As an initial step in that exercise, Labour has committed to commissioning a supply-chain task force to identify weaknesses in critical areas in government. But seeking to achieve this resilience by onshoring up domestic supply chains will clearly have its limits. Growing the UK's manufacturing capacity in electric vehicles, for example, will require affordable but reliable sources of critical minerals which can only be acquired from suppliers in a limited number of countries.

That's why another key pillar of Janet Yellen's supply side approach is 'friend-shoring': countries with shared political values and economic interests deepening their coordination to ensure access to critical materials needed to achieve the ambitions of their domestic industrial strategies. As Canada's deputy prime minister Chrystia Freedland put it, 'Where democracies must be strategically vulnerable, we should be vulnerable to each other'.[16]

Clearly, the political challenge of formalising the opportunities of friend-shoring in Labour's vision for long-term industrial strategy is building partnerships which can survive disruptive political events, including elections which lead to changes of administrations in the governments of trusted partner states. That is why instruments of international law will be essential to cementing and articulating the expectations that these friends place on each other, including at moments when those relationships are under strain.

There are a number of developments which an incoming Labour government could build on. For example, the Minerals Security Partnership is an association launched in July 2022 by 14 countries (including the UK) and the EU which aims to accelerate the development of diverse and sustainable critical energy minerals supply chains. Through the Minerals Security

---

[16] Deputy Prime Minister of Canada Chrystia Freeland, 'Remarks by the Deputy Prime Minister at the Brookings Institution in Washington, D.C.', 11 October, 2022, at https://deputypm.canada.ca/en/news/speeches/2022/10/11/remarks-deputy-prime-minister-brookings-institution-washington-dc.

Partnership, the UK and its partners will facilitate commercial agreements and secure financing, including from multilateral development banks, for projects which achieve the association's economic objectives and meet high environment, social and governance standards.

Labour has already recognised the need for new international alliances and agreements in meeting its missions of securing the highest sustained growth in the G7 and delivering clean power by 2030. In November 2022, Shadow Climate Change Secretary Ed Miliband announced that an incoming Labour government would work with international partners to form an 'inverse-OPEC' group of countries with shared commitments to renewable energy and clean technology. While the details of this clean power alliance are still to be announced, it is envisaged that members of the coalition would share information and cooperate on investment with the objective of driving down global energy prices. In other words, the Alliance would facilitate 'friend-vestment' to meet the shared objectives of participating countries.

In order to maintain the trust and confidence of partners in the Global South, it is essential that initiatives and agreements forming form part of what the Carnegie Endowment refers to as 'joint industrial policy' are open to countries from across Africa, Asia and Latin America in addition to our G7 and NATO partners. In a speech given by Shadow Foreign Secretary David Lammy to Chatham House in January 2023, it was suggested that the Labour's Clean Power Alliance would be drawn from nations committed to 100 per cent clean power by 2030. Using this narrow criteria for entry risks excluding least developed and middle-income countries who are committed to the phase-out of fossil fuels but over a timeframe which extends beyond the end of this decade. For example, the Colombian government has set out plans for an ambitious energy transition, with a 70 per cent renewable energy target by 2030. For a country which currently produces 800,000 barrels of crude oil a day and 85 million metric tons of coal a year, this is a significant commitment.

Friend-shoring has faced criticism as undermining the principles of the multilateral rules-based trading system. As WTO Director General Ngozi Okonjo-Iweala recently put it, 'We must now figure out how to operate a multilateral system designed to foster interdependence and peace when some of our members are at war.'[17] It is arguably both a response to, and a contributor to, the perilous circumstances in which the WTO now finds itself. Commentators have pointed to the US refusal to appoint judges to the WTO's appellate body, US tariffs on China and retaliatory measures imposed in response and the exponential increase in unilateral economic sanctions as evidence that the WTO is in deep trouble.

Some economic and security experts believe that postwar rules governing multilateral trade are beyond redemption and that the fundamental incompatibility of the US and Chinese systems leads to a conclusion that further 'decoupling' is the only way to break the current impasse. But, the economic consequences of a complete decoupling would be severe, reducing global GDP by 5 per cent. It would be a particular threat to 'non-aligned' countries, including in the Global South, which are reliant on strong trade with and investment from both the US and China for their own economic development. That is why creative proposals are needed to save the WTO with more flexible trading rules, in which improved rules dealing with systemic frictions are designed and safeguarded, but with greater scope for differentiated national policies and agreements between countries who are willing to make deeper agreements.[18]

If Labour is to succeed in finding a new role as a 'rule shaper', it should advocate a new role for the WTO, alongside international agreements and institutions with its partners which are robust and broad-based. The Clean Power Alliance which a Labour government would look to establish with international partners should give a seat at the table to countries in the Global South which are leading the way on the green transition and develop an institutional framework in which those states have a meaningful voice.

---

[17] DG Ngozi Okonjo-Iweala, 'National Foreign Trade Council: strengthening the WTO and the global trading system', WTO, 27 April 2022, at https://www.wto.org/english/news_e/spno_e/spno25_e.htm.

[18] R.Z. Lawrence, 'Policy Brief 22-15: How to save the WTO with more flexible trading rules', Pieterson Institute for International Economics, December 2022, at https://www.piie.com/sites/default/files/2022-12/pb22-15.pdf.

The future of sanctions

Russia's invasion of Ukraine in February 2022 has highlighted the deep dysfunction within the UN. Russia has used its veto power as a permanent member of the UN Security Council to block any efforts to end the conflict or hold the Kremlin accountable for its actions. Countries in the Global South have long called for membership of the highest UN body to be more representative, with it lacking any permanent member from Africa or Latin America or reflecting regional powers from Japan to India. But, the Russia–Ukraine conflict has added a sense of urgency to these calls for reform. That is why Labour is right to commit to an 'open ended campaign to reform the UN Security Council [and support] a coalition of like-minded countries supporting the suspension of the veto in cases of mass atrocities'.[19]

While the ambition behind this commitment is commendable and the scale of the challenge should not negate efforts for reform, it is clear that Russia itself would be resistant to any expansion of the Security Council.[20] That's why alternative fora to impose pressure on Putin and those who have supported and funded his war in Ukraine are essential: from the arrest warrant issued by the International Criminal Court in March 2023 to the establishment of a special tribunal to hold Russia accountable for its actions.

Economic sanctions have been another tool the UK and its allies have deployed in this conflict. While there is a long history of states deploying coercive economic measures both as an alternative to war, and to bolster those war efforts, the use of sanctions in response to Russia's invasion of Ukraine have been unprecedented, both in terms of their scope and complexity. Economic analysis conducted by the US Department of Treasury suggests that Russia's macroeconomic performance is suffering as a

---

[19] D. Lammy, 'Britain reconnected, for security and prosperity at home', Chatham House, 23 January 2023, at https://www.chathamhouse.org/sites/default/files/2023-01/David%20Lammy-Chatham-House-speech-2023-01-23.pdf.

[20] P. Niland, 'Russia's Ukraine invasion highlights the need for fundamental UN reform', Atlantic Council, 12 October 2023, at https://www.atlantic council.org/blogs/ukrainealert/russias-ukraine-invasion-highlights-the-need-for-fundamental-un-reform/.

consequence of these measures, coupled with the costs of waging the largest armed conflict in Europe since 1945.[21]

The high-level political coordination between the UK, EU and US in imposing further rounds of restrictive measures on Russia has held over the last two years. However, there are further, practical steps that a Labour government could take with its international partners to ensure that this political will translates into effective implementation and, therefore, impact.

This includes closer working on key sanctions concepts, including ownership and control. To provide a specific example, so-called asset-freezing measures prohibit any transactions with a specified individual or entity as well as any entity which that sanctioned person owns or controls. The EU and US both make clear in their sanctions guidance that shareholdings should be 'accumulated' to assess whether or not an entity meets the relevant 50 per cent ownership threshold. By contrast, UK guidance suggests that accumulation should not generally be applied. This means that two sanctioned persons could each own 49 per cent of the shares in an entity and under UK sanctions that company would not itself need to be treated as sanctioned unless there is evidence of joint arrangements between those sanctioned persons. This reduces the scope, and therefore effectiveness, of UK sanctions given the practical challenges for UK banks and firms trying of proving or disproving the existence of agreements between sanctioned persons.

Another area which requires further attention is the use of third countries as gateways for the circumvention of these sanctions. There is significant evidence that jurisdictions in the Middle East and Central Asia have been used as transit routes for components for military equipment and other materials required to sustain Putin's war effort. This requires stronger action against UK companies which do not conduct adequate due diligence on the end-use and end-users of their products. The EU has imposed a strict requirement on its companies to contractually

---

21 R. Lyngaas, 'Sanctions and Russia's war: limiting Putin's capabilities', U.S. Department of the Treasury, 14 December 2023, at https://home.treasury. gov/news/featured-stories/sanctions-and-russias-war-limiting-putins-capabilities.

prohibit re-export of sensitive goods and technology to Russia. The UK government chose not to introduce equivalent measures in its latest round of sanctions in December 2023. This should be reconsidered if the existing restrictions are to be as effective as possible. In government, Labour should also be unafraid to target companies and individuals in those third countries which are identified as enablers of Russian sanctions circumvention, to ensure that all loopholes are closed.

Finally, UK regulators need the resources and political support to take enforcement action against those who breach sanctions. The UK sanctions regulators' most recent annual report, published in December 2023, confirmed that no fines have been handed out for breaches of Russian sanctions since the full-scale invasion. In 2022/2023, the UK government imposed two fines worth £45,000 for breaches of all sanctions regimes. In the same period. The US Office for Foreign Assets Control issued 19 fines with a total value of US$72 million. It is critical that the unprecedented sanctions targeting Russia translate into meaningful enforcement action if there is to be a genuine deterrent under which companies know that failing to take adequate steps to comply with sanctions has real consequences. Labour has announced a whistle-blower regime with financial rewards for those who come forward with details of sanctions violations. It must also ensure that regulators have the personnel required to investigate and act on those reports.

Conclusion

The idea that the UK should be a 'rule shaper' not a 'rule breaker' of international law should not be a radical statement, given its pivotal role in helping build many of the world's leading international institutions. Yet sustained policies of the Conservative government over the last 14 years have fundamentally damaged that reputation.

This chapter has outlined policies which could put the UK back front and centre of the global policy debate:

- taking the initiative in placing due diligence requirements on corporate supply chains;
- placing environmental damage front and centre of international criminal law; and

- securing our key industries from hostile states by partnering with democratic allies.

Reform in each of these priorities will help foster a UK that is confident, progressive and delivering for the British people.

This is a crucial time for international law; in an era of regional conflict and economic polarisation its role has only become more important. And yet, the rules based international order faces unprecedented threats. From the smouldering embers of the forest fire that has engulfed Britain's international reputation, it is possible to imagine green shoots appearing. It is high time the UK regained its position as a forward-thinking, internationally minded country, providing a greener, and more economically secure, system in the UK and beyond.

Summary of key proposals

- The UK should introduce a new corporate due diligence law to safeguard supply chains from human rights abuses.
- Labour must push for mass environmental harm, or 'ecocide', to be criminalised in both international and domestic law.
- The UK must work with its international partners and allies to secure vulnerable supply chains and create a bullet-proof sanctions regime.

Index